THE LION
GRAPHIC

BIBLE

Illustrations by Jeff Anderson
Script by Mike Maddox
Lettering by Steve Harrison

A LION BOOK

Contents

This edition copyright © 2001 Lion Publishing
Text copyright © 1998 Mike Maddox
Illustrations copyright © 1998 Jeff Anderson
Lettering copyright © 1998 Steve Harrison

The moral rights of the author, illustrator
and letterer have been asserted

Published by
Lion Publishing plc
Mayfield House, 256 Banbury Road,
Oxford OX2 7DH, England
www.lion-publishing.co.uk
ISBN 0 7459 4598 8

First hardback edition 1998
First paperback edition 2001
10 9 8 7 6 5 4 3 2

A catalogue record for this book is available
from the British Library

Printed and bound in Spain by
Artes Gráficas Toledo, S.A.U.
D.L. TO: 142-2002

IN THE BEGINNING, GOD CREATED THE HEAVENS AND THE EARTH.

THEN GOD SAID, 'LET THE LAND PRODUCE PLANT LIFE: GRASSES, HERBS, SEED-BEARING PLANTS, FRUIT-BEARING TREES, PLANTS OF EVERY KIND.' AND GOD SAW THAT IT WAS GOOD.

THERE WAS EVENING AND MORNING, AND THAT WAS THE THIRD DAY.

AND GOD SAID, 'LET THERE BE LIGHTS IN THE SKY TO SEPARATE DAY FROM NIGHT, AND TO SERVE AS SIGNS MARKING THE SEASONS, DAYS AND YEARS.'

SO GOD MADE TWO GREAT LIGHTS, ONE TO SHINE BY DAY, AND ONE TO SHINE BY NIGHT.

HE ALSO MADE THE STARS.

AND GOD SAW THAT IT WAS GOOD. THERE WAS EVENING AND MORNING, AND THAT WAS THE FOURTH DAY.

AND GOD SAID, 'LET THE OCEANS TEEM WITH LIFE, AND LET BIRDS FLY IN THE SKIES.'

SO GOD CREATED THE GREAT SEA CREATURES, AND EVERY LIVING THING IN THE OCEAN.

AND GOD WAS PLEASED WITH WHAT HE SAW, AND SAW THAT IT WAS GOOD.

GOD BLESSED THEM AND SAID, 'BE FRUITFUL AND INCREASE TO FILL THE SEAS AND SKIES.' THERE WAS EVENING AND MORNING, AND THAT WAS THE FIFTH DAY.

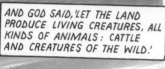

AND GOD SAID, 'LET THE LAND PRODUCE LIVING CREATURES, ALL KINDS OF ANIMALS: CATTLE AND CREATURES OF THE WILD.'

AND IT WAS SO.

GOD SAW THAT IT WAS GOOD.

AND GOD SAID, 'LET US MAKE HUMAN BEINGS IN OUR IMAGE TO HAVE CHARGE OVER ALL CREATURES ON THE EARTH, IN THE SKIES AND IN THE OCEANS.'

SO GOD CREATED HUMAN BEINGS IN HIS OWN IMAGE.

MALE AND FEMALE HE CREATED THEM.

GOD BLESSED THEM AND SAID, 'BE FRUITFUL AND INCREASE ON THE EARTH. FILL THE EARTH AND TAKE CHARGE OF EVERY LIVING CREATURE.'

'I GIVE YOU ALL SEED-BEARING PLANTS AND EVERY KIND OF FRUIT TO EAT AS FOOD. EVERY GREEN PLANT I GIVE TO EAT.' AND SO IT WAS.

GOD SAW THE WHOLE OF CREATION. IT WAS VERY GOOD. THERE WAS EVENING AND MORNING. AND THAT WAS THE SIXTH DAY.

SO GOD'S WORK OF CREATION WAS COMPLETE AND ON THE SEVENTH DAY GOD RESTED. SO GOD BLESSED THE SEVENTH DAY AND MADE IT HOLY.

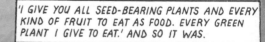

THAT IS THE ACCOUNT OF THE UNIVERSE, AND OF HOW THE HEAVENS AND EARTH WERE CREATED.

WHEN GOD MADE THE EARTH, HE MADE A MAN - 'ADAM' - FROM THE DUST OF THE DRY GROUND, BREATHING LIFE INTO HIM.

GOD PLANTED A GARDEN IN EDEN, AND THERE HE PUT THE MAN HE HAD CREATED. THE GARDEN WAS FULL OF BEAUTIFUL TREES THAT BORE DELICIOUS FRUIT.

IN THE MIDDLE OF THE GARDEN GOD SET THE TREE OF LIFE AND THE TREE OF THE KNOWLEDGE OF GOOD AND EVIL.

GOD GAVE ADAM CHARGE OF THE GARDEN, TO TAKE CARE OF IT AND TEND IT, SAYING; 'YOU ARE FREE TO EAT FROM ANY TREE IN THE GARDEN, EXCEPT THE TREE OF THE KNOWLEDGE OF GOOD AND EVIL.'

'IF YOU EAT ITS FRUIT, YOU ARE SURELY DOOMED TO DIE.'

GOD BROUGHT ALL THE BIRDS AND ANIMALS TO ADAM TO GIVE THEM THEIR NAMES.

THEN GOD SAID, 'IT'S NOT GOOD FOR ADAM TO BE ALONE. HE NEEDS A FITTING PARTNER TOO.'

SO GOD PUT ADAM INTO A DEEP SLEEP, AND WHILE HE WAS SLEEPING TOOK A RIB FROM HIS SIDE.

WITH THE RIB GOD MADE A WOMAN.

WHEN HE WOKE AND SAW WHAT GOD HAD DONE, ADAM SAID:

AT LAST! ONE OF MY OWN KIND.

BONE TAKEN FROM MY BONE, FLESH FROM MY FLESH, I WILL CALL YOU 'WOMAN' BECAUSE YOU WERE TAKEN OUT OF MAN.

THE MAN AND WOMAN WERE BOTH NAKED, BUT HAD NO FEELING OF SHAME.

A RIVER FLOWED FROM EDEN TO WATER THE GARDEN. FROM THERE IT BRANCHED INTO FOUR STREAMS.

THE MAN AND THE WOMAN CULTIVATED THE GARDEN, AND CARED FOR ALL THE ANIMALS.

IN THE CENTRE OF THE GARDEN WERE THE TWO SPECIAL TREES GOD HAD PLANTED. THE FIRST WAS CALLED THE TREE OF LIFE.

THE SECOND WAS THE TREE GOD HAD WARNED THEM OF — THE TREE WHOSE FRUIT WOULD CAUSE THEIR DEATHS IF THEY ATE IT.

THIS WAS THE TREE OF KNOWLEDGE — KNOWLEDGE NOT ONLY OF WHAT WAS GOOD —

BUT ALSO OF EVIL...

NOW, THE SERPENT WAS THE MOST CUNNING OF ALL THE CREATURES GOD HAD MADE, AND HE SPOKE TO THE WOMAN, SAYING:

IS IT *REALLY* TRUE THAT GOD HAS FORBIDDEN YOU TO EAT THE FRUIT OF ANY TREE?

OH, I'M SSORRY, I SSTARTLED YOU.

I WAS SURPRISED BY YOUR QUESTION.

GOD TOLD US WE CAN EAT THE FRUIT OF ANY TREE, EXCEPT THE ONE THAT GROWS IN THE MIDDLE OF THE GARDEN. IF WE EAT ITS FRUIT OR EVEN TOUCH IT WE ARE SURELY DOOMED TO DIE!

HOW INTERESSTING.

YOU SSEE, THAT'SS JUSST NOT TRUE. YOU WON'T DIE.

GOD HASS LIED TO YOU!

SO GOD BANISHED THE MAN AND THE WOMAN FROM HIS PRESENCE IN THE GARDEN. FOR LIGHT AND GOODNESS CANNOT COEXIST WITH DARKNESS AND EVIL.

AN ANGEL WITH A FLAMING SWORD WAS SET TO GUARD THE ENTRANCE, BARRING THE WAY TO THE TREE OF LIFE FOR EVER.

THEN ADAM NAMED HIS WIFE 'EVE', WHICH MEANS 'LIVING', BECAUSE SHE WOULD BE THE MOTHER OF THE HUMAN RACE.

BEFORE THEY LEFT, GOD MADE GARMENTS OF ANIMAL SKIN FOR ADAM AND EVE TO WEAR.

THEIR LIFE FROM NOW ON WOULD BE EXACTLY AS GOD SAID: A STRUGGLE TO SURVIVE IN A WORLD TURNED HOSTILE AND DANGEROUS.

THEY WOULD KNOW TOIL AND PAIN UNTIL THE DAY THEY DIED AND THEY RETURNED TO THE DUST THEY WERE MADE FROM.

15

THE WORLD THEY KNEW NOW WAS A HARD, COLD PLACE COMPARED WITH THE BEAUTY OF EDEN.

ADAM AND EVE SLEPT TOGETHER. EVE BECAME PREGNANT AND GAVE BIRTH TO A SON, CALLED CAIN.

LATER SHE HAD ANOTHER SON, ABEL.

CAIN GREW UP TO WORK THE SOIL; ABEL BECAME A SHEPHERD.

IN TIME, CAIN BROUGHT SOME OF HIS HARVEST AS AN OFFERING TO GOD. ABEL BROUGHT THE BEST LAMB OF HIS FLOCK.

GOD WAS PLEASED WITH ABEL'S OFFERING, BUT NOT WITH CAIN'S. ABEL WAS A GOOD MAN, A MAN OF FAITH, BUT GOD COULD SEE THE DARKNESS IN CAIN'S HEART.

CAIN WAS FURIOUS.

AND SO GOD SAID:

BUT CAIN REFUSED TO LISTEN TO GOD. HE BURNED WITH RAGE.

WHY SO ANGRY, CAIN? NO NEED TO SCOWL IF YOU HAVE DONE RIGHT.

IF NOT, SIN IS CROUCHING BY THE DOOR OF YOUR LIFE. IT WANTS TO CONTROL YOU.

BUT YOU MUST FIGHT IT!

ALLOWING HIS ANGER TO RULE HIM, HE PLOTTED AGAINST HIS BROTHER...

ABEL, COME OUT TO THE FIELDS WITH ME. THERE'S SOMETHING I WANT TO SHOW YOU.

WHAT IS IT?

IT'S A SURPRISE. YOU'LL SEE.

CAIN LED ABEL WELL AWAY FROM ANY WITNESSES, AND, AFTER MAKING SURE THEY WERE QUITE ALONE —

HE KILLED HIM.

IT WAS COLD, DELIBERATE MURDER.

THEN GOD SAID:

CAIN? WHERE IS YOUR BROTHER?

HOW SHOULD I KNOW?

AM I ABEL'S KEEPER?

WHAT HAVE YOU DONE?

YOUR BROTHER'S BLOOD CRIES OUT TO ME FROM THE VERY GROUND YOU TILL.

BECAUSE OF IT YOU ARE UNDER A CURSE! THE GROUND WILL NO LONGER GIVE YOU CROPS. YOU SHALL BE A WANDERER AND A FUGITIVE ON EARTH.

YET GOD PUT HIS MARK OF PROTECTION ON CAIN. HE MUST NOT BE KILLED.

SO CAIN LEFT HOME AND WENT EAST, FAR FROM GOD'S PRESENCE.

YET HE TOO HELPED TO PEOPLE THE EARTH. CAIN'S CHILDREN BUILT CITIES AS THEY GREW IN NUMBER. HIS OFFSPRING LEARNED HOW TO FORGE IRON AND BRONZE, TO MAKE MUSIC AS WELL AS VIOLENCE.

ADAM HAD ANOTHER SON, WHOM HE CALLED **SETH**, AND WHO IN TURN BECAME THE FATHER OF **ENOSH**. IN THIS WAY THEY MULTIPLIED AND GREW IN NUMBERS, INCREASING THEIR POPULATION ALL THE WHILE.

ADAM LIVED 930 YEARS, AND THEN HE **DIED**, AS GOD HAD SAID.

ENOSH HAD MANY CHILDREN, AND THEN LIKE HIS PARENTS BEFORE HIM, HE **DIED**. THE PATTERN OF BIRTH, LIFE AND DEATH WAS SET. THE FIRST PEOPLE LIVED TO A VERY GREAT AGE, PRODUCING MANY CHILDREN, WHO IN TURN GAVE BIRTH TO OTHER CHILDREN; AND SO THEIR NUMBERS SPREAD.

BUT AS THEY INCREASED, THEY BECAME **CORRUPTED** BY THE WORLD. THEY FELL INTO **EVIL WAYS**, AND THE STREETS OF THE FIRST CITIES WERE FULL OF TERRIBLE CRUELTY AND UNBEARABLE VIOLENCE.

HUMANKIND SPREAD, NOT LIKE A TREE PRODUCING FRUIT, BUT LIKE A DISEASE, BLIGHTING EVERYTHING IT TOUCHED.

HELP ME! PLEASE, SOMEONE HELP ME!

FIFTY?

ONE HUNDRED.

SIXTY-FIVE?

ONE HUNDRED.

SEVENTY, **AND** I KILL YOUR PARENTS?

DONE.

MONEY FOR FOOD!

LOOK YOU STUPID HAG, EAT THE BOY! OR SELL HIM TO ME!

HOW MUCH WILL YOU PAY?

WHEN GOD LOOKED AT THE WORLD, HE COULD ONLY FIND **ONE MAN** WHO REMAINED UNTOUCHED BY THE ATROCITIES, AND REFUSED TO ACCEPT THE DARKNESS THAT SURROUNDED HIM.

AND AS GOD LOOKED AT THE PEOPLE OF EARTH, HE KNEW THEY COULD NOT BE ALLOWED TO SURVIVE. **HUMANKIND WAS ALREADY DOOMED.**

WHICH LEADS US TO NOAH.

THE EARTH WAS SOON POPULATED, BUT BECAME SO CORRUPT AND FULL OF EVIL THAT GOD REGRETTED MAKING HUMANKIND IN THE FIRST PLACE.

EXCEPT FOR A MAN CALLED NOAH, THAT IS. IN A CRUEL AND VIOLENT WORLD NOAH ALONE VALUED HIS RELATIONSHIP WITH GOD, AND SO PLEASED GOD.

THIS IS NOAH'S STORY...

YOU SENT FOR ME FATHER? YOU HAVE NEWS?

I'VE SPOKEN WITH GOD! STRANGE DAYS LIE AHEAD FOR US, AND WE MUST PREPARE FOR THEM.

SOMETHING TERRIBLE IS GOING TO HAPPEN.

THE LORD GOD HAS DECIDED TO PUT AN END TO EVIL.

EVERY LIVING CREATURE ON EARTH WILL DIE.

EVERYTHING?

SURELY THERE MUST BE SOME OTHER WAY? THERE MUST STILL BE HOPE – THERE'S SUCH GREAT BEAUTY IN THE WORLD.

AND WHAT ABOUT US? ARE WE TO DIE TOO?

ARE WE GOING TO DIE BECAUSE ALL THE REST ARE STUPID AND GREEDY?

EVERY LIVING BEING, EVERY MAN, WOMAN, CHILD AND ANIMAL WILL DIE.

WE ALONE WILL SURVIVE.

AND SO THEY BEGAN THE GREAT WORK – A MASSIVE BOAT RESTING ON DRY GROUND BENEATH THE BURNING SUN.

IT WAS HIS FAITH THAT MADE H DO THIS. NOAH HAD NO WAY O PREDICTING THE FUTURE. INSTEA HE TOOK GOD SERIOUSLY, EVEN WHEN TOLD TO UNDERTAKE SUCH AN ENORMOUS TASK.

ALL OF WHICH MUST HA SEEMED VERY ODD INDE TO THE PEOPLE NEARBY.

GOD WILL REMAKE THE WORLD, BUT WE HAVE TO TRUST HIM. WE ARE TO BUILD A BOAT – A VERY LARGE BOAT.

BUT FATHER, WE LIVE MILES FROM THE SEA!

NOT FOR MUCH LONGER IT WOULD SEEM!

LOOK OUT! THE TIDE'S COMING IN!

EVERYONE IN THE BOAT BEFORE OLD NOAH GETS HIS BEARD WET!

QUICK, BEFORE IT STARTS RAINING FISH!

FOR THE LAST TIME, LEAVE US ALONE!

IS THAT FIGHTING TALK? I DO HOPE SO. IT WOULD BE MORE ... ENTERTAINING IF YOU WOULD FIGHT INSTEAD OF BUILDING FLOATING FARMYARDS.

BAH! HIS GOD'S WARPED HIS BRAIN. IF HE TOLD HIM TO BALANCE GOATS ON HIS NOSE HE'D DO IT.

EITHER THAT OR TIE PADDLES TO THEIR LEGS!

BUT NOAH DID AS GOD HAD TOLD HIM.

450 FEET LONG, 75 FEET WIDE AND THREE STOREYS HIGH, THE BOAT WAS EVENTUALLY FINISHED.

WATERPROOF AND WITH A LOADING RAMP TO TAKE THE HEAVIEST LIVING CREATURES, IT HAD NO KEEL, NO SAILS NOR RUDDER — THIS WASN'T A SHIP BUILT FOR A VOYAGE OF DISCOVERY.

THIS WAS A LIFEBOAT.

BUT EVEN WITH THE BOAT COMPLETED, THE WORK WAS FAR FROM OVER FOR NOAH AND HIS FAMILY.

THE GATHERING AND STOCKING OF PROVISIONS FOR A LONG STAY WAS A TASK IN ITSELF. ESPECIALLY CONSIDERING THE NEEDS OF THEIR CARGO —

A BREEDING PAIR OF EVERY ANIMAL IN CREATION, ALL TO BE TAKEN INTO THE BOAT, CARED FOR AND FED — EACH WITH ITS OWN DIET AND NEEDS.

ALL OF THEM — TWO BY TWO.

THEY CALLED THE BOAT 'THE ARK', MEANING 'CHEST' OR 'BOX', FOR IT CONTAINED THE FUTURE OF ALL LIFE ON EARTH.

THE ARK FINISHED, THE SKIES BECAME HEAVY AND STRANGE...

IS THIS THE TIME, FATHER?

I THINK SO. ARE THE ANIMALS SECURE IN THEIR STALLS?

YES FATHER.

THEN IT'S BEST WE GO BELOW. WE WILL BE SAFE ENOUGH — GOD WILL SEE TO IT THAT THE DOORS REMAIN SEALED.

SEE? THE RAINS BEGIN. QUICKLY, LET'S GO BELOW.

ON THAT DAY THE RAINS BEGAN.

THE RIVERS BURST THEIR BANKS, AND THE SEAS ROSE.

GOD LOOKED AT THE WORLD AND SAW THAT THE PEOPLE WERE UTTERLY CORRUPT. THEIR HEARTS AND MINDS WERE FULL OF WICKEDNESS, VIOLENCE AND EVIL.

GOD, WHO BREATHED LIFE INTO A STERILE WORLD, REGRETTED MAKING ANY OF THEM.

SO THE WATERS ROSE ABOVE THEIR FIELDS, THEIR CITIES AND THEIR HISTORIES.

THEIR MEMORIES PERISHED WITH THEM, UNTIL THE STAIN OF LIFE WAS WASHED FROM THE EARTH COMPLETELY.

EVEN THE HIGHEST MOUNTAI[N]S WERE COVERED, AND APART F[ROM] THE RAIN THERE WAS SILEN[CE] ON EARTH AGAIN.

BUT GOD REMEMBERED NOAH.

NOAH, AND THOSE WITH HIM IN THE ... WERE SPARED. NOAH HAD THREE ...; THEY AND THEIR FAMILIES WOULD ...INUE THE HUMAN RACE.

AND THE ANIMALS WOULD BREED AGAIN.

THIS WAS GOD'S PLAN, NOT NOAH'S. GOD KNEW THEIR NEEDS AND HOW BEST TO CARE FOR THEM.

AFTER ALL, THEY WERE THE WORK OF THE SAME CREATOR.

RAINS FELL LIKE NO RAIN BEFORE OR SINCE, ...LLOWING CITIES, TOWNS AND MOUNTAINS.

FOR FORTY DAYS —

AND FORTY NIGHTS.

AND THEN, ALMOST AS SUDDENLY AS IT BEGAN —

IT STOPPED.

ABOUT TIME TOO!

IT'S OVER! HAVE ONE OF THE BOYS BRING A RAVEN UP FROM THE CARRION BIRDS SECTION — LET'S SEE IF THE WATERS ARE SHRINKING YET.

THE RAVEN FLEW AROUND THE ARK, BUT IT DID NOT STRAY FAR — MEANING THAT LAND HAD NOT YET APPEARED.

IT WAS LATE IN THE EVENING WHEN IT RETURNED.

IN ITS BEAK IT CARRIED A FRESH OLIV
BRANCH, THE FIRST GREENERY THE
CREW HAD SEEN SINCE THEIR VOYAGE
BEGAN. THE WATERS HAD BEGUN TO RECE

HE WAITED, AND THEN SENT THE BIRD OUT AGAIN.

THEN NOAH RELEASED A DOVE. AT FIRST IT RETURNED AS THERE WAS NOWHERE FOR IT TO REST.

THEIR TIME TOGETHER ON THE ARK WAS ALMOST OVER.

FREE AT LAST THE ANIMALS EXPLODED OUTWARDS IN A DAZZLING BLAZE OF FUR AND FEATHERS. ALL SHAPES AND SIZES, COLOURS AND SOUNDS, THEY SPREAD TO THE FAR CORNERS OF THE WORLD.

NOAH AND HIS FAMILY WORSHIPPED THEIR GOD ON THAT DAY, AND GOD ANSWERED THEM, SAYING:

NEVER AGAIN WILL I CURSE THE EARTH BECAUSE OF WHAT PEOPLE HAVE DONE. AS LONG AS THE WORLD LASTS, THERE WILL BE SPRING AND HARVEST, NIGHT AND DAY, SUMMER AND WINTER, DAY AND NIGHT.

GO: HAVE MANY CHILDREN, AND ALL THE WORLD WILL BE YOURS.

THEN GOD AND NOAH MADE AN AGREEMENT, A FORMAL COVENANT.

NEVER AGAIN WOULD GOD SEND A FLOOD TO DESTROY THE EARTH, AND AS A SIGN HE SET THE RAINBOW IN THE SKY SO THAT ALL LIVING CREATURES COULD SEE GOD'S PROMISE.

NOAH'S SONS AND FAMILIES MOVED OUT INTO THE WORLD WITH GOD'S BLESSING, AND AS THEY MULTIPLIED THEY BUILT CITIES.

THE STORY OF ABRAHAM

CENTURIES HAVE PASSED. THE EARTH HAS BEEN REPEOPLED AND THE FIRST GREAT CIVILIZATIONS ARE ON THE RISE.

ABRAHAM, A WEALTHY SHEPHERD AND DISTANT DESCENDANT OF NOAH, IS LEAVING THE CITY OF UR, HOME TO THE CHALDEAN PEOPLE. TOGETHER WITH HIS WIFE, SARAH, AND HIS SERVANTS, ABRAHAM IS LEAVING A LIFE OF SAFETY AND COMFORT FOR A GREAT JOURNEY INTO THE UNKNOWN.

GOD HAS CALLED HIM, AT THE AGE OF SEVENTY-FIVE, TO START A NEW LIFE IN THE WEST.

I TELL YOU SARAH, I FEEL THIS JOURNEY IS THE START OF SOMETHING WONDERFUL. GOD HAS PROMISED US SO MUCH. HE SAYS WE WILL HAVE A CHILD AND THAT –

A CHILD?! GOD SAID I'LL BEAR A CHILD?

YES. AND THAT CHILD WILL BE THE START OF A GREAT NATION WHICH WILL –

A NATION NOW, IS IT? A MINUTE AGO IT WAS A CHILD, NOW IT'S A WHOLE NATION?

YES. A NATION, AND THROUGH THEM THE WHOLE WORLD WILL BE TOUCHED BY GOD.

FORGETTING ONE THING.

GOD FORGETS NOTHING.

GOD HAS LOOKED AFTER US SO FAR, GOD PROVIDES FOR US ON OUR JOURNEY, AND IF WE'RE TOLD WE'LL HAVE A CHILD, THEN WE WILL.

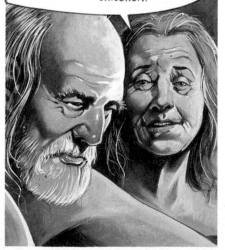

ABRAHAM, IT'S TOO LATE FOR US. YOU'RE AN OLD MAN AND WE'VE BEEN MARRIED FOR YEARS. IF THERE ARE CHILDREN TO BE HAD THEY ARE OTHER PEOPLE'S CHILDREN.

IF I WAS GOING TO HAVE CHILDREN, I'D HAVE HAD THEM BY NOW. BUT YOU CAN STILL HAVE CHILDREN, AS OTHERS DO - JUST SLEEP WITH ONE OF MY SERVANTS. PERHAPS SHE WILL GIVE US CHILDREN.

PEOPLE LAUGH AT US, ABRAHAM.

ABRAHAM WAS AN OLD MAN AND CHILDLESS, YET HE REMEMBERED GOD'S WORDS TO HIM.

YOU PROMISED ME CHILDREN. BUT MY ONLY HEIR IS A STRANGER. LORD GOD, WHAT CAN YOU GIVE ME NOW?

BUT GOD SAID AGAIN:

YOUR HEIR WILL BE YOUR OWN SON, COMING FROM YOUR OWN BODY. LOOK UP AT THE STARS - COUNT THEM IF YOU CAN.

YOU WILL HAVE AS MANY DESCENDANTS AS THERE ARE STARS IN THE SKY.

AND SO ABRAHAM TRUSTED GOD. BUT STILL THEY HAD NO CHILDREN.

SARAH, MEANWHILE, WAS PUSHING HER OWN SOLUTION.

HER SERVANT-GIRL, HAGAR, WAS OF CHILDBEARING AGE. AND SARAH WAS NOW SO DESPERATE FOR A CHILD SHE WAS ALMOST BEYOND CARING HOW SHE CAME BY IT.

IT'S ONE THING FOR GOD TO TELL YOU WE'RE GOING TO HAVE A CHILD, BUT IT'S ANOTHER ACTUALLY HAVING IT. THE ONLY REASON I CAN THINK OF WHY WE HAVEN'T CHILDREN IS BECAUSE GOD IS STOPPING ME FROM HAVING THEM!

SO WHAT DO YOU SUGGEST?

HAGAR.

AND SO ABRAHAM DID WHAT SARAH SAID. HE SLEPT WITH HAGAR, HER SERVANT.

IT WAS SARAH'S IDEA, AFTER ALL.

HAGAR BECAME PREGNANT ALMOST AT ONCE, AND BEGAN TO FEEL SOMEHOW SUPERIOR TO HER MISTRESS, FUELLING POOR SARAH'S FEELINGS OF INADEQUACY.

FRUSTRATED AND JEALOUS, SHE TOOK HER ANGER OUT ON HAGAR, TREATING HER CRUELLY.

BY TAKING MATTERS INTO THEIR OWN HANDS, ABRAHAM AND SARAH HAD INTERFERED WITH GOD'S PLAN.

PREGNANT AND DESPERATELY UNHAPPY, HAGAR RAN AWAY ALONE, OUT INTO THE DESERT.

IT WAS TIME FOR GOD TO INTERVENE...

THE ANGEL OF THE LORD MET HAGAR OUT IN THE DESERT.

HAGAR! THE LORD KNOWS HOW UNHAPPY YOU ARE.

GO BACK TO SARAH. YOU WILL CALL YOUR CHILD 'ISHMAEL': THROUGH HIM YOU WILL HAVE TOO MANY DESCENDANTS TO COUNT. GOD KNOWS. HE CARES. GO BACK.

SO HAGAR RETURNED, TO GIVE BIRTH TO ISHMAEL. AT LAST ABRAHAM HAD A SON OF HIS OWN. COULD THIS HAVE BEEN WHAT GOD MEANT?

ABRAHAM WAS EIGHTY-SIX WHEN ISHMAEL WAS BORN. THE PAIN WAS ALMOST TOO MUCH FOR SARAH TO BEAR.

ONE DAY, AS ABRAHAM SAT RESTING FROM THE MIDDAY SUN, HE SAW THREE FIGURES IN THE DISTANCE, MAKING THEIR WAY TOWARDS HIM.

THE SUN WAS MERCILESSLY HOT, AND IT WAS HARD TO SEE PROPERLY THROUGH THE HEAT-HAZE AT FIRST.

BUT EVEN SO, ABRAHAM COULD TELL THERE WAS SOMETHING *DIFFERENT* ABOUT THESE VISITORS.

WHO ON EARTH'S THIS, WALKING AROUND IN THE SUN LIKE THAT?

SOMETHING -VERY- *STRANGE*..!

MY LORDS! *MY LORDS!* SIRS, PLEASE WAIT!

MY LORD, IF I HAVE EVER PLEASED YOU, FOUND ANY FAVOUR *AT ALL* IN YOUR EYES, PLEASE STAY A WHILE AND EAT WITH US!

LET ME BRING SOME WATER FOR YOU, AND A LITTLE SOMETHING TO EAT, PERHAPS? HMM?

VERY WELL, WE SHALL. THANK YOU.

SARAH! *SARAH!!* WE'VE GOT *VISITORS!*

WHO IS IT?

OH! *IT'S UNBELIEVABLE!* WHY, IT'S...

QUICKLY, MAKE UP SOME *CAKES.* USE ONLY THE *BEST* FLOUR! USE A WHOLE *SACKFUL!*

I THOUGHT WE WERE SAVING THAT FOR A SPECIAL OCCASION!

THIS *IS* A SPECIAL OCCASION! HAVE THE BEST CALF SLAUGHTERED TOO, AND COOKED FOR A FEAST! COOK IT AS IF THIS WERE A *PARTY!*

MY LORDS, PLEASE ALLOW ME TO WAIT ON YOU *MYSELF!*

WHATEVER *HAS* GOT INTO HIM...?

TELL ME, WHERE IS SARAH, YOUR WIFE?

ABRAHAM, THROUGH YOU WILL COME A GREAT NATION. ALL THE PEOPLE ON EARTH WILL BE BLESSED THROUGH THEM.

IN THE TENT, COOKING. WHY?

THIS TIME NEXT YEAR, I WILL COME BACK TO VISIT YOU. I WILL COME BACK TO SEE YOU AND SARAH - AND YOUR SON.

OUR... SON?

OUR SON? NOW? WHEN WE'RE OLD AND WORN OUT? I'M TOO OLD TO GET PREGNANT! AND EVEN IF I WAS STILL ABLE, ABRAHAM IS PAST IT!

HA! IF IT WASN'T SO SAD IT'D BE FUNNY! PREGNANT AT MY AGE!

WHY DO YOU LAUGH, SARAH?

OH! I - I DIDN'T! HONESTLY!

PLEASE DON'T LIE. I HEARD YOU.

TELL ME SARAH, IS ANYTHING TOO DIFFICULT FOR GOD?

AND IT WAS THEN THAT SARAH ALSO KNEW WHO THE STRANGE VISITOR REALLY WAS.

GOD HAD KEPT HIS PROMISE. ALTHOUGH OLD IN THE EYES OF THE WORLD, THROUGH ISAAC, ABRAHAM AND SARAH WOULD HAVE AS MANY DESCENDANTS AS THERE WERE PEBBLES ON THE BEACH, OR STARS IN THE CLEAR NIGHT SKY.

NINE MONTHS LATER, EXACTLY AS THEY WERE TOLD, SARAH GAVE BIRTH TO A SON, WHOM THEY CALLED ISAAC.

28

ISAAC WAS THE ANSWER TO YEARS OF PAINFUL LONGING.

HE WAS THEIR JOY, THEIR LOVE, THEIR FAITH IN GOD REALIZED, AND ALL THEIR DREAMS COME TRUE.

HE WAS ALMOST LIFE ITSELF TO THEM.

GOD WANTED ABRAHAM TO BE THE FATHER OF A PEOPLE THROUGH WHOM THE WORLD WOULD BE BLESSED. BUT FIRST THERE WOULD BE ONE MORE TEST...

AND SO ONE DAY ABRAHAM RECEIVED A MESSAGE FROM GOD. IT WAS THE MOST APPALLING NEWS.

WITH A HEAVY HEART ABRAHAM OBEYED THE MESSAGE, AND SET OFF WITH HIS YOUNG SON.

HE WAS TO TAKE THE BOY TO THE TOP OF A MOUNTAIN, AND SACRIFICE HIM AS A BURNT OFFERING TO GOD.

ABRAHAM HAD WANTED THIS SON SO BADLY, IT WAS AGONY TO LOSE HIM IN SUCH A HORRIFYING WAY.

ISAAC KNEW NOTHING OF ALL THIS. TO HIM THE DAY WAS A GREAT ADVENTURE WITH HIS FATHER.

SEE, FATHER? ALL THAT WOOD I CARRIED WILL BURN WELL! ALL WE NEED NOW IS A LAMB.

HERE. LET ME HELP YOU UP. THERE WE GO. YOU'RE GETTING BIG NOW, I CAN HARDLY LIFT YOU!

FATHER? WE'VE BUILT THE ALTAR, WE'VE GOT THE KNIFE, BUT WHERE'S THE LAMB TO BE SACRIFICED?

GOD WILL PROVIDE IT.

HERE. SIT STILL WHILE I DO THIS.

ABRAHAM! DO NOT HARM THE CHILD!

ABRAHAM STOPPED. IT WAS GOD WHO SAID: 'DO NOTHING TO HARM THE CHILD. NOW I KNOW YOU TRUST ME, FOR YOU DID NOT EVEN WITHHOLD YOUR ONLY SON.'

ABRAHAM LOOKED — AND THERE WAS A RAM CAUGHT IN THE BUSHES BEHIND HIM. HE TOOK THE RAM AND SACRIFICED THAT INSTEAD.

THEN ABRAHAM HEARD GOD'S VOICE AGAIN.

BY MY OWN NAME I SWEAR THAT YOU WILL HAVE YOUR REWARD. BECAUSE YOU KEPT NOTHING BACK FROM ME, I WILL GIVE YOU AS MANY DESCENDANTS AS THERE ARE STARS IN THE SKY.

AS MANY AS THERE ARE GRAINS OF SAND ON THE SEASHORE.

EVERY NATION ON EARTH WILL ASK ME TO BLESS THEM AS I WILL BLESS YOUR DESCENDANTS.

THE STORY OF ISAAC

ISAAC GREW TO BE A MAN. HIS MOTHER DIED.

ISAAC HAD LOVED HER DEARLY AND TOOK HER DEATH HARD. ABRAHAM SET ABOUT CHOOSING HIM A WIFE.

THE LOCAL CANAANITE WOMEN WORSHIPPED OTHER GODS. SO ABRAHAM LOOKED TO THE LAND OF HIS OWN PEOPLE — FAR-OFF MESOPOTAMIA.

HE SENT A SERVANT, EQUIPPED WITH CAMELS AND SUPPLIES FOR THE LONG JOURNEY. RE-TRACING THE ROUTE ABRAHAM HAD TAKEN DECADES BEFORE, THE SERVANT WOULD TRY TO FIND A SUITABLE WIFE.

GIVEN THE ENORMITY OF THE TASK, THE SERVANT DID THE WISEST THING HE COULD: HE PRAYED, ASKING GOD FOR HELP IN FINDING THE RIGHT PERSON.

OUTSIDE THE CITY OF HARAN, THE SERVANT SAT BY THE WELL AND PRAYED AGAIN...

LORD GOD, BE KIND TO MY MASTER, AND HELP ME. AS THE GIRLS COME OUT FROM THE CITY TO DRAW WATER I'LL ASK THEM FOR A DRINK. IF ONE OFFERS WATER FOR MY CAMELS TOO, I'LL KNOW THAT SHE'S YOUR CHOICE, AND THAT —

HELLO?

YOU LOOK THIRSTY. DO YOU WANT ME TO GIVE YOUR CAMELS A DRINK TOO?

THAT WAS QUICK!

THE GIRL WAS EVEN A DISTANT RELATIVE! GOD HAD LED THE SERVANT TO SOMEONE WHO WOULD BE THE PERFECT MATCH FOR ISAAC.

HER NAME WAS REBEKAH, AND SHE WAS VERY BEAUTIFUL.

THE SERVANT MET WITH HER FATHER, BETHUEL, AND HER BROTHER, LABAN. THEY WERE DELIGHTED TO HEAR NEWS OF ABRAHAM, AND OF HOW HE WAS PROSPERING.

GOD HAD CLEARLY BEEN AT WORK IN LEADING THE SERVANT TO THEM. SO THEY GAVE HIM PERMISSION TO ASK REBEKAH IF SHE WOULD GO WITH HIM.

THE FINAL CHOICE WAS HERS.

REBEKAH AGREED TO THE MATCH AND, TAKING HER MAIDS, SET OFF FOR THE LAND OF CANAAN AND A NEW LIFE...

ISAAC WAS OUT IN THE FIELDS EARLY ONE EVENING, WHEN HE SAW CAMELS IN THE DISTANCE. THEY WERE HEADING DIRECTLY FOR HIS CAMP.

REBEKAH SAW ISAAC FROM AFAR, A LONE FIGURE, WALKING TOWARDS THEM THROUGH THE FIELDS.

ISAAC BROUGHT REBEKAH TO THE TENT OF HIS MOTHER, SARAH, AND THERE HE MARRIED HER.

THE PAIN HE FELT AT HIS MOTHER'S DEATH WAS REPLACED BY HIS LOVE FOR REBEKAH.

GOD HAD NOT ONLY FOUND HIM A WIFE, BUT HEALED HIS BROKEN HEART.

IN TIME, REBEKAH GAVE BIRTH TO TWINS, ALTHOUGH THEY WERE AS UNLIKE AS TWO BROTHERS COULD BE.

ESAU WAS THE ELDER. WHEN HE WAS BORN, HIS WHOLE BODY WAS COVERED IN HAIR, ALMOST AS IF HE WERE WEARING ROUGH CLOTHES.

HE BECAME A GREAT HUNTER, A MAN WHO LOVED THE HILLS, FIELDS, AND THE OPEN SKIES. ISAAC, WHO HAD A TASTE FOR WILD GAME, LOVED HIS SON GREATLY.

THE YOUNGER TWIN, JACOB, WAS THE EXACT OPPOSITE. A QUIET MAN WHO ENJOYED THE COMPANY OF OTHERS, HE WAS HIS MOTHER'S FAVOURITE.

GOD HAD TOLD ISAAC THAT THE TWO BOYS WOULD BE THE FATHERS OF TWO NATIONS, AND THAT THE FIRSTBORN WOULD BE SUBJECT TO THE OTHER.

ESAU LIVED ONLY FOR THE MOMENT. A FACT WHICH COST HIM DEAR AS HE GREW OLDER —

WHATEVER IS IT THAT YOU'RE COOKING, JACOB? IT SMELLS WONDERFUL. GIVE ME SOME BEFORE I STARVE TO DEATH!

YOU CAN SMELL FOOD A MILE AWAY.

ONLY WHEN I'M HUNGRY.

LIKE NOW FOR INSTANCE. COME ON, BEFORE IT GOES COLD!

BUT I'VE SPENT ALL DAY MAKING THIS. I KNOW IT'S YOUR FAVOURITE FOOD BUT I CAN'T JUST GIVE IT AWAY.

CAN I?

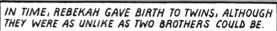

RED STEW, DONE JUST THE WAY YOU LIKE IT AND – OH! IS THAT THUNDER I CAN HEAR?

NO – IT'S YOUR STOMACH RUMBLING, MY MISTAKE.

I'LL TELL YOU WHAT, GIVE ME YOUR BIRTHRIGHT AND WE'LL CALL IT QUITS.

... MY BIRTHRIGHT?

MY, THAT DOES SMELL GOOD!

YES, YOUR BIRTHRIGHT. I MEAN, IT'S NOT AS IF YOU CAN EAT YOUR BIRTHRIGHT, IS IT? IT'S NOT AS IF YOUR BIRTHRIGHT WAS HERE IN FRONT OF YOU, DONE TO PERFECTION.

GOING COLD.

ALL RIGHT, ALL RIGHT! YOU CAN HAVE MY BIRTHRIGHT, JUST GIVE ME SOME STEW!

CERTAINLY. WOULD YOU LIKE SOME BREAD TOO?

HMMPH.

JACOB'S ACTIONS WERE RUTHLESS.

BUT ESAU, IN CARING MORE ABOUT HIS STOMACH THAN HIS RIGHTS AS FIRSTBORN SON, HAD BEHAVED AS IF HIS FAMILY MEANT NO MORE TO HIM THAN A BOWL OF STEW.

JACOB NOW BELIEVED HE HAD A LEGITIMATE CLAIM TO ESAU'S INHERITANCE. THE FIRSTBORN SON WOULD HAVE A GREATER SHARE OF THE WILL, AND THIS WAS NOW JACOB'S.

BUT HIS SCHEMING WAS FAR FROM OVER.

ISAAC WAS AN OLD MAN. BLIND, AND EXPECTING TO DIE SOON, HE CALLED FOR ESAU, HIS FAVOURITE SON.

ISAAC HAD LIVED HIS WHOLE LIFE TRUSTING HIS OWN SENSES. HE RELIED ONLY ON WHAT HE COULD SEE, SMELL, HEAR, TOUCH AND TASTE. ONE BY ONE THESE SENSES BEGAN TO FAIL HIM...

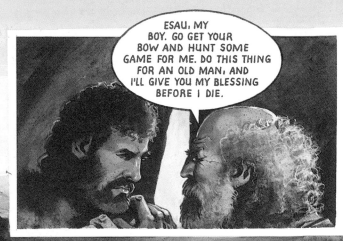

ESAU, MY BOY. GO GET YOUR BOW AND HUNT SOME GAME FOR ME. DO THIS THING FOR AN OLD MAN, AND I'LL GIVE YOU MY BLESSING BEFORE I DIE.

AND SO ESAU WENT AWAY, TO HUNT SOMETHING SPECIAL FOR THE OLD MAN. NO HARM IN THAT — HAD REBEKAH NOT OVERHEARD THEIR CONVERSATION.

WHETHER OR NOT ESAU HAD BEEN RIGHT TO SELL HIS BIRTHRIGHT, WHETHER OR NOT JACOB HAD BEEN RIGHT TO COERCE HIM, THAT SALE WAS LEGALLY BINDING.

WHICH GAVE REBEKAH AN IDEA...

JACOB? COME HERE A MOMENT, PLEASE!

WILL YOU DO AS YOU'RE TOLD? I'VE THOUGHT THIS THROUGH, AND BELIEVE ME, IT'LL WORK. IF ANYTHING GOES WRONG I'LL TAKE THE BLAME.

NOW, DO AS I SAY.

NOW LISTEN TO ME: GO AND SLAUGHTER TWO KID GOATS AND BRING THEM TO ME. WHILE ESAU'S AWAY I'LL MAKE YOUR FATHER HIS FAVOURITE DISH — I KNOW THE SORT OF THING HE LIKES. THEN HE'LL GIVE THE BLESSING TO YOU.

WHY WOULD HE DO THAT?

BECAUSE HE'LL THINK YOU'RE ESAU.

THINK I'M ESAU? MOTHER, EVEN A BLIND MAN COULD TELL THAT I'M NOTHING LIKE MY BROTHER! I DON'T EVEN FEEL THE SAME!

AND SO JACOB DID AS HIS MOTHER TOLD HIM...

WAKE UP FATHER — IT'S ME, ESAU, WITH YOUR STEW. EAT UP, I WANT TO RECEIVE YOUR BLESSING.

ESAU? YOU WERE QUICK! AND WHAT'S WRONG WITH YOUR VOICE? YOU SOUND LIKE JACOB!

REBEKAH HAD MADE JACOB A SUIT OF GOATSKIN. TO A BLIND, DEAF OLD MAN, HE MIGHT JUST PASS AS ESAU.

HMM. COME CLOSER, ERM... ESAU. LET ME TOUCH YOU.

YOU FEEL LIKE HIM, EVEN IF YOUR VOICE IS JACOB'S. ARE YOU REALLY MY SON ESAU?

I AM.

THEN YOU HAVE MY BLESSING.

QUICK? YES, ERM... GOD HELPED ME. HERE, EAT THIS STEW. I CAUGHT THE GAME MYSELF LIKE YOU SAID, SO THAT YOU'D GIVE ME YOUR BLESSING.

MAY GOD GIVE YOU HEAVEN'S DEW, AND PLENTY OF GRAIN AND NEW WINE. MAY NATIONS SERVE YOU AND BOW DOWN BEFORE YOU.

RULE OVER EVERY MEMBER OF THIS FAMILY FOR EVER. MAY THOSE WHO CURSE YOU BE CURSED, AND THOSE WHO BLESS YOU BE BLESSED.

WELL, THAT WASN'T TOO HARD, WAS IT?

GOD HAD TOLD ISAAC THAT HIS FIRSTBORN SON WOULD BE SUBJECT TO THE YOUNGER TWIN. YET ISAAC GAVE ESAU THE BIRTHRIGHT ANYWAY. AND REBEKAH DECEIVED HER HUSBAND.

JACOB HAD HIS FULL INHERITANCE, BUT LIED AND CHEATED TO WIN WHAT HE SAW AS HIS BY RIGHT.

A FACT WHICH WOULD NOT ESCAPE ESAU WHEN HE RETURNED FROM HUNTING...

WAKE UP FATHER. IT'S ME, ESAU. SIT UP AND EAT THIS, THEN YOU CAN GIVE ME YOUR BLESSING.

WHAT DO YOU MEAN? YOU HAVEN'T ALREADY GIVEN ME THE BLESSING. I'VE ONLY JUST GOT HERE!

AFTER THE FIRST CONFUSION, ISAAC AND ESAU SOON PUT TWO AND TWO TOGETHER. BUT IT WAS TOO LATE — ISAAC HAD FORMALLY GIVEN THE FULL INHERITANCE TO JACOB.

JACOB! I'LL KILL HIM!

AND SO ESAU MADE PLANS. ISAAC WOULDN'T LIVE FOR EVER AND SO, AFTER A RESPECTABLE PERIOD OF MOURNING, ESAU WOULD MURDER HIS BROTHER.

JACOB HAD RECEIVED THE BIRTHRIGHT AS GOD INTENDED, BUT THE WHOLE FAMILY HAD LIED AND DECEIVED EACH OTHER IN THE PROCESS.

JACOB, THE QUIET HOME-LOVER, RAN AWAY INTO EXILE THROUGH FEAR OF HIS BROTHER. LEAVING THE CAMPS HE HAD LIVED IN ALL HIS LIFE, HE SET OUT FOR THE HOME OF HIS UNCLE LABAN, REBEKAH'S BROTHER.

HE NEVER SAW HIS BELOVED MOTHER AGAIN.

ALONE IN THE HILLS, JACOB TOOK A ROCK FOR A PILLOW AND LAY DOWN TO SLEEP.

HE WAS NEVER THE OUTDOORS MAN HIS BROTHER WAS, BUT SOON FELL ASLEEP.

WHICH IS WHEN SOMETHING STRANGE HAPPENED.

JACOB DREAMED OF A LADDER, A STAIRWAY REACHING FROM EARTH UP TO HEAVEN, AND ANGELS OF GOD WERE ASCENDING AND DESCENDING.

I AM THE LORD, THE GOD OF ABRAHAM AND ISAAC.

I AM GIVING YOU THIS LAND YOU ARE LYING ON. YOUR DESCENDANTS WILL BE MORE NUMEROUS THAN THE DUST OF THE EARTH, AND THROUGH THEM I WILL BLESS THE WHOLE WORLD.

AND AT THE VERY TOP OF THE STAIRWAY, STOOD GOD.

AND GOD LOOKED AT JACOB. AND GOD SPOKE.

I AM WITH YOU, WATCHING OVER YOU WHEREVER YOU GO, AND I WILL BRING YOU BACK TO THIS PLACE ONE DAY. I WILL NOT LEAVE YOU UNTIL I HAVE DONE WHAT I HAVE PROMISED.

I AM WITH YOU, JACOB.

THEN JACOB AWOKE, AND WAS AFRAID —

I HAVE SLEPT AT THE GATES OF HEAVEN! GOD IS HERE AND I DIDN'T KNOW IT!

IF GOD WILL BE WITH ME AND WATCH OVER ME, IF GOD WILL CLOTHE ME AND FEED ME, THEN THE LORD WILL BE MY GOD TOO.

GOD HAD GIVEN JACOB THE SAME PROMISE GIVEN TO ABRAHAM AND ISAAC EVEN THOUGH HE'D DONE NOTHING TO DESERVE IT.

JACOB NAMED THE PLACE BETHEL, WHICH MEANS 'HOUSE OF GOD', THEN CONTINUED ON HIS JOURNEY TOWARDS THE COUNTRY OF HIS MOTHER.

AS JACOB APPROACHED THE CITY OF HARAN, HE MET SOME SHEPHERDS IN OUTLYING FIELDS.

HELLO, I'M (UMPH!) JACOB, THE SON OF REBEKAH, YOUR FATHER'S SISTER.

HEAVY THIS, ISN'T IT ?

I'M LOOKING FOR A MAN CALLED LABAN. DO YOU KNOW HIM ?

LABAN? LOOK, HERE COMES HIS DAUGHTER RACHEL TO WATER THE SHEEP. YOU CAN ASK HER YOURSELF. WE'RE JUST WAITING TO ROLL THE STONE AWAY FROM THE WELL SO THE SHEEP CAN DRINK.

ALLOW ME.

I THINK YOU'D BETTER COME AND MEET MY FATHER.

AND SO AT LAST JACOB WAS TAKEN TO THE HOUSE OF HIS UNCLE, LABAN.

MY BOY! MY OWN FLESH AND BLOOD! WELCOME !

AND IT WAS HERE THAT JACOB'S TROUBLES REALLY BEGAN. JACOB, THE TRICKSTER, WAS ABOUT TO BE OUTDONE...

JACOB WAS IN LOVE WITH RACHEL RIGHT FROM THE START. WHEN LABAN ASKED WHAT WAGES HE WOULD WANT FOR WORKING FOR HIM, JACOB OFFERED SEVEN YEARS' LABOUR IN RETURN FOR HER HAND IN MARRIAGE.

THIS WAS AN OFFER TOO GOOD FOR LABAN TO TURN DOWN.

HOWEVER... RACHEL HAD AN OLDER SISTER, NAMED LEAH, AND BY ALL ACCOUNTS SHE WASN'T QUITE THE BEAUTY RACHEL WAS.

FINDING A HUSBAND FOR RACHEL HAD BEEN EASY, AND LABAN HAD DONE VERY WELL OUT OF THE ARRANGEMENT, BUT THINGS WOULDN'T BE SO EASY ONCE JACOB'S SEVEN-YEAR CONTRACT WAS UP.

AND SO JACOB SERVED SEVEN YEARS FOR RACHEL, BUT THE YEARS SEEMED NO MORE THAN DAYS, SO GREAT WAS HIS LOVE FOR HER.

IF JACOB WAS A SCHEMER, HE'D MET HIS MATCH IN LABAN.

ANYWAY, THE SEVEN YEARS WERE UP, THE WEDDING BETWEEN RACHEL AND JACOB CAME AROUND, AND THERE WAS MUCH CELEBRATING AND FEASTING.

AND POSSIBLY DRINKING.

THE BRIDE LOOKED BEAUTIFUL IN HER WEDDING DRESS.

IN HER VEIL.

AT THE END OF THE EVENING, LABAN GAVE HIS DAUGHTER IN MARRIAGE TO JACOB AND WATCHED AS THEY WENT OFF TO BED.

IT WAS DARK.

SHE WORE A VEIL.

WHATEVER THE REASON, IT WASN'T UNTIL MORNING LIGHT THAT JACOB LOOKED AT HIS WIFE, AND SAID —

LEAH?! WHAT ARE YOU DOING HERE?!

I'M YOUR WIFE.

YOU MOST CERTAINLY ARE NOT!

I AM NOW.

LABAN! WHAT HAVE YOU DONE TO ME?! I WORK SEVEN YEARS FOR YOU, AND YOU MARRY ME TO THE WRONG DAUGHTER!

YOU MEAN LEAH? WHAT'S SO TERRIBLE ABOUT THAT?

THERE'S REALLY NO NEED TO GET UPSET LIKE THIS.

YOU HAVE TO MARRY THE ELDER SISTER BEFORE YOU CAN MARRY THE YOUNGER ONE. I THOUGHT EVERYONE KNEW THAT. IT'S THE TRADITION.

WELL, I'VE NEVER HEARD OF IT.

THERE YOU ARE THEN. NOW YOU'VE MARRIED LEAH, ALL YOU HAVE TO DO IS WAIT A WEEK AND THEN, IF YOU WANT, YOU CAN MARRY RACHEL.

OF COURSE, THAT WILL COST ANOTHER SEVEN YEARS' WORK.

AND SO JACOB SERVED ANOTHER SEVEN YEARS, ALTHOUGH THERE'S NO MENTION OF THEM SEEMING LIKE DAYS THIS TIME.

MARRIED TO TWO SISTERS, JACOB'S FAMILY LIFE PROVED FAR FROM IDYLLIC...

JACOB, WE'VE BEEN MARRIED FOR AGES AND I'M STILL NOT PREGNANT. GIVE ME CHILDREN, OR I'LL DIE!

WELL, IT'S NOT MY FAULT! I MEAN, LEAH HAS HAD PLENTY AND —

HER AGAIN! FORGET HER, IT'S NOT HER I'M INTERESTED IN!

IF YOU CAN'T GIVE ME CHILDREN, YOU'LL HAVE TO SLEEP WITH MY MAIDSERVANT. PERHAPS I CAN BUILD A FAMILY THROUGH HER.

SO JACOB DID AS RACHEL ASKED, AND SOON THE MAIDSERVANT BECAME PREGNANT.

OF COURSE, ONCE HE HAD SLEPT WITH RACHEL'S MAIDSERVANT, LEAH INSISTED HE SLEEP WITH HERS TOO, AND SOON SHE BECAME PREGNANT AS WELL.

THE TWO SISTERS ARGUED CONSTANTLY, WHILE JACOB'S FAMILY GREW AND GREW.

AT LAST RACHEL CONCEIVED, AND GAVE BIRTH TO A SON.

JACOB LOVED RACHEL MUCH MORE THAN LEAH, AND AT LAST SHE HAD GIVEN HIM A SON. HE LOVED THAT SON MORE THAN ALL HIS OTHER CHILDREN.

THEY CALLED THE CHILD JOSEPH.

AS IF JACOB DIDN'T HAVE ENOUGH TROUBLE AT HOME, HIS FATHER-IN-LAW, LABAN, BEGAN TO TAKE ADVANTAGE OF JACOB'S SUCCESS AS A FARMER.

YOUR FATHER'S ATTITUDE TOWARDS ME IS CHANGING. I'VE WORKED AS HARD AS I CAN, YET HE'S CHANGED MY WAGES FOR THE TENTH TIME.

GOD HAS MADE US PROSPER AND KEPT US FROM HARM. NOW HE SAYS WE SHOULD LEAVE THIS PLACE.

OUR OWN FATHER TREATS US AS IF WE WERE FOREIGNERS. HE SOLD US TO YOU, AND THEN SPENT ALL THE MONEY. WHATEVER PROFITS WE MAKE BELONG TO US NOW, NOT HIM.

DO WHATEVER GOD TELLS YOU.

AND SO JACOB PUT HIS WIVES AND CHILDREN ON CAMELS AND, DRIVING HIS FLOCKS AND HERDS BEFORE HIM, SET OFF HOME, BACK TO THE LAND OF CANAAN.

FOR THE SECOND TIME IN HIS LIFE JACOB WAS RUNNING AWAY. WHEN JACOB FIRST CAME THIS WAY, HE WAS ALONE, FLEEING FROM HIS BROTHER. NOW HE WAS RETURNING AS THE HEAD OF A LARGE FAMILY.

OF COURSE, JACOB COULDN'T JUST TAKE ALL THIS OUT FROM UNDER LABAN'S NOSE WITHOUT HIM NOTICING AND, AS THEY CAMPED IN THE HILL COUNTRY OF GILEAD, LABAN AND HIS MEN FINALLY CAUGHT UP WITH THEM.

THEY HAD BEEN TRACKING THEM FOR A WHOLE WEEK.

HOWEVER, THE NIGHT BEFORE, LABAN HAD BEEN TROUBLED BY A STRANGE DREAM, IN WHICH GOD WARNED HIM NOT TO THREATEN JACOB.

DESPITE HIS ANGER, IT WAS THEREFORE WITH SOME CAUTION THAT LABAN APPROACHED JACOB.

JUST WHAT IS GOING ON HERE?

YOU'VE CARRIED OFF MY DAUGHTERS LIKE HOSTAGES, YOU'VE TAKEN MY FLOCKS, YOU'VE EVEN TAKEN MY GRANDCHILDREN WITHOUT LETTING ME SAY GOODBYE TO THEM!

BELIEVE ME, JACOB, I COULD DO YOU GREAT HARM IF I CHOSE TO.

LABAN AND JACOB BUILT A PILLAR FROM STONES, AND MADE A FORMAL AGREEMENT THERE AND THEN. LABAN MADE JACOB PROMISE TO TREAT HIS DAUGHTERS WELL, AND TO TAKE NO OTHER WIVES.

LABAN WOULD NOT PASS BEYOND THE PILLAR TO HARM JACOB AND JACOB WOULD NOT PASS BEYOND THE PILLAR TO HARM LABAN, AS GOD WAS THEIR WITNESS.

WHEN JACOB FIRST CROSSED THE RIVER JORDAN, HE WAS RUNNING FROM HIS BROTHER, ESAU, AND OWNED NOTHING BUT THE STAFF HE LEANED ON. NOW, RETURNING HOME, HE HAD WIVES, CHILDREN, FLOCKS AND SERVANTS TO CARE FOR.

JACOB WAS SCARED OF TROUBLE AHEAD. EVERY STEP THEY TOOK TOWARDS CANAAN BROUGHT THEM CLOSER TO THE LANDS BELONGING TO ESAU.

ADVANCE SCOUTS AHEAD OF THEM REPORTED THAT ESAU HAD HEARD OF JACOB'S RETURN AND WAS RIDING TOWARDS THEM WITH 400 MEN.

THERE WAS UNFINISHED BUSINESS BETWEEN THE TWO BROTHERS, AND ESAU'S DEATH THREATS STILL HUNG HEAVY IN THE AIR.

JACOB FEARED THE WORST.

SPLITTING HIS PEOPLE INTO GROUPS, EACH LADEN WITH GIFTS FOR ESAU, HE SENT THEM ON AHEAD OF HIM. IN THIS WAY HE HOPED TO PACIFY HIS BROTHER, OR AT THE VERY LEAST GIVE THEM A BETTER CHANCE OF SURVIVAL SHOULD ESAU ATTACK.

HIS HERDS AND SERVANTS SENT ON, JACOB THEN SENT HIS WIVES, MAIDSERVANTS AND ALL ELEVEN SONS OVER THE RIVER.

AND SO HE WAS ALONE ONCE MORE.

JACOB HAD PRAYED TO THE GOD OF HIS FATHERS TO SAVE HIM FROM HIS BROTHER'S VENGEANCE.

THEN, AS NOW, JACOB HAD BEEN ALONE AND SCARED, TERRIFIED OF HIS BROTHER AND FEARING FOR HIS LIFE. BUT GOD HAD NOT FORGOTTEN JACOB, NOR THE PROMISES MADE ALL THOSE YEARS BEFORE.

AND NOW, AS BEFORE, GOD SPOKE TO JACOB...

A MAN CAME TO HIM IN THE NIGHT, AND THEY FOUGHT UNTIL DAYBREAK.

ALL HIS LIFE JACOB HAD STRUGGLED AGAINST GOD. NOW THAT STRUGGLE TOOK ON A NEW, LITERAL MEANING.

THEY FOUGHT ALL THROUGH THE NIGHT, NEITHER GAINING ANY GROUND.

WHEN THE MAN REALIZED THAT HE COULD NOT OVERCOME JACOB, HE TOUCHED THE SOCKET OF JACOB'S HIP. JACOB'S HIP WAS WRENCHED, BUT STILL HE FOUGHT ON.

LET ME GO! IT'S NEARLY DAYBREAK!

I WON'T LET GO OF YOU UNTIL YOU BLESS ME!

THEN TELL ME YOUR NAME.

JACOB. MY NAME IS JACOB.

THEN YOU ARE JACOB NO LONGER. FROM NOW ON YOUR NAME WILL BE 'ISRAEL'.

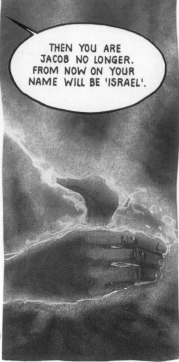

AND WITH THAT THE MAN WAS GONE. JACOB REALIZED THAT HE HAD SEEN GOD FACE TO FACE AND YET LIVED.

AND SO HE WAS CALLED 'ISRAEL' - THE HEBREW WORD MEANS 'HE STRUGGLES WITH GOD'.

FOR THE REST OF HIS LIFE, JACOB WALKED WITH A LIMP FROM THE WRESTLER'S TOUCH. BUT NOW HE NO LONGER PRAYED TO 'THE GOD OF MY FATHERS'. NOW HE PRAYED TO 'THE GOD OF ISRAEL'; GOD HAD BECOME HIS GOD.

OF COURSE, THERE WAS STILL THE MATTER OF ESAU TO ATTEND TO...

WEAK FROM HIS STRUGGLE AND LEANING HEAVILY ON HIS STAFF, JACOB FELT HIS HEART SINK WHEN HE SAW THAT AT LONG LAST HIS BROTHER HAD CAUGHT UP WITH HIM.

AFTER EVERYTHING HE HAD BEEN THROUGH, TO DIE NOW! JACOB HADN'T ESCAPED DEATH FROM THE HANDS OF HIS BROTHER, HE'D MERELY DELAYED IT.

AS ESAU RAN TOWARDS HIM, JACOB BOWED DOWN TO THE GROUND BEFORE HIM.

I SAW A FAMILY ON THE ROAD AHEAD OF ME. WHO ARE THEY?

THEY ARE THE CHILDREN GOD HAS GIVEN ME, YOUR SERVANT.

I SAW FLOCKS AND HERDS DRIVEN AHEAD OF THEM. WHAT ARE THEY DOING HERE?

THEY ARE A GIFT, MY LORD, FROM YOUR SERVANT. PLEASE - TAKE THEM.

JACOB, I ALREADY HAVE EVERYTHING I NEED. KEEP WHAT YOU HAVE. I HAVE MORE THAN ENOUGH.

NO! PLEASE TAKE THEM! SEEING YOU LIKE THIS IS LIKE SEEING THE FACE OF GOD. IF I HAVE FOUND ANY FAVOUR IN YOUR EYES, PLEASE ACCEPT THEM.

AND SO, BECAUSE JACOB HAD INSISTED, ESAU ACCEPTED, AND THEIR RECONCILIATION WAS COMPLETE. JACOB HAD DONE NOTHING TO DESERVE SUCH FORGIVENESS, AND YET HIS BROTHER OFFERED IT ANYWAY.

WHERE JACOB HAD EXPECTED VIOLENCE, ESAU HAD EMBRACED HIM AND WEPT WITH JOY AT HIS RETURN. HAPPY TO HAVE HIS BROTHER BACK ALIVE, ESAU SET OFF ONCE MORE.

WHY NOT COME WITH ME NOW?

I HAVE SHEEP AND COWS TO THINK OF, MANY OF THEM WITH YOUNG. WE'LL FOLLOW YOU AT OUR OWN PACE. ALL I WANT NOW IS FOR THINGS TO BE RIGHT BETWEEN US.

AND SO JACOB WAS HOME AT LAST.

HE BOUGHT FIELDS IN THE LAND OF CANAAN, AND THERE HE BUILT AN ALTAR TO THE GOD OF ISRAEL — **HIS** GOD.

ALTHOUGH SAFE IN THE LAND OF CANAAN, JACOB'S FAMILY LIFE WAS NO MORE PEACEFUL THAN IT HAD BEEN BEFORE. SINCE HE HAD CHILDREN BY FOUR WOMEN, TWO OF WHOM WERE SISTERS, HOW COULD IT BE?

RACHEL, JACOB'S BELOVED WIFE, DIED GIVING BIRTH TO A SECOND SON, CALLED BENJAMIN.

RACHEL WAS BURIED ON THE ROAD TO BETHLEHEM, AND OVER HER TOMB JACOB SET A PILLAR.

BENJAMIN WAS THE LAST OF JACOB'S CHILDREN.

GOD HAD GIVEN JACOB MANY SONS, YET JACOB WAS BLIND TO THEIR FEELINGS AND OPENLY FAVOURED JOSEPH ABOVE THE REST. HE HAD BEEN BORN TO HIM LATE IN LIFE, AND WAS RACHEL'S FIRST SON.

AS A SIGN OF AFFECTION, JACOB GAVE JOSEPH A COAT, RICHLY DECORATED WITH MANY COLOURS.

HIS BROTHERS BECAME INCREASINGLY WORRIED. DID THIS MEAN THAT JACOB INTENDED TO GIVE EVERYTHING TO JOSEPH, WHEN IT WAS THEY WHO HAD DONE ALL THE HARD WORK?

AS IF THIS WEREN'T BAD ENOUGH, JOSEPH STARTED HAVING STRANGE DREAMS...

THE STORY OF JOSEPH

LAST NIGHT I HAD THE MOST INCREDIBLE DREAM. IT WAS SO VIVID, IT SEEMED REAL.

WE WERE OUT IN THE FIELDS GATHERING CORN, WHEN SUDDENLY YOUR SHEAVES OF CORN ALL BOWED DOWN TO MINE.

I DREAMED THAT THE SUN, THE MOON AND ELEVEN STARS WERE ALL BOWING DOWN TO ME. WHAT DO YOU THINK IT MEANS?

WHAT KIND OF A DREAM IS THAT, JOSEPH? DO YOU THINK YOUR MOTHER AND I AND ALL YOUR BROTHERS ARE GOING TO COME AND BOW DOWN TO YOU?

I THINK IT BEST IF WE ALL JUST FORGET ABOUT THESE DREAMS.

BUT JACOB DID NOT FORGET.

AND NEITHER DID JOSEPH'S BROTHERS.

AS A FAMILY OF SHEPHERDS, MUCH OF THEIR TIME WAS SPENT AWAY IN THE HILLS, TENDING THE SHEEP.

SENT BY JACOB TO SEE HOW HIS BROTHERS WERE, JOSEPH FOUND THEM AT LAST. THEY WERE WAITING FOR HIM.

ALL OF THEM.

HERE COMES LITTLE DREAMER BOY NOW.

LET'S DO IT LIKE WE AGREED. ONCE HE'S DEAD WE'LL DROP THE BODY DOWN A WELL AND SAY WILD ANIMALS MUST HAVE TAKEN HIM.

LET'S DO IT.

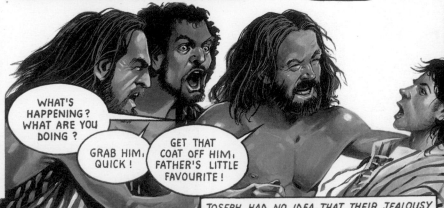

WHAT'S HAPPENING? WHAT ARE YOU DOING?

GRAB HIM, QUICK!

GET THAT COAT OFF HIM, FATHER'S LITTLE FAVOURITE!

JOSEPH HAD NO IDEA THAT THEIR JEALOUSY STRETCHED AS FAR AS MURDER.

WAIT! WE CAN'T KILL HIM, HE'S STILL OUR BROTHER!

REUBEN, WE ALL AGREED!

IT'S TOO LATE TO TURN BACK NOW!

THEN LET'S JUST THROW HIM DOWN THIS DRY WELL. IF THE FALL KILLS HIM, IT WON'T HAVE BEEN US.

REUBEN COULDN'T BRING HIMSELF TO KILL JOSEPH. HE SECRETLY PLANNED TO COME BACK LATER AND RESCUE HIM.

STRIPPED OF THE HATED COAT, JOSEPH WAS FLUNG INTO THE WELL.

MERCIFULLY THE FALL WAS NOT GREAT ENOUGH TO KILL HIM.

ALL ALONE, AND TERRIFIED BY HIS BROTHERS' BRUTALITY, JOSEPH SAT IN THE DARKNESS LISTENING TO THE SOUNDS OF HIS BROTHERS EATING AND ARGUING ABOVE HIM.

SOON THE SOUNDS GAVE WAY TO VOICES HE DIDN'T RECOGNIZE—STRANGERS WITH THICK FOREIGN ACCENTS.

WE'VE DECIDED WE'D GAIN NOTHING FROM YOUR DEATH. YOU ARE OUR OWN BROTHER, AFTER ALL.

WE'RE GOING TO SELL YOU TO THESE TRADERS INSTEAD.

AND SO JOSEPH WAS SOLD FOR TWENTY SHEKELS. LIKE A HORSE, LIKE A CAMEL, LIKE A SACK OF GRAIN. HE WAS THEIR OWN BROTHER, AFTER ALL.

THE BROTHERS SPLIT THE MONEY BETWEEN THEM, AND WATCHED THE CARAVAN DEPART. JOSEPH WAS OUT OF THEIR LIFE NOW AND WOULD TROUBLE THEM NO MORE.

NONE OF THEM COULD HAVE KNOWN THEN THAT THEIR PATHS WOULD CROSS AGAIN, AND IN THE MOST INCREDIBLE CIRCUMSTANCES...

JOSEPH WAS TAKEN TO EGYPT AND SOLD TO A HIGH-RANKING OFFICIAL IN THE COURT OF THE PHARAOH – A MAN NAMED POTIPHAR.

POTIPHAR WAS QUICK TO REALIZE THAT THERE WAS SOMETHING SPECIAL ABOUT HIS NEW SLAVE. GOD WAS WITH JOSEPH AND HELPED HIM TO EXCEL AT EVERYTHING HE DID.

POTIPHAR WAS NO FOOL. HE KNEW A GOOD THING WHEN HE SAW IT! SOON HE ENTRUSTED THE RUNNING OF HIS WHOLE ESTATE TO JOSEPH.

THE MORE RESPONSIBILITY HE WAS GIVEN, THE BETTER HE DID. GOD BLESSED JOSEPH WITH A GREAT MANY GIFTS...

... INCLUDING HIS GOOD LOOKS – A FACT WHICH DIDN'T ESCAPE POTIPHAR'S WIFE.

JOSEPH, NO ONE IN THE ENTIRE HOUSEHOLD IS AS HIGHLY THOUGHT OF AS YOU. MY HUSBAND WITHHOLDS NOTHING FROM YOU.

EXCEPT **ME**, OF COURSE. COME TO BED WITH ME.

HOW CAN YOU SAY THAT ?! MY MASTER TRUSTS ME WITH EVERYTHING. IT WOULD BE A SIN AGAINST GOD TO REPAY HIM LIKE THIS !

REMEMBER YOU ARE STILL A SLAVE. YOU CAN'T AVOID ME FOR EVER, JOSEPH. I WANT YOU, AND I SHALL HAVE YOU.

I DON'T KNOW HOW YOU CAN EVEN SAY SUCH THINGS.

OH, I GIVE UP! THIS HEBREW HAS BEEN SENT TO MAKE FUN OF ME! HAVE IT YOUR WAY!

POTIPHAR, I WAS ALONE IN THE HOUSE AND YOUR SERVANT TRIED TO RAPE ME! I SCREAMED AND HE RAN AWAY! LOOK, HE LEFT HIS CLOAK BEHIND !

OF COURSE, NO ONE WOULD BELIEVE THE WORD OF A SLAVE AGAINST THAT OF AN OFFICIAL'S WIFE. IN A RAGE, POTIPHAR HAD JOSEPH THROWN IN JAIL.

JOSEPH WAS SCARED, ALONE, AND IN THE DARK ONCE MORE.

HEY, JOSEPH! WE'VE SOME COMPANY FOR YOU!

BUT I'M *INNOCENT*! THERE'S BEEN A TERRIBLE *MISTAKE*!

THAT'S WHAT THEY *ALL* SAY! YOU'LL LIKE THESE TWO, JOSEPH! FORMER KING'S OFFICIALS, LIKE YOU!

WELL, WE'RE STUCK HERE TOGETHER, WE MAY AS WELL *TRY* TO GET ALONG.

WHAT'S THE POINT? I'M HAUNTED BY *DREAMS*. I CAN'T GET THEM OUT OF MY *HEAD*.

ME TOO. THE SAME DREAM EVERY NIGHT, AND THERE'S NO ONE HERE TO INTERPRET THEM FOR US.

INTERPRETATIONS BELONG TO *GOD*. IT WAS DREAMS THAT GOT ME IN TROUBLE IN THE FIRST PLACE; BUT SEEING AS WE'RE ALREADY *IN* TROUBLE, WHY DON'T YOU TELL ME ABOUT THEM?

I USED TO BE THE PHARAOH'S *CUPBEARER*, BEFORE I OFFENDED HIM. IN MY DREAM I SAW THREE GRAPEVINES. I SQUEEZED THE GRAPES INTO MY MASTER'S CUP, AND GAVE IT TO HIM. I DON'T KNOW WHAT IT MEANS, AND THE WORRY IS MAKING ME SICK.

I HAD A DREAM TOO. I WAS THE PHARAOH'S MASTER *BAKER*, BEFORE I OFFENDED HIM. I DREAMT I HAD THREE BREADBASKETS. ONE WAS FULL OF BREAD FOR THE PHARAOH, BUT BIRDS CAME AND ATE *EVERYTHING*.

THE THREE *GRAPEVINES* REPRESENT THREE *DAYS*. IN THREE DAYS' TIME THE PHARAOH WILL RESTORE YOU TO YOUR POSITION, AND YOU WILL CARRY HIS CUP AS BEFORE.

THE THREE BASKETS *ALSO* REPRESENT THREE DAYS. THREE DAYS FROM NOW THE PHARAOH WILL HAVE YOUR SENTENCE CHANGED FROM LIFE IMPRISONMENT TO *DEATH*.

THE THIRD DAY WAS THE PHARAOH'S BIRTHDAY, AND HE GAVE A GREAT FEAST FOR ALL HIS OFFICIALS. HE PARDONED THE CUPBEARER AND RESTORED HIM TO HIS FORMER OFFICE: BUT THE BAKER HE HAD *HANGED*.

THE CUPBEARER DIDN'T GIVE JOSEPH A SECOND THOUGHT...

UNTIL SOME YEARS LATER...

GOD HAD BEEN AT WORK IN EGYPT. WHILE JOSEPH WAS IN PRISON, EVENTS HAD TAKEN PLACE THAT WOULD NOT ONLY CHANGE JOSEPH'S FUTURE, BUT HIS PEOPLE'S, AND THROUGH THEM, THE *WORLD*...

JOSEPH! ON YOUR FEET, MAN, *QUICKLY*!

ARE YOU MY *EXECUTIONER*?

HARDLY. YOU'LL NEED A SHAVE AND A CLEAN CHANGE OF CLOTHES. WE'RE TAKING YOU TO SEE THE *PHARAOH*!

AND SO THE SON OF JACOB CAME FACE TO FACE WITH THE MOST POWERFUL MAN ON EARTH — THE *PHARAOH!*

MY CUPBEARER HAS CONFESSED THAT HE HAS DONE YOU A GREAT *DISSERVICE*, HEBREW. YOU SHOWED HIM A KINDNESS, AND YET HE SOON *FORGOT* YOU. HE HAS SINCE BEEN *REMINDED* OF HIS SHORTCOMINGS. I AM TOLD YOU CAN INTERPRET *DREAMS*, JOSEPH. IS THIS *TRUE*?

NO, YOUR MAJESTY. IT IS *NOT*.

BUT GOD WILL GIVE PHARAOH THE ANSWER HE DESIRES.

YOUR *GOD*? VERY WELL.

I DREAMT I STOOD ON THE BANKS OF THE RIVER *NILE*, WHEN SEVEN COWS, SLEEK AND FATTENED, EMERGED FROM THE WATERS TO GRAZE AMONG THE REEDS.

BUT THE SEVEN FAT COWS WERE PURSUED BY SEVEN THIN COWS. UGLY, WASTED AND ULCEROUS, THEY ATE THE SEVEN FATTENED COWS, BUT LOOKED NO BETTER FOR IT. THEY LOOKED AS *DISEASED* AS THEY HAD BEFORE.

I DREAMT OF SEVEN HEALTHY EARS OF CORN, WITHERED AND STRANGLED BY SEVEN BLIGHTED EARS OF CORN, SCORCHED BY THE WIND.

I AM TROUBLED, JOSEPH. I HAVE CONSULTED THE MAGICIANS AND WISE MEN, BUT THEY HAVE BEEN NO HELP TO ME. TELL ME, WHAT DOES THIS MEAN?

FAMINE IS ON THE WAY. EGYPT WILL **DIE** UNLESS YOU ACT QUICKLY. THE COWS AND CORN MEAN THE SAME THING. SEVEN YEARS OF ABUNDANT HARVESTS WILL COME, BUT THEY WILL BE FOLLOWED BY SEVEN YEARS OF DROUGHT, PESTILENCE AND BLIGHT. THE FAMINE THAT FOLLOWS WILL **DESTROY** EGYPT!

FIND A MAN YOU CAN **TRUST** AND PUT HIM IN CHARGE OF ALL EGYPT. LET HIM GATHER **GRAIN**, AND STOCKPILE FOOD. APPOINT COMMISSIONERS TO TAKE A FIFTH OF EVERYTHING THAT GROWS, AND **SAVE** IT FOR THE BAD YEARS TO COME.

AND I HAVE **FOUND** HIM! GOD HAS SHOWN YOU ALL THIS, AND SO I APPOINT **YOU**, JOSEPH. I AM PHARAOH, BUT I COMMAND THAT IN ALL EGYPT NO ONE WILL SO MUCH AS LIFT A HAND WITHOUT **YOUR** PERMISSION!

JOSEPH WAS THIRTY YEARS OLD WHEN HE ENTERED PHARAOH'S SERVICE. HE WAS GIVEN THE ROYAL CHARIOT TO RIDE IN, AND EVERYWHERE HE WENT, PEOPLE BOWED BEFORE HIM.

JOSEPH WORKED TIRELESSLY THROUGHOUT THE SEVEN YEARS, GATHERING AND STORING GRAIN. HE BUILT MASSIVE STOREHOUSES IN EACH OF THE MAJOR CITIES, AND SAW THAT THEY WERE FILLED BEYOND CAPACITY.

BUT EVEN SO, IT WOULD ONLY JUST BE ENOUGH.

BUT EGYPT SURVIVED.

AT LONG LAST JOSEPH OPENED THE STOREHOUSES, AND PEOPLE CAME FROM ALL EGYPT TO BUY GRAIN FROM PHARAOH'S RESERVES.

THE FAMINE SPREAD BEYOND THE BORDERS OF EGYPT, AND SOON VISITORS WERE ARRIVING FROM NEIGHBOURING COUNTRIES TO BUY FOOD. ONE DAY SOME PEOPLE ARRIVED WHO JOSEPH HAD NEVER EXPECTED TO SEE AGAIN AS LONG AS HE LIVED...

SEVEN YEARS, TO THE DAY, THE DROUGHT CAME. THE RIVER DRIED UP AND THE CROPS FAILED. THE ANIMALS STARVED AND DIED IN THE BLISTERING HEAT.

THE LAND GAVE UP ON LIFE.

HERE, TAKE THIS. I NEED TO SPEAK TO THESE **FOREIGNERS**.

YES SIR.

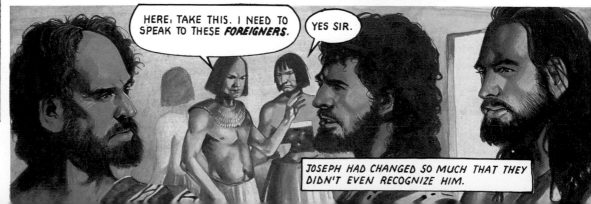

JOSEPH HAD CHANGED SO MUCH THAT THEY DIDN'T EVEN RECOGNIZE HIM.

YOU THERE! WE'RE ON THE LOOKOUT FOR ENEMY *SPIES!* *IDENTIFY* YOURSELVES AT ONCE!

WE COME FROM THE LAND OF *CANAAN,* SIR. ALL BROTHERS OF THE SAME FATHER. HONEST MEN, COME TO BUY FOOD. PLEASE, OUR PEOPLE ARE *STARVING!*

WHY SO MANY OF YOU THEN?

THERE WERE *TWELVE* OF US, BUT ONE DIED. THE YOUNGEST IS STILL WITH HIS FATHER.

THEN *PROVE* YOUR INNOCENCE! ONE OF YOU MUST REMAIN HERE AS *PRISONER,* THE REST OF YOU RETURN AND *BRING* ME YOUR YOUNGEST BROTHER AS A TOKEN OF TRUST.

I *TOLD* YOU THIS WOULD HAPPEN! GOD IS PUNISHING US FOR WHAT WE DID TO *JOSEPH!*

AND SO JOSEPH KEPT SIMEON AS PRISONER, BUT IT CAUSED HIM SO MUCH PAIN THAT HE COULD NOT LOOK THE BROTHERS IN THE FACE FOR FEAR OF THEM SEEING HIS TEARS.

SO YOU CAME BACK TO RESCUE YOUR BROTHER?

WE HAVE LOST ONE BROTHER ALREADY. IF WE WERE TO LOSE ANOTHER IT WOULD BREAK OUR FATHER'S HEART.

AND THIS IS THE YOUNGEST?

IT IS, SIR. HIS NAME IS *BENJAMIN.*

I SEE. WELL, I'M SORRY FOR MY EARLIER HARSHNESS, I WAS OBVIOUSLY WRONG ABOUT YOU.

THIS BOY IS THE SPY! HE STAYS WITH ME!

NO!
PLEASE MY
LORD, WE'VE DONE
ALL THAT YOU
ASKED!

PLEASE,
IF YOU HAVE
ANY PITY AT ALL,
TAKE ME
INSTEAD!

OUR FATHER LOVED HIS WIFE RACHEL
SO VERY MUCH, AND SHE BORE HIM
TWO SONS. THE FIRST IS DEAD, AND
IF HE WERE TO LOSE BENJAMIN AS
WELL, THE PAIN WOULD KILL HIM!

SO HE STILL
LIVES THEN?
JACOB, I MEAN?
MY - OUR
FATHER?

YOU SEE, I
NOW HIS NAME.
T THEN I WOULD,
WOULDN'T I?

MY NAME
IS JOSEPH.

WHAT?
JOSEPH!

IT CAN'T
BE! HE'LL
KILL US!

EVERYBODY
RUN!

IT'S TRUE. JOSEPH, WHO YOU SOLD
AS A SLAVE. LOOK AT ME, LOOK
AT MY FACE!

...JOSEPH?

DON'T BLAME YOURSELVES, AND
DON'T BE AFRAID. I BELIEVE IT WAS
REALLY GOD WHO SENT ME HERE.

THIS IS ONLY THE SECOND YEAR
OF THE FAMINE, AND THE WORST
IS YET TO COME. GOD HAS
PROVIDED A WAY FOR US TO SURVIVE.

GO BACK TO CANAAN AND
BRING OUR FATHER,
JACOB. BRING THE FLOCKS,
THE WIVES, THE SERVANTS,
THE CHILDREN. BRING
EVERYONE. DON'T YOU
SEE? GOD HAS SAVED US!

AND SO IT WAS THAT IN THE SECOND YEAR OF THE GREAT FAMINE, JACOB TOOK HIS WHOLE HOUSEHOLD, AND SET OUT ON ONE LAST GREAT JOURNEY.

ALTHOUGH THE LAND HAD GIVEN UP ON LIFE, GOD STILL STUCK TO THE PROMISES HE HAD MADE TO JACOB.

GOD APPEARED TO JACOB IN A DREAM ONE MORE TIME. 'DO NOT BE AFRAID OF GOING TO EGYPT,' GOD TOLD HIM. 'YOUR CHILDREN WILL BE A GREAT NATION, AND ONE DAY I SHALL LEAD YOUR PEOPLE BACK TO CANAAN.'

IT WAS ALL TOO WONDERFUL FOR WORDS.

JOSEPH WAS NOT DEAD, BUT RULED OVER THE MOST POWERFUL NATION ON EARTH.

FATHER?

IS THAT YOU? IS IT **REALLY** YOU?

HERE, LET ME LOOK AT YOU. IT'S BEEN SO VERY LONG, AND YOU'VE CHANGED SO MUCH. I NEVER THOUGHT I'D SEE YOU AGAIN. I WAS SURE YOU MUST BE DEAD.

I LIVE, FATHER. IT'S REALLY ME.

I'M **JOSEPH**.

OH MY BOY! I AM READY TO DIE NOW THAT I'VE SEEN YOU WITH MY OWN EYES! THE GOD OF YOUR FATHER, THE GOD OF ISAAC AND ABRAHAM HAS SAVED US!

THE FAMINE RAVAGED THE LAND, AND THE SOIL REFUSED TO YIELD CROPS. ALL AROUND, HARVESTS FAILED, LIVESTOCK PERISHED AND PEOPLE STARVED.

AND YET EGYPT SURVIVED. AND BECAUSE JOSEPH SURVIVED HIS FAMILY DID TOO.

ALL THROUGH THE FAMINE YEARS THE CHILDREN OF JACOB, ALSO CALLED **ISRAEL**, LIVED ON IN EGYPT. THE TWELVE SONS OF ISRAEL WOULD BECOME TWELVE TRIBES, AND THEIR PEOPLE CALLED THE **ISRAELITES**, THE CHILDREN OF ISRAEL.

AS A YOUNG MAN JACOB HAD FLED HIS FAMILY IN TERROR, FLEEING FOR HIS LIFE WITH NO POSSESSIONS, FRIENDS NOR FUTURE.

YET NOW HE WAS THE FATHER OF PHAROAH'S RIGHT-HAND MAN.

WHEN JACOB DIED, HE WAS GIVEN A **KING'S** BURIAL.

HIS BODY WAS RETURNED TO CANAAN, WHERE IT WAS LAID BESIDE ABRAHAM AND SARAH, AND ISAAC AND REBEKAH.

JOSEPH HIMSELF LIVED TO BE VERY OLD. AND DESPITE HIS BROTHERS' FEARS, HE FORGAVE THEM COMPLETELY FOR THEIR EARLIER CRUELTY.

ALTHOUGH JOSEPH WAS BURIED IN EGYPT, HIS WILL INSTRUCTED THE ISRAELITES TO TAKE HIS BONES WITH THEM WHEN THEY FINALLY RETURNED HOME. HE WOULD BE LAID TO REST WITH HIS FORBEARS.

AND SO THE ISRAELITES GREW IN NUMBERS IN EGYPT. AND WHILE THE YEARS TURNED TO DECADES —

AND THE DECADES TO **CENTURIES** —

THE JOURNEYS WERE FAR FROM OVER FOR THE CHILDREN OF ISRAEL.

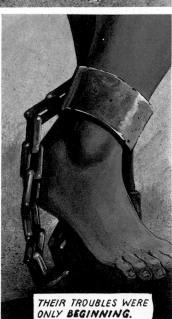

THEIR TROUBLES WERE ONLY **BEGINNING**.

THE STORY OF MOSES

NEARLY 300 YEARS HAVE PASSED SINCE THE TIME OF JOSEPH AND THE GREAT FAMINE. DARK TIMES HAVE FALLEN ON EGYPT.

JACOB'S RACE, THE ISRAELITES, HAVE BECOME SLAVES TO THE EGYPTIANS. DESPITE THIS THEY STILL CLING TO LIFE, AND EVEN INCREASE IN NUMBERS.

THE NEW PHARAOH ORDERS A FINAL SOLUTION TO THE ISRAELITE 'PROBLEM' — ALL NEWBORN BABY BOYS ARE TO BE DROWNED AT BIRTH IN THE RIVER NILE.

THIS IS THE STORY OF A MAN CALLED MOSES, AND OF HOW HE LED HIS PEOPLE TO FREEDOM.

BORN AT THE TIME OF THE PERSECUTION, THE BABY MOSES WAS KEPT UNDETECTED FOR THREE MONTHS. HIS MOTHER KNEW IT WAS ONLY A MATTER OF TIME BEFORE HE WAS DISCOVERED.

IN THE END SHE TOOK HIM TO THE NILE HERSELF.

BUT NOT TO BE DROWNED. PLACING HIM IN A BASKET WATERPROOFED WITH TAR, SHE PUSHED HIM OUT INTO THE REEDS.

IT HAPPENED THAT ONE OF THE PHARAOH'S DAUGHTERS HAD GONE DOWN TO THE RIVER TO BATHE. IT WAS TOWARDS HER THAT THE LITTLE BASKET GENTLY FLOATED, TAKING WITH IT THE BABY INSIDE.

THE PHARAOH'S DAUGHTER HEARD THE BABY CRYING.

SHE HAD NO IDEA WHERE THE BABY HAD COME FROM. BUT WATCHING FROM CLOSE BY TO MAKE SURE THE BABY WAS SAFE WAS AN OLDER SISTER OF MOSES.

PHARAOH'S DAUGHTER DECIDED TO MAKE THE CHILD HER OWN. AND SO THE ABANDONED CHILD OF AN OPPRESSED SLAVE WAS TAKEN OUT OF DANGER, AND INTO THE VERY HEART OF PHARAOH'S PALACE.

MOSES GREW UP IN THE PHARAOH'S PALACE, SAFE FROM HARM IN THE HOUSE OF THE VERY MAN WHO WANTED TO EXTERMINATE HIS RACE.

IF HE'D ANY IDEA OF THE TROUBLE MOSES WOULD CAUSE EGYPT LATER, THE PHARAOH WOULD PROBABLY HAVE KILLED HIM WITH HIS OWN HANDS, THERE AND THEN.

YOUNG MOSES LIVED A PRIVILEGED LIFE IN THE ROYAL HOUSEHOLD, WHILE ALL AROUND HIM HIS FELLOW ISRAELITES SUFFERED AT THE HANDS OF THEIR MASTERS.

HE WATCHED AS HE GREW, WAITING FOR THE CHANCE TO STRIKE BACK.

ONE DAY HE SAW AN EGYPTIAN SAVAGELY BEATING AN ISRAELITE — AND SOMETHING INSIDE HIM SNAPPED...

HE'S HAD ENOUGH! STOP IT!

PLEASE! NO MORE!

DIDN'T YOU HEAR ME?

I SAID STOP!

WHO DO YOU THINK YOU ARE? HE'S MY SLAVE! AND ANYWAY HE'S ONLY AN ISRAELITE!

IT WAS ONLY AFTERWARDS THAT MOSES REALIZED WHAT HE HAD DONE...

MOSES HAD MADE SURE THERE WERE NO WITNESSES BEFORE CALLING TO THE MAN, AND THINKING NO ONE WAS LOOKING, HE STRUCK THE MAN DEAD.

QUICKLY HE BURIED THE BODY IN THE DESERT SAND. THINKING HIS CRIME WOULD GO UNDETECTED, HE RETURNED TO THE CITY.

THE NEXT DAY HE SAW TWO ISRAELITES ARGUING...

WHY ARE YOU FIGHTING EACH OTHER WHEN IT'S THE EGYPTIANS WHO ARE YOUR REAL PROBLEM? WHY DON'T YOU TAKE IT OUT ON THEM?

LOOK, YOU OWE ME THREE LOAVES!

AND I SAID YOU'D HAVE TO WAIT FOR THEM, UNLESS YOU WANT BROKEN LEGS AS WELL!

DON'T YOU THREATEN ME!

AND WHAT ARE YOU GOING TO DO TO STOP US? KILL US LIKE YOU DID THAT SLAVE-DRIVER YESTERDAY? BURY US IN THE SAND?

HORROR.

THE CRIME HE THOUGHT SO SECRET, SO WELL HIDDEN, WAS COMMON KNOWLEDGE. EVEN MEN BRAWLING IN THE STREETS KNEW ABOUT IT.

TERRIFIED, MOSES RAN FOR HIS LIFE.

HE ROAMED FAR INTO THE DESERT, WHERE THE MIDIANITE PEOPLE LIVED, THEMSELVES DESCENDANTS OF ABRAHAM.

ONE DAY AS HE SAT BY A WELL, THE DAUGHTERS OF JETHRO, THE MIDIANITE PRIEST, CAME TO DRAW WATER.

AS MOSES WATCHED, SOME SHEPHERDS ARRIVED AND BEGAN TO HARASS THE WOMEN.

MOSES' SENSE OF INJUSTICE HAD ALREADY CAUSED HIM TO KILL ONE MAN. NOW IT GOT HIM INVOLVED IN YET ANOTHER DISPUTE.

WHY? WHAT'LL YOU GIVE ME IF I DO?

GIVE THAT BACK!

HEY! WHY DON'T YOU JUST LEAVE THEM ALONE?

DIDN'T YOU HEAR ME?

I SAID LEAVE THEM ALONE!

WE WERE ONLY HAVING A BIT OF FUN!

I DON'T CARE.

THE WOMEN WENT BACK TO THEIR FATHER AND TOLD HIM OF THE STRANGER WHO HAD COME TO THEIR RESCUE AS IF FROM NOWHERE.

LIFE WAS OFTEN HARD FOR THE DESERT DWELLERS, SO A KINDNESS RARELY WENT UNREWARDED. MOSES WAS TAKEN TO JETHRO, THE PRIEST AND BECAME PART OF HIS FAMILY, MARRYING ONE OF HIS DAUGHTERS.

THE ISRAELITE FOREMEN SOON CAME TO RESENT MOSES' INTERFERENCE. PHARAOH NOW HAD EVEN MORE REASON TO HATE THEM. THE MORE THEY BEGGED FOR MERCY, THE HARDER PHARAOH WORKED THEM.

SO MOSES PRAYED ONCE MORE —

LORD GOD, WHY HAVE YOU CAUSED SO MUCH TROUBLE FOR US? SINCE I WENT TO SEE PHARAOH, THINGS HAVE ONLY GOT WORSE.

I AM THE LORD WHO SPOKE TO ABRAHAM, TO ISAAC AND JACOB. I MADE A PROMISE TO THEM, AND I HAVE NOT FORGOTTEN IT. GO BACK TO THE PHARAOH AND TELL HIM TO RELEASE MY PEOPLE.

BUT HE WON'T LISTEN TO ME!

TAKE AARON, YOUR BROTHER. HE WILL SPEAK FOR YOU AND PHARAOH WILL LISTEN. I WILL PUNISH THE EGYPTIANS FOR WHAT THEY HAVE DONE. THEY WILL RELEASE YOU.

AND SO MOSES WENT TO SEE THE PHARAOH. HE WOULD TELL HIM STRAIGHT: RELEASE THE ISRAELITES, OR UNIMAGINABLE PLAGUES AND DISASTERS WOULD RAVAGE HIS COUNTRY. GOD'S PLANS HAD TO BE FULFILLED. BUT THE PHARAOH JUST LAUGHED...

MOSES, YOU AMUSE ME! I HAVE MAGICIANS WHO CAN DO ALL THE THINGS YOU DESCRIBE, I'M NOT AFRAID OF CONJURING TRICKS!

COME AARON, WE'VE WARNED HIM. WE CAN DO NO MORE.

AND SO IT STARTED. TEN PLAGUES IN ALL CAME ON EGYPT, EACH WORSE THAN THE LAST. FIRST WAS THE PLAGUE OF BLOOD — THE RIVER NILE, LIFELINE OF THE EGYPTIAN PEOPLE, TURNED TO BLOOD.

THEN A PLAGUE OF FROGS, DRIVEN FROM THE FILTHY WATERS AND THE ROTTING FISH. THEY INVADED THE STREETS AND HOUSES, WHERE THEY DIED, ADDING TO THE STENCH.

THEN A PLAGUE OF GNATS, AND A PLAGUE OF FLIES, FEEDING ON THE ROTTING FISH AND FROGS.

BUT STILL PHARAOH REFUSED TO LET THE ISRAELITES GO.

60

THEN CAME A PLAGUE ON THE LIVESTOCK, FOLLOWED BY A PLAGUE OF BOILS AND SKIN INFECTIONS ON THE PEOPLE.

A PLAGUE OF HAILSTONES FELL, DESTROYING CROPS THE LENGTH OF THE COUNTRY. THEN A PLAGUE OF LOCUSTS, FINISHING OFF WHAT THE HAILSTONES HAD LEFT.

STILL PHARAOH REFUSED TO LET THE ISRAELITES GO.

THEN CAME A PLAGUE OF DARKNESS. NINE PLAGUES HAD FALLEN SO FAR, BUT ONE WAS STILL TO COME. AND IT WOULD BE THE WORST...

PHARAOH HAS BEEN GIVEN ONE FINAL CHANCE, BUT HE HAS REFUSED. HE TOLD ME TO GET OUT OF HIS SIGHT, AND I INTEND TO DO JUST THAT! ONE MORE PLAGUE WILL COME, AND THEN HE WILL RELEASE US. BUT WE MUST BE PREPARED.

TONIGHT IS A SPECIAL NIGHT. FROM NOW ON WE WILL MARK THIS AS THE FIRST DAY IN OUR CALENDAR, IT'S SO IMPORTANT.

EVERY ISRAELITE FAMILY MUST TAKE THEIR BEST LAMB, AND SLAUGHTER IT ~ IF THEY'RE TOO POOR, THEN SHARE WITH THEIR NEIGHBOUR. THEY MUST TAKE SOME BLOOD AND MAKE A MARK ON THEIR DOORFRAMES.

THEY MUST ROAST THE LAMB AND EAT IT WITH BREAD MADE WITHOUT YEAST. IT'S VITAL WE DO THIS TONIGHT, AND THROUGHOUT ALL GENERATIONS TO COME.

SOMETHING DREADFUL IS GOING TO HAPPEN TO EGYPT, BUT THOSE OF US WHO FOLLOW THESE INSTRUCTIONS WILL BE LEFT UNHARMED.

THIS WAS THE PLAGUE OF THE FIRSTBORN, AND THE WORST OF ALL.

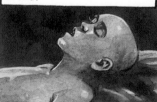

AT MIDNIGHT GOD STRUCK EGYPT. THE ELDEST CHILD OF EVERY EGYPTIAN, FROM THE PHARAOH ON HIS THRONE TO THE LOWEST PRISONER IN HIS DUNGEON, DIED.

WAILING AND CRYING FILLED THE STREETS.

BUT DEATH PASSED OVER THE ISRAELITES.

AT LAST PHARAOH LET THEM GO.

THE EGYPTIAN PEOPLE WERE SO KEEN TO SEE THE BACK OF THE ISRAELITES THAT THEY EVEN GAVE THEM GOLD AND SILVER, FOOD AND LIVESTOCK.

AARON, TELL THE PEOPLE TO REMEMBER THIS DAY. EVERY YEAR ON THIS DAY WE WILL EAT BREAD WITHOUT YEAST TO REMIND US THAT OUR GOD RESCUED US.

IT WILL BE A SIGN, AS PLAIN AS IF WE'D TIED A NOTE TO OUR FOREHEADS OR WRISTS.

THE FIRSTBORN OF ALL ISRAEL, EVEN THE LIVESTOCK, NOW BELONG TO GOD. WE ARE ALL UNDER HIS PROTECTION.

ALL ISRAEL LEFT EGYPT. EVEN JOSEPH'S BONES WERE CARRIED WITH THEM. AT LONG LAST HE COULD BE BROUGHT HOME FOR BURIAL. THE LONG JOURNEY HOME HAD BEGUN.

BACK IN EGYPT, THE NATION SLOWLY RECOVERED FROM THE RAVAGES OF THE PLAGUES, GIVING SOME PEOPLE TIME TO THINK CLEARLY AGAIN...

HE'S BEEN LIKE THIS FOR DAYS. HE'S NEVER BEEN SO QUIET.

IT WON'T LAST.

AFTER ALL THE TROUBLE THEY CAUSED, I SIMPLY LET THEM GO? HAVE I LOST MY MIND?

GUARDS! SUMMON THE CHARIOTEERS! CALL THE FASTEST MEN IN THE LAND! I WANT THE ISRAELITES BROUGHT BACK!

I WANT THEM BACK!

62

THE ISRAELITES CAMPED AND RESTED. HEMMED IN BY MOUNTAINS ON ONE SIDE AND THE RED SEA ON THE OTHER, THEY WERE AN EASY TARGET FOR THE EGYPTIAN SOLDIERS.

THESE WERE FOOTSORE SLAVES, STILL ACHING FROM FORCED LABOUR. ALTHOUGH ARMED, THEY WOULD BE NO MATCH FOR PHARAOH'S ELITE CHARIOTEERS.

THE EGYPTIANS ARE COMING !

CALL THE GUARDS ! SOMEONE TELL MOSES AND AARON !

MOSES! COME QUICKLY !

SO THE EGYPTIANS HAVE COME AFTER US AT LAST.

MOSES, WHAT'S WRONG WITH YOU ?

WE WERE BETTER OFF UNDER PHARAOH! HE WOULD HAVE KILLED US THERE AND THEN, NOT DRAGGED US OUT INTO THE DESERT TO DIE.

TELL THE PEOPLE NOT TO BE AFRAID. GOD IS WITH US.

BUT MOSES, THE EGYPTIANS—

THE EGYPTIANS WILL NEVER BE SEEN AGAIN.

AS THE EGYPTIANS APPROACHED THE ISRAELITE CAMP, THE TWO SIDES WERE HIDDEN FROM EACH OTHER BY A CLOUD.

IN AN OTHERWISE EMPTY DESERT, PHARAOH'S FINEST TROOPS FAILED TO LOCATE AN ENTIRE NATION CAMPED RIGHT IN FRONT OF THEIR EYES.

BUT THE ISRAELITES WERE STILL TRAPPED: THE EGYPTIANS BEHIND THEM AND THE SEA IN FRONT. THEN GOD SPOKE TO MOSES:

WHY DO THE PEOPLE CRY OUT TO ME? RAISE YOUR STAFF AND YOU WILL CROSS THE SEA ON DRY LAND.

SO MOSES RAISED HIS STAFF OVER THE SEA AS GOD SAID.

AND AS HE DID SO A STRONG WIND CAME IN FROM THE EAST.

MOSES STOOD THERE ALL NIGHT, HIS STAFF OVER THE SEA, AND IN THE MORNING

THE WATERS

HAD PARTED.

I DON'T BELIEVE IT.

AND SO THEY PASSED UNHARMED ACROSS THE SEA. EVERY MAN, WOMAN AND CHILD, THEIR FLOCKS AND HERDS, AND WHAT POSSESSIONS THEY COULD CARRY.

ALL PASSED SAFELY ACROSS THE SEA.

WHO IS LIKE YOU, MY GOD?

THE NATIONS WILL HEAR OF THIS, AND OUR ENEMIES WILL MELT BEFORE US! YOUR UNFAILING LOVE WILL LEAD US, AND YOU WILL REIGN FOR EVER!

AFTER THEM! FOLLOW THEM ACROSS!

AFTER ALL, IF AN ARMY OF SLAVES COULD CROSS THE RED SEA UNHARMED, WHY SHOULDN'T THEY? IN THEIR CHARIOTS THEY WOULD BE ACROSS IN NO TIME AT ALL.

ONWARD! DRAW YOUR SWORDS AND CHARGE! WE HAVE THEM!

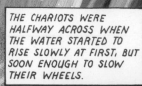

THE CHARIOTS WERE HALFWAY ACROSS WHEN THE WATER STARTED TO RISE SLOWLY AT FIRST, BUT SOON ENOUGH TO SLOW THEIR WHEELS.

WHAT?!

NO! NOT NOW!!

TURN BACK! THE WATER IS RISING! TURN BACK!

LOOK! THE WATERS HAVE SWALLOWED THE WHOLE ARMY!

THEY WANTED US DEAD, NOW THEY'RE GONE! ONLY GOD COULD HAVE SAVED US.

NOT ONE OF THEM SURVIVED.

WHO INDEED, IS LIKE YOU, LORD GOD? IN YOUR UNFAILING LOVE YOU WILL LEAD YOUR PEOPLE AND PROTECT US.

THEN THE PROPHETESS MIRIAM, MOSES' AND AARON'S SISTER, TOOK HER TAMBOURINE, AND ALL THE WOMEN OF ISRAEL FOLLOWED HER, REJOICING.

AND AS THEY DANCED THEY SANG:

'SING TO THE LORD, FOR HE HAS WON A GREAT VICTORY, THE HORSES AND RIDERS HE HAS THROWN INTO THE SEA.'

FORTY YEARS HAVE PASSED.

FORTY YEARS OF JOURNEYING, OF FIGHTS AND DISAGREEMENTS, OF GREAT VICTORIES AND GREAT DISAPPOINTMENTS.

BUT ABOVE ALL, FORTY YEARS OF GOD KEEPING THE PROMISES MADE TO HIS PEOPLE.

THE ISRAELITES HAVE AT LAST REACHED THE BORDERS OF CANAAN, THE PROMISED LAND.

AS THEY PREPARE FOR THE FINAL STAGE OF THEIR JOURNEY, MOSES, NOW AN OLD MAN, MAKES HIS WAY TO THE TOP OF MOUNT NEBO, WHICH OVERLOOKS THE PROMISED LAND ITSELF...

LOOK AT THEM. THEY WERE BAD ENOUGH WHEN I WAS THERE TO LEAD THEM, BUT NOW THEY'RE ON THEIR OWN WHO KNOWS WHAT THEY'LL DO...

...FOOLS, THE LOT OF THEM — FOOLS WHO CAN'T SEE WHERE THEIR OWN STUPIDITY WILL LEAD THEM.

AND I'M SO TIRED.

FORTY YEARS, ALWAYS ON THE MOVE — NO WONDER I'M TIRED. BACK THERE IN THE DESERT, WHEN WE WERE HUNGRY, GOD SENT US **MANNA** — FOOD SENT FROM HEAVEN TO FEED US. EVERY MORNING WE WOULD GATHER IT, AND EAT UNTIL WE WERE FULL.

I WISH THE EGYPTIANS **HAD** CAUGHT US AFTER ALL!

BUT OF COURSE, THAT WASN'T GOOD ENOUGH FOR THEM.

IN EGYPT WE HAD FISH AND FRESH VEGETABLES, MELON AND CUCUMBER. NOW IT'S MANNA, MANNA, MANNA! WE'RE SICK TO DEATH OF THE STUFF! WE WANT MEAT AGAIN!

SO GOD SENT US MEAT. FLOCKS OF QUAILS THAT VIRTUALLY FLEW INTO OUR ARMS.

BUT THE PEOPLE BECAME GREEDY, GATHERING MORE THAN THEY REALLY NEEDED.

QUAIL FOR SUPPER, QUAIL FOR BREAKFAST, SOON WE HAD QUAIL COMING OUT OF OUR EARS! BUT OF COURSE, SOON THEY WERE SICK OF THE SIGHT OF IT.

AND IF THEY WEREN'T HUNGRY, THEY WERE THIRSTY.

DID I CREATE THESE PEOPLE? DO I HAVE TO CARRY THEM IN MY ARMS THE WHOLE DISTANCE? NO. BUT IT FELT LIKE IT AT TIMES.

MOSES, THERE'S NO WATER OUT HERE!

DID YOU BRING US HERE SO WE COULD DIE OF THIRST? DO YOU WANT TO KILL OUR CHILDREN? WE HOLD YOU RESPONSIBLE!

LORD GOD, WHAT AM I GOING TO DO WITH ALL THESE PEOPLE? IF I DON'T FIND THEM WATER SOON THEY'LL SURELY STONE ME TO DEATH!

BUT GOD SPOKE TO ME, EVEN AS THE PEOPLE PICKED UP STONES TO KILL ME.

GOD TOLD ME TO GO WITH THE ELDERS, AND STRIKE THE ROCKS WITH MY STAFF. GOD WOULD STAND BEFORE ME, AND WATER WOULD COME OUT OF THE GROUND.

SO I TOOK MY STAFF, AND RAISED IT HIGH IN THE AIR —

CRACK! I BROUGHT IT DOWN ON THE ROCKS!

AND WATER CAME OUT.

THEN THERE WERE THE BATTLES. AFTER ALL, WE WEREN'T THE ONLY PEOPLE IN THE DESERT. THE AMALEKITES CAME AND ATTACKED US, BUT GOD WAS WITH US.

I SENT JOSHUA TO LEAD OUR FORCES, AND THEN WENT TO THE TOP OF THE HILL OVERLOOKING THE BATTLE.

IT WAS THEN I HAD A WELCOME VISITOR — JETHRO, MY FATHER-IN-LAW. HE HAD HEARD OF ALL THAT HAD HAPPENED SINCE WE LEFT EGYPT, AND CAME TO JOIN US, BRINGING ME SOME ADVICE...

MOSES, WHY DO YOU INSIST ON DOING EVERYTHING YOURSELF? THERE'S TOO MUCH WORK FOR ONE MAN. THERE ARE OTHERS WHO CAN HELP.

IT'S RIGHT THAT [...] REPRESENT THE P[...] BEFORE GOD, AND T[...] THEM, BUT APPO[...] PEOPLE TO SORT OU[...] MINOR ARGUME[...] FOR YOU.

AS LONG AS I HELD MY STAFF IN THE AIR, WE TRIUMPHED. BUT IF I LOWERED MY ARMS, WE WOULD START TO LOSE. I BECAME SO TIRED THAT AARON AND HUR HAD TO HOLD MY ARMS UP FOR ME.

JOSHUA AND HIS MEN FOUGHT WELL, BUT IT WAS ONLY BECAUSE GOD WAS WITH US THAT WE WON.

FIND GOD-FEARING MEN WHO CAN'T BE BRIBED, WHO CAN DECIDE WHICH CASES TRULY DESERVE YOUR ATTENTION, AND LET THEM SORT OUT THE REST THEMSELVES.

THREE MONTHS TO THE DAY AFTER LEAVING EGYPT, WE CAME TO THE SINAI DESERT AND CAMPED AT THE FOOT OF MOUNT SINAI ITSELF.

IT WAS ON MOUNT SINAI THAT GOD FIRST SPOKE FROM THE BURNING BUSH, TELLING ME TO GO AND BRING THE ISRAELITES FROM EGYPT. NOW I HAD RETURNED, BRINGING ALL ISRAEL WITH ME.

THERE WE CAMPED AND WAITED.

ON THE MORNING OF THE THIRD DAY WE WERE WOKEN BY THE SOUND OF THUNDER.

THE MOUNTAIN WAS ALIVE WITH THUNDER AND LIGHTNING — THE NOISE WAS INDESCRIBABLE. PEOPLE WOKE IN TERROR, RUNNING THIS WAY AND THAT, CRYING AND SCREAMING.

AND ALL WERE SAYING THE SAME THING: 'FIND MOSES! WHERE IS MOSES? SAVE US!'

AND THEY HAD GOOD REASON TO BE AFRAID: WITH A TRUMPET BLAST LOUDER THAN THUNDER, GOD HIMSELF HAD COME DOWN ONTO THE MOUNTAIN.

SO I WENT UP THE MOUNTAINSIDE. UP INTO THE SMOKE AND CLOUD, THOUGH THE GROUND TREMBLED AND SMOKE BILLOWED OUT AS FROM A FURNACE.

AND THERE I SAW GOD FACE TO FACE.

AND GOD SPOKE TO ME.

AND THEN I WENT BACK TO THE PEOPLE, AND TOLD THEM EVERYTHING GOD HAD SAID.

THE LORD, OUR GOD BROUGHT US OUT OF EGYPT! IF WE OBEY HIS COMMANDMENTS THEN OUT OF ALL THE PEOPLE ON EARTH HE WILL TREASURE US THE MOST!

THESE ARE HIS RULES THAT WE MUST OBEY IF WE ARE TO BE HIS PEOPLE. LISTEN TO WHAT HE SAYS:

ONE: 'YOU SHALL HAVE NO OTHER GODS BESIDE ME.'

TWO: 'YOU SHALL NOT MAKE IDOLS IN THE SHAPE OF ANYTHING IN HEAVEN, OR ON THE EARTH, OR BELOW THE WATERS. YOU SHALL NOT BOW DOWN TO THEM OR WORSHIP THEM.'

THREE: 'DO NOT TAKE THE LORD'S NAME IN VAIN, FOR GOD WILL PUNISH ANYONE WHO MISUSES HIS NAME.'

FOUR: 'REMEMBER THE SEVENTH DAY AND KEEP IT HOLY. YOU SHALL WORK FOR SIX DAYS BUT YOU MUST DO NO WORK ON THE SEVENTH'

FIVE: 'HONOUR YOUR FATHER AND YOUR MOTHER, SO THAT YOU MAY LIVE LONG IN THE LAND THE LORD IS GIVING YOU.'

SIX: 'YOU SHALL NOT MURDER.'

SEVEN: 'YOU SHALL NOT COMMIT ADULTERY.'

EIGHT: 'YOU SHALL NOT STEAL.'

NINE: 'YOU SHALL NOT GIVE FALSE TESTIMONY AGAINST YOUR NEIGHBOUR.'

TEN: 'YOU SHALL NOT COVET YOUR NEIGHBOUR'S HOUSE. YOU SHALL NOT COVET YOUR NEIGHBOUR'S WIFE, OR MANSERVANT OR MAIDSERVANT, OR HIS OX OR DONKEY, OR ANYTHING THAT BELONGS TO YOUR NEIGHBOUR.'

THEY SAW THE LIGHTNING AND HEARD THE THUNDER, AND WERE SO AFRAID THAT THEY **BEGGED** ME TO SPEAK TO GOD FOR THEM.

IT WASN'T TO LAST OF COURSE – THE COMPLAINING RETURNED! BUT NOW WE HAD GOD'S LAW TO LIVE BY – THE TEN COMMANDMENTS, AND HUNDREDS OF OTHER LAWS GIVEN BY GOD, COVERING ALL OF LIFE.

GOD WANTED US TO LOVE HIM AND OBEY HIS LAWS. WE WERE TO CARE FOR ONE ANOTHER, AND HIS LAWS SHOWED US HOW. THE LAW PROVIDED FOR THE POOR AND PROTECTED THE LAND; NOT JUST A SET OF RESTRICTIONS, BUT A TOOL FOR LIVING – A GIFT FROM GOD.

AND THE PEOPLE ACCEPTED IT GLADLY.

I BUILT AN ALTAR WITH TWELVE STONES, TO REPRESENT THE TWELVE TRIBES OF ISRAEL, DESCENDED FROM JACOB'S TWELVE SONS. I READ ALOUD TO THEM THE TERMS OF THE COVENANT WITH GOD, AND THEY REPLIED 'WE WILL DO EVERYTHING OUR GOD SAYS. WE WILL OBEY.'

AND SO I WENT TO TALK WITH GOD ONCE MORE, TAKING WITH ME JOSHUA, WHO HAD FOUGHT THE AMALEKITES. TOGETHER, WE MADE OUR WAY BACK UP THE MOUNTAIN.

WE WERE GONE FOR FORTY DAYS.

IN THAT TIME GOD TOLD US HOW TO BUILD THE ARK OF THE COVENANT, THE BOX THAT WOULD HOLD THE FORMAL AGREEMENT BETWEEN GOD AND HIS PEOPLE. WE WERE TOLD TO BUILD THE TABERNACLE, THE TENT WHERE GOD WOULD DWELL DURING OUR JOURNEY.

WHEN GOD HAD FINISHED, HE GAVE ME THE TEN COMMANDMENTS, WRITTEN ON STONE. AND THEN WE WENT BACK DOWN TO THE PEOPLE.

MOSES, I CAN HEAR SHOUTING! IS THERE WAR IN THE CAMP? WHAT'S HAPPENED?

THAT'S NOT SHOUTING JOSHUA – IT'S SINGING.

IT TURNED OUT WE HAD BEEN GONE LONG ENOUGH FOR THE PEOPLE TO THINK WE WOULD NEVER RETURN...

MOSES! WE THOUGHT YOU MUST BE DEAD! I CAN EXPLAIN EVERYTHING! YOU KNOW WHAT THE PEOPLE ARE LIKE, AND WITH YOU GONE THEY SAID THEY WANTED GODS TO GO BEFORE THEM.

NO! I LEFT AARON IN CHARGE, THIS SHOULDN'T HAVE HAPPENED! THEY'RE COMPLETELY OUT OF CONTROL!

THEY'RE WORSHIPPING THAT GOLDEN COW, THE FOOLS! DON'T THEY UNDERSTAND ANYTHING? AARON, WHAT HAVE YOU DONE?

I TOOK THEIR GOLD AND JEWELLERY, AND THREW IT IN THE FIRE, AND LOOK! THIS COW CAME OUT!

'THIS COW CAME OUT?!' YOU MADE IT WITH TOOLS! YOU MADE IT!

I DON'T KNOW WHAT I WAS EXPECTING FROM THEM, BUT IT CERTAINLY WASN'T THIS!

THEY'D AGREED TO WORSHIP NO OTHER GODS, AND YET AS SOON AS I LEFT THEM ALONE, THEY ACTUALLY WENT AND MADE ONE!

I WAS SO ENRAGED, I SMASHED THE STONE TABLETS – THE TABLETS THAT GOD HAD WRITTEN ON WITH HIS OWN HAND!

I TOOK THE WRETCHED COW THEY'D MADE, AND BURNED IT IN THE FIRE! I GROUND IT INTO POWDER, MIXED IT WITH WATER AND MADE THEM DRINK IT!

I PLEADED WITH GOD TO SPARE THEM, REMINDING HIM OF THE PROMISES MADE TO ABRAHAM, ISAAC AND JACOB: THAT FROM THEM WOULD COME A WHOLE NATION.

AND HE FORGAVE THEM. HE GAVE THEM CHANCE AFTER CHANCE TO ACCEPT HIS WAYS BUT THE ISRAELITES WERE NEVER SATISFIED. AND THEN, WHEN WE WERE WITHIN SIGHT OF THE PROMISED LAND, THE PEOPLE PROVOKED GOD'S ANGER *AGAIN*.

I SENT TWELVE SPIES TO SURVEY THE LAND AHEAD. CALEB, FROM THE TRIBE OF JUDAH, AND JOSHUA, REPORTED THAT THE LAND WAS JUST AS GOD SAID IT WOULD BE.

PEOPLE FLED IN TERROR WHENEVER THEY SAW THEM BECAUSE OF WHAT OUR GOD HAD DONE. THE PEOPLE WE WOULD HAVE TO FIGHT WERE FAINTING AT THE SIGHT OF US!

BUT THE OTHER SPIES EXAGGERATED AND LIED, SAYING THE PEOPLE THERE WERE TOO STRONG FOR US, AND THE LAND TOO POOR TO SUSTAIN LIFE. ALL THAT NIGHT WE ARGUED WITH THEM...

JOSHUA AND CALEB SAY THE LAND HERE IS GOOD. IF IT PLEASES GOD, HE WILL LEAD US INTO THE LAND HE PROMISED US.

BUT WE'LL HAVE TO FIGHT! WE'LL DIE IN BATTLE, OUR WIVES AND CHILDREN WILL BE KIDNAPPED! I SAY WE SHOULD GO BACK TO EGYPT!

EGYPT?! BUT WE HAVE NOTHING TO FEAR! IF GOD IS WITH US, THEN THESE PEOPLE CAN DO NOTHING AGAINST US!

WE DON'T CARE. PEOPLE SAY THERE ARE GIANTS ROAMING LOOSE, AND WE'RE LIKE GRASSHOPPERS TO THEM! OUR LEADERS HAVE LED US TO CERTAIN DEATH. STONE THEM! STONE THEM TO DEATH, APPOINT NEW LEADERS AND RETURN TO EGYPT!

ENOUGH!

YOU WERE *SLAVES* IN EGYPT! HAVE YOU FORGOTTEN ALREADY WHAT GOD HAS DONE FOR YOU?

IS YOUR FAITH SO WEAK? I WILL APPEAL TO GOD TO SAVE YOUR LIVES.

GOD SENTENCED THE UNBELIEVING ISRAELITES TO WANDER IN THE DESERT UNTIL THAT WHOLE GENERATION HAD DIED.

WE BUILT THE TABERNACLE – THE TENT WHERE GOD LIVED WITH US DURING OUR JOURNEY AND PLACED THE ARK OF THE COVENANT INSIDE. WHEN WE FINISHED, GOD COVERED THE TENT WITH A CLOUD BY DAY AND A FIRE ABOVE IT BY NIGHT. DURING ALL OUR TRAVELS WE COULD CLEARLY SEE THAT GOD WAS WITH US.

BUT STILL THE PEOPLE HAD NO FAITH...

THERE'S NO WATER HERE! THIS IS A DREADFUL PLACE TO CAMP. ARE YOU TRYING TO GET US KILLED?

LACK OF WATER WAS A SERIOUS THING, BUT GOD SPOKE TO ME SAYING:

TAKE YOUR STAFF, AND GATHER EVERYONE IN FRONT OF THIS ROCK. SPEAK TO THE ROCK AND WATER WILL COME OUT OF IT, ENOUGH FOR THE PEOPLE AND THEIR LIVESTOCK.

EVEN WITH ALL THE MIRACLES GOD PERFORMED, THE PEOPLE STILL COMPLAINED! I WAS FURIOUS.

I HAVE HAD ENOUGH! YOU WERE HUNGRY AND I FED YOU, YOU WERE LOST AND I LED YOU, AND STILL YOU COMPLAIN.

NOW YOU SAY YOU'RE THIRSTY.

YOU WANT WATER? HERE, DRINK UNTIL YOU BURST! I'LL GIVE YOU WATER!

I HAD NEVER BEEN ANGRIER.

MY ANGER COST ME DEAR. IN MY RAGE I HAD TAKEN CREDIT FOR THINGS THAT GOD HAD DONE. I HAD SEEN GOD'S HOLINESS WITH MY OWN EYES AND KNEW HE COULDN'T MAKE COMPROMISES, NOT EVEN FOR ME...

TOMORROW YOU TAKE POSSESSION OF THE LAND GOD PROMISED YOU. I APPOINT JOSHUA AS MY SUCCESSOR. OBEY HIM AS YOU WOULD ME.

MOSES, WHAT ARE YOU SAYING? YOU MAKE IT SOUND LIKE YOU WON'T BE COMING WITH US.

I HAVE SINNED, AND GOD CAN MAKE NO EXCEPTIONS. AS MY PUNISHMENT I CAN COME NO FURTHER.

NOW LISTEN TO ME: I'M GIVING YOU A COMMAND, BUT IT'S NOT DIFFICULT.

IT'S HERE WITH YOU NOW, YOU KNOW IT AND CAN QUOTE IT, AND IT'S SIMPLY THIS:

CHOOSE LIFE!

IF YOU OBEY GOD, AND KEEP HIS COMMANDS, THEN GOD WILL BLESS YOU. BUT IF YOU DISOBEY AND WORSHIP OTHER GODS, THEN YOU WILL BE DESTROYED.

I'M GIVING YOU THAT CHOICE. CHOOSE WELL, AND GOD WILL GO BEFORE YOU.

BE STRONG, JOSHUA, BE BRAVE. GOD GOES WITH YOU. HE WILL NEVER LEAVE YOU OR FORSAKE YOU. TAKE TO HEART ALL THE THINGS I HAVE SAID TO YOU. THEY'RE NOT IDLE WORDS – THEY ARE YOUR LIFE!

BLESSED ARE YOU, ISRAEL! WHO ELSE IS LIKE YOU, A PEOPLE SAVED BY GOD?

AND SO MOSES CLIMBED THE MOUNTAIN, AND LOOKED DOWN OVER THE PROMISED LAND.

MOSES WAS 120 YEARS OLD WHEN THE ISRAELITES LEFT HIM TO GO ON TO THE LAND GOD HAD PROMISED, BUT HIS EYES WERE NOT WEAK, AND HIS STRENGTH HAD NOT GONE.

HE DIED IN OLD AGE AND ALTHOUGH HE NEVER ENTERED THE PROMISED LAND, HE SAW IT SPREAD OUT BEFORE HIM FROM THE MOUNTAIN-TOP OF NEBO.

NEITHER BEFORE, NOR AFTER, WAS THERE A PROPHET LIKE MOSES, WHO KNEW GOD FACE TO FACE.

THE STORY OF JOSHUA

WITH HEAVY HEARTS THE ISRAELITES LEFT MOSES AND MADE THEIR WAY TOWARDS THE RIVER JORDAN, AND THE WAY TO THEIR NEW HOME.

AHEAD LAY THE CITY OF JERICHO, GUARDING THE FORDS OVER THE RIVER JORDAN — IT WAS THERE THAT RESISTANCE WAS EXPECTED TO BE FIERCEST.

ANY INFORMATION ABOUT TROOP MOVEMENTS, THE MORALE OF THE DEFENDERS, OR WEAKNESSES IN THE FORTIFICATIONS MIGHT PROVE CRUCIAL IN THE BATTLE TO COME.

THE TWO SPIES LODGED IN THE ONE PLACE IN THE CITY WHERE STRANGERS MIGHT COME AND GO AT ANY TIME WITH NO QUESTIONS ASKED AND NONE EXPECTED; THE HOUSE OF RAHAB THE PROSTITUTE.

DESPITE BEING SO CLOSE TO THE PROMISED LAND, THE DANGERS THAT HAD BESET THEIR JOURNEY WERE STILL FAR FROM OVER, SO JOSHUA SENT TWO SPIES OUT FROM THE MAIN GROUP.

ANXIETY HUNG OVER THE CITY LIKE A SHROUD — NEWS OF THE ISRAELITES' ADVENTURES TRAVELLED BEFORE THEM. THOSE WHO MIGHT OPPOSE THEM WERE IN MORTAL FEAR.

TRY AND ACT NATURAL AND THEY WON'T GUESS A THING.

IN SUCH A TENSE ATMOSPHERE, THE TWO STRANGERS STOOD OUT LIKE SORE THUMBS...

YOU TWO! WE'RE ROUNDING UP ALL FOREIGNERS. YOU'RE TO COME WITH US!

I THINK NOW WOULD BE A GOOD TIME TO RUN.

SO MUCH FOR ACTING NATURAL.

SHUT UP AND KEEP RUNNING!

RAHAB! HIDE US!

QUICK, INSIDE!

SO WHO ARE YOU REALLY?

ISRAELITE SPIES, SENT TO SURVEY THE LAND AHEAD OF THE MAIN PARTY.

PEOPLE HERE HAVE HEARD OF YOU AND ARE TERRIFIED.

THEY ARE?

SSSHHH. THERE ARE PEOPLE OUTSIDE.

WE'VE SEARCHED EVERY HOUSE IN THIS DISTRICT. THERE'S ONLY ONE LEFT!

THE PROSTITUTE'S HOUSE! KICK THE DOOR DOWN IF YOU HAVE TO! **FIND THEM!**

FOLLOW ME. SOMETIMES MY 'GUESTS' LEAVE IN A HURRY: I HAVE AN ESCAPE ROUTE.

IF YOU ATTACK JERICHO, PROMISE ME YOU'LL SPARE ME AND MY FAMILY.

WE SWEAR IT.

HURRY! BEFORE THE GUARDS RETURN! AND REMEMBER YOUR PROMISE!

WE WON'T FORGET YOU!

AND SO THE PROSTITUTE HELPED THE SPIES TO ESCAPE. THEY RETURNED WITH THEIR NEWS: THE PEOPLE OF JERICHO WERE AFRAID, THEY WERE SCARED OF THE ISRAELITES... AND GOD.

THAT WAS ALL THE CONFIRMATION JOSHUA NEEDED.

JOSHUA SUMMONED HIS OFFICERS...

GOD HAS GIVEN THE CITY OF JERICHO INTO OUR HANDS. THE PEOPLE ARE TERRIFIED: AND WE'VE YET TO RAISE A SWORD OR SHOOT ONE ARROW.

TOMORROW WE CROSS THE JORDAN. WE MUST KEEP THE PEOPLE IN ORDERED RANKS.

THE ISRAELITES HAD WANDERED THE DESERT FOR FORTY YEARS. ALL THE MEN OF MILITARY AGE WHEN THEY LEFT EGYPT WERE NOW DEAD. ONLY JOSHUA AND CALEB, THE TWO WHO TRUSTED GOD, LIVED TO ENTER THE PROMISED LAND.

IT WAS A NEW GENERATION WHO CROSSED THE RIVER.

NOW ONLY THE CITY OF JERICHO STOOD BETWEEN THEM AND GOD'S PROMISE.

ON THE EVENING OF THE FOURTEENTH DAY OF THE MONTH, WHEN CAMPED ON THE PLAIN BEFORE THE CITY, THE ISRAELITES CELEBRATED THE PASSOVER. THE MANNA STOPPED THE NEXT DAY. FROM NOW ON THEY WOULD EAT FOOD FROM THE LAND OF CANAAN.

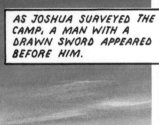

AS JOSHUA SURVEYED THE CAMP, A MAN WITH A DRAWN SWORD APPEARED BEFORE HIM.

HALT! YOU THERE! ARE YOU WITH US, OR FOR OUR ENEMIES?

NEITHER.

- REPLIED THE MAN -

I AM THE COMMANDER OF THE ARMY OF GOD.

TAKE OFF YOUR SHOES JOSHUA, SON OF NUN, FOR YOU ARE STANDING ON HOLY GROUND.

JERICHO IS YOURS. AS LONG AS YOU FOLLOW GOD'S INSTRUCTIONS TO THE LETTER, ITS WALLS WILL CRUMBLE BEFORE YOU.

LISTEN CAREFULLY TO WHAT YOU MUST DO:

MARCH YOUR MEN AROUND THE CITY ONCE A DAY FOR SIX DAYS. SEVEN PRIESTS CARRYING TRUMPETS ARE TO WALK AHEAD OF THE ARK OF THE COVENANT. ON THE SEVENTH DAY MARCH SEVEN TIMES ROUND — WITH THE PRIESTS BLOWING THEIR TRUMPETS.

LET THE WHOLE ARMY GIVE A GREAT SHOUT. THEN THE WALLS WILL COLLAPSE AND YOUR MEN WILL BE FREE TO ENTER.

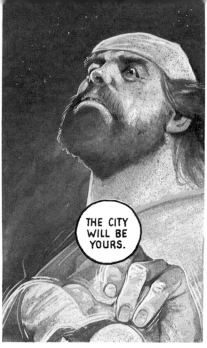

THE CITY WILL BE YOURS.

JOSHUA GOT UP EARLY THE NEXT MORNING, AND SUMMONED THE PRIESTS WHO HAD CARRIED THE ARK.

DESPITE THE STRANGE INSTRUCTIONS FROM THE COMMANDER OF GOD'S ARMY, JOSHUA TRUSTED GOD COMPLETELY.

AND SO THEY MARCHED AROUND THE CITY, THE SOLDIERS IN THE LEAD, FOLLOWED BY THE SEVEN PRIESTS BLOWING THE TRUMPETS, THE PRIESTS CARRYING THE ARK, AND A REARGUARD OF TROOPS BEHIND THEM.

AROUND THE CITY THEY MARCHED, EVERY DAY FOR SIX DAYS, THE SOLDIERS MARCHING IN THE SHADOW OF THE DEFENCES, THE SOUND OF TRUMPETS ECHOING OFF THE UNYIELDING WALLS. EVERY DAY FOR A WHOLE WEEK THEY MARCHED, BENEATH THE WATCHING EYES OF THE DEFENDERS.

IT WOULD BE FAIR TO SAY THAT THIS WASN'T REALLY WHAT THE SOLDIERS ON THE BATTLEMENTS OF JERICHO WERE EXPECTING...

HERE THEY COME AGAIN.

THIS IS THE SEVENTH TIME THIS WEEK. WHAT ARE THEY DOING OUT THERE? ALL THAT WANDERING AROUND IN THE DESERT MUST HAVE ADDLED THEIR BRAINS!

WHAT'S THE MATTER, TOO SCARED TO FIGHT?

DON'T YOU KNOW ANY OTHER TUNES? YOU'RE STARTING TO BORE US!

WHY DON'T YOU SHOW US WHAT'S IN THE BOX YOU'RE CARRYING? IT'S GOT TO BE MORE INTERESTING THAN LISTENING TO THIS ALL WEEK!

THE PEOPLE DID AS JOSHUA COMMANDED. AND WHEN THE PRIESTS BLEW THE TRUMPETS, THE ARMY GAVE A GREAT SHOUT —

AND AT THAT MOMENT, THE WALLS STARTED TO CRUMBLE...

THE ARMIES OF THIRTY-ONE KINGS FELL BEFORE JOSHUA'S ARMY, THE SHRINES OF THE PAGAN IDOLS **DESTROYED**. THE PROMISED LAND WAS TO BE HOME TO A PEOPLE CHOSEN BY A GOD WHO TOLERATES NO RIVALS.

THE ISRAELITES PUT AN END TO THE CHILD SACRIFICE AND THE SHRINE PROSTITUTES, TO THE EVIL THAT LAY ON THE LAND.

AND THEN JOSHUA SPOKE TO THE PEOPLE ONE LAST TIME. NEVER AGAIN WOULD ALL ISRAEL BE GATHERED IN ONE PLACE. THESE WERE HIS WORDS:

'THIS IS WHAT THE LORD, OUR GOD, SAYS: "LONG AGO YOUR FATHERS LIVED FAR BEYOND THE RIVER EUPHRATES AND WORSHIPPED STRANGE GODS. BUT I TOOK YOUR FATHER, **ABRAHAM**, AND BROUGHT HIM TO THIS LAND, CALLED **CANAAN**.

'"I GAVE HIM **ISAAC**, AND TO ISAAC HIS SONS **ESAU** AND **JACOB**, BUT JACOB WENT TO EGYPT. SO I SENT **MOSES**, AND I BROUGHT YOU OUT! YOU SAW WITH YOUR **OWN EYES** WHAT I DID TO THE EGYPTIANS!"

'THROW AWAY THE GODS YOUR FATHERS WORSHIPPED BEYOND EUPHRATES AND IN EGYPT. AND SERVE GOD ONLY. CHOOSE **NOW** WHOM YOU WILL SERVE.

'AS FOR ME AND MY FAMILY, WE WILL SERVE THE LORD.'

THE PEOPLE CHOSE GOD THAT DAY, AS JOSHUA CHOSE, AND THE TWELVE TRIBES WENT EACH TO THE SECTION OF LAND THAT JOSHUA HAD APPORTIONED. JOSEPH'S BONES, CARRIED FROM EGYPT, WERE BURIED.

THEY WERE HOME AT LAST...

IN THE YEARS AFTER JOSHUA'S DEATH, A NEW GENERATION AROSE, WHO KNEW NOTHING OF GOD, OR WHAT HE HAD DONE FOR ISRAEL.

AND THOSE WHO DID KNOW, SIMPLY DIDN'T CARE. LIFE WAS GOOD, AND **WHILE** LIFE WAS GOOD, THE PEOPLE DID AS THEY WANTED. COMFORTABLE IN THEIR NEW LAND, THEY GREW LAZY AND COMPLACENT... AND ULTIMATELY, **DECADENT**.

THEY BECAME ATTRACTED TO PAGAN RELIGIONS, AND WORSHIPPED **BAAL** AND **ASHTAROTH**, THE GODS OF THEIR ENEMIES.

THEIR OWN GOD FORGOTTEN, THEY LOST THEMSELVES TO REVELRY AND ORGIES.

THEY EMBRACED THE FERTILITY CULTS OF THEIR NEIGHBOURS, THEY BOWED TO STATUES MADE OF STONE AND WOOD, AND CELEBRATED THE OBSCENE RITES OF DARKNESS IN PLACE OF GOD'S LIGHT...

THEY BROKE EVERY LAW KNOWN TO THEM. RELIGIOUS, SOCIAL ...

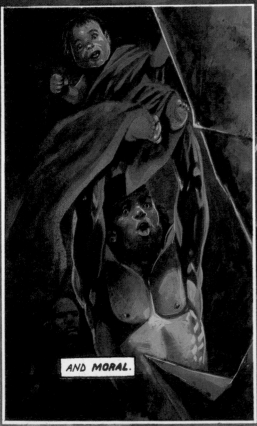

AND **MORAL**.

THE COUNTRY BECAME GRIPPED BY REAL, TANGIBLE **EVIL**.

THESE WERE DARK TIMES FOR ISRAEL.

BUT ALTHOUGH THEY REJECTED GOD, GOD STILL HAD PLANS TO SAVE THEM. IT WAS TO THIS END THAT HE SENT PEOPLE WHO, DESPITE THE DANGERS, WOULD RESCUE ISRAEL FROM THEIR ENEMIES.

THIS WAS THE DAY OF THE **JUDGES**.

THE STORY OF GIDEON

THE PEOPLE REJECT GOD, THEN THEY'RE SURPRISED WHEN THINGS FALL APART!

FLAMES IN THE DISTANCE AGAIN. ANOTHER TOWN GONE.

WITHOUT GOD'S PROTECTION, ISRAEL WAS LEFT WIDE OPEN TO ATTACK. THE MIDIANITE PEOPLE, EAGER TO TAKE ADVANTAGE OF ISRAEL'S WEAKENED STATE, SWARMED LIKE LOCUSTS ALONG THE EASTERN BORDERS, LEAVING NO LIVING THING IN THEIR WAKE...

AND WHAT DO WE DO? BURY FOOD IN THE GROUND TO HIDE IT. WE'RE REDUCED TO LIVING LIKE ANIMALS! *WHY DOESN'T GOD DO SOMETHING?!*

IN FAIRNESS, GIDEON WASN'T REALLY EXPECTING AN ANSWER THERE AND THEN...

GOD IS WITH YOU, GIDEON, FOR YOU ARE BRAVE INDEED — A MIGHTY WARRIOR!

BRAVE AND *MIGHTY*? I'M UP HERE GROVELLING AROUND IN THE DIRT, TRYING TO THRESH GRAIN IN A WINEPRESS SO THE MIDIANITES WON'T FIND IT!

NO, NOT BRAVE AND MIGHTY.

BESIDES, HOW CAN YOU SAY 'GOD IS WITH YOU'? IF GOD *WERE* WITH US, HE'D SEND SOMEONE TO SAVE HIS PEOPLE.

BUT GOD *WILL* SAVE THEM. HE IS SENDING THEM *YOU* GIDEON! AND THROUGH YOU, GOD WILL SAVE ISRAEL!

WAIT A MOMENT — WHO AM I TALKING TO?

EITHER I'VE GONE COMPLETELY MAD, OR I'M HAVING A CONVERSATION WITH... WITH *GOD*?

ME?! WHAT DOES HE WANT TO SEND *ME* FOR?

IF THIS IS *REALLY* HAPPENING, IF YOU *ARE* GOD'S MESSENGER, THEN GIVE ME THIS SIGN!

I'LL LEAVE THIS FLEECE ON THE GROUND. IF IN THE MORNING ALL THE GROUND IS DRY, BUT THE FLEECE IS WET, THEN I'LL KNOW!

AND SO, THE NEXT MORNING...

WELL, I'D SAY THAT WAS WET ENOUGH.

AND THE GROUND'S AS DRY AS A BONE... I SUPPOSE IT MUST BE GOD!

I'D BETTER GET STARTED THEN.

FIRST THING WE DO, GET RID OF THE IDOLS!

AND SO GIDEON TOOK HIS SERVANTS AND *SMASHED* HIS FATHER'S IDOLS TO PIECES!

QUIETLY.

WHEN HE WAS SURE NO ONE WAS LOOKING.

BUT IN A SMALL TOWN SECRETS DON'T STAY SECRET ALL THAT LONG...

JOASH! OPEN UP BEFORE WE BREAK THIS DOOR DOWN!

YOUR SON'S SMASHED THE STATUE OF BAAL! *AND* THE ASHERAH POLE! HE MUST *DIE!*

DIE? YOU'RE GOING TO KILL HIM BECAUSE HE BROKE A STATUE?

JOASH, YOU OLD FOOL! HE'S ANGERED THE GODS! IF WE DON'T KILL HIM WE'LL ALL SUFFER!

IF BAAL REALLY *IS* A GOD THEN HE'S PERFECTLY CAPABLE OF FIGHTING HIS *OWN* BATTLES.

ARE *YOU* GOING TO FIGHT FOR HIM? ARE YOU WILLING TO DIE TO DEFEND A STATUE?

PAH! LET BAAL SORT HIM OUT.

LET BAAL DEAL WITH HIM!

I DON'T KNOW WHAT YOU THINK YOU'RE DOING, GIDEON, BUT YOU'D BETTER TAKE MORE CARE THAN *THAT!*

DON'T WORRY, FATHER. GOD IS MOVING THROUGH ISRAEL. THINGS WILL CHANGE. YOU'LL SEE.

WITHIN A FEW SHORT WEEKS, GIDEON GATHERED ENOUGH MEN FROM NEIGHBOURING TRIBES TO MAKE A STAND. AND NOT A MOMENT TOO SOON...

TODAY WE FIGHT BACK!

THE MIDIANITES HAVE JOINED WITH PEOPLE FROM THE EAST AND EVEN NOW STAND READY TO INVADE!

GOD HAS TOLD ME WE SHALL WIN, BUT WE MUST *TRUST* HIM, WHATEVER HE ORDERS!

GOD COMMANDS THAT YOU DRINK WATER BEFORE WE FIGHT.

AS THEY DRANK, GIDEON SORTED THEM INTO TWO GROUPS: THOSE WHO GOT DOWN ON THEIR KNEES TO DRINK, AND THOSE WHO CUPPED WATER IN THEIR HANDS.

IT WAS IN *THIS* WAY THAT GOD CHOSE THE MEN WHO WOULD FIGHT – THE REST WERE TO RETURN HOME.

THIS DOESN'T MAKE *SENSE!* WHY LEAVE US WITH ONLY THREE HUNDRED MEN?

THIS WAY EVERYONE WILL KNOW IT WAS GOD WHO SAVED THEM!

THE STORY OF SAMSON

GRANDFATHER, YOU PROMISED US A STORY BEFORE BED.

A STORY? YOU MEAN A ROMANCE WITH LOVE AND WEDDINGS AND A HAPPY ENDING?

NO WAY! GIVE US ONE WITH BATTLES AND LOTS OF FIGHTING! TELL US ABOUT ONE OF THE JUDGES!

THE JUDGES? WELL, THERE WERE ABOUT A DOZEN OF THEM. THEY RULED ISRAEL BEFORE WE HAD A KING, AND THEY WEREN'T ALL AS REASONABLE AS GIDEON!

LET ME SEE NOW ~ THERE WAS DEBORAH THE PROPHETESS, EHUD THE ASSASSIN, AND THEN THERE WAS SAMSON... WHERE DO I EVEN BEGIN WITH SAMSON?!

HE WAS BORN A NAZARITE. THAT MEANS HE WAS SET APART FOR GOD, A SPECIAL PERSON. HE WASN'T SUPPOSED TO DRINK, TO TOUCH DEAD BODIES OR CUT HIS HAIR.

BUT SAMSON DIDN'T CARE ABOUT THAT, HE HARDLY CARED ABOUT ANYTHING! THE PHILISTINES WERE RAVAGING OUR BORDERS, AND SAMSON WAS JUST THE MAN TO SORT THEM OUT!

THE STORIES THAT PEOPLE TOLD ABOUT HIM..! HOW HE WOULD BURST OUT OF ROPES, WRESTLE WITH LIONS, TIE THREE HUNDRED JACKALS TOGETHER BY THEIR TAILS, AND STROLL AWAY FROM DANGER WITH THE TOWN GATES SLUNG OVER HIS SHOULDERS!

ANOTHER TIME HE KILLED A THOUSAND MEN, ARMED ONLY WITH A DONKEY'S JAWBONE! THERE WAS NOTHING THE PHILISTINES COULD DO TO STOP HIM. NOTHING! FOR TWENTY YEARS HE FOUGHT THEM. THEIR EVERY PLAN, EVERY SCHEME, EVERY CAMPAIGN WOULD FAIL, AND ALL BECAUSE OF SAMSON.

BUT SAMSON HAD A WEAKNESS.

HER NAME WAS DELILAH, AND SHE WAS THE MOST BEAUTIFUL WOMAN ON EARTH. OR AT LEAST SAMSON THOUGHT SO.

I MEAN, WOULD YOU ARGUE WITH HIM?

POOR SAMSON. IF HE KNEW SHE SECRETLY SERVED HER PHILISTINE MASTERS, HE DIDN'T CARE. AFTER ALL, HE WAS **SAMSON** — WHAT COULD HARM HIM?

THEY OFFERED HER A FORTUNE, IF ONLY SHE WOULD FIND THE SECRET OF HIS STRENGTH, AND THE WAY TO ROB HIM OF IT. AND SO SHE BEGAN...

WHY WON'T YOU TELL ME YOUR SECRET? YOU WOULD IF YOU REALLY LOVED ME.

IT'S NO SECRET. TIE ME UP WITH SOGGY BOWSTRINGS AND I'LL BE LIKE A KITTEN.

YOU'RE LAUGHING AT ME!

I'M SORRY. ONLY UNUSED ROPE CAN HOLD ME AND —

WHY DO YOU KEEP LYING?

ALL RIGHT THE TRUTH — WEAVE MY HAIR INTO A LOOM AND THEN — WHERE ARE YOU GOING?

IN THE END HE GAVE IN.

IT'S MY HAIR.

SHE WAS SO PERSISTENT. BUT THEN SHE WOULD BE — THEY'D OFFERED HER A **FORTUNE**.

HIS STRENGTH CAME FROM GOD.

HIS LONG HAIR WAS A SYMBOL, A SIGN OF HIS DEVOTION. IF HIS HAIR WAS CUT, GOD WOULD TAKE HIS STRENGTH AWAY.

HE SHOULD NEVER HAVE TOLD HER, BECAUSE WHILE HE SLEPT (WORN OUT BY HER CONSTANT NAGGING, NO DOUBT), SHE CUT OFF ALL HIS HAIR.

IT WAS ALL HE HAD LEFT OF HIS VOWS AS A NAZARITE. HE'D ALREADY BROKEN THE OTHERS, AND NOW THAT HE HAD ALLOWED THIS WOMAN TO CUT HIS HAIR, HE WAS NO DIFFERENT FROM ANYONE ELSE.

HE WAS NO STRONGER THAN AN ORDINARY MAN. AND THE PHILISTINES CAPTURED HIM JUST AS EASILY.

YOU CAN'T IMAGINE HOW MUCH THE PHILISTINES HATED SAMSON. THEY GOUGED HIS EYES OUT AND MADE HIM WORK LIKE A COMMON OX.

HE HAD ONCE BEEN ISRAEL'S DEFENDER, CHOSEN BY GOD HIMSELF! NOW HE WAS NO BETTER THAN A FARM ANIMAL.

NOW, THE PHILISTINES WORSHIPPED A GOD THEY CALLED DAGON, AND WITH SAMSON NOT ONLY THEIR PRISONER, BUT UTTERLY HUMILIATED INTO THE BARGAIN, THEY DECIDED TO HOLD A GREAT FEAST IN CELEBRATION, TO THANK THEIR GOD.

WE CAN DO WHAT WE LIKE WITH ISRAEL NOW! WHO'S TO STOP US? THE FOOLS PUT THEIR TRUST IN ONE MAN, AND NOW HE'S OURS!

HAVE THE GUARDS BRING SAMSON OUT SO WE CAN ALL HAVE A GOOD LOOK AT HIM. I THINK IT WOULD BE MOST... *ENTERTAINING*.

BUT AS SAMSON HAD LANGUISHED IN THE DUNGEON, HIS HAIR HAD GRADUALLY STARTED TO GROW BACK.

AND AS HIS HAIR GREW BACK, HE STARTED TO THINK CLEARLY, PERHAPS FOR THE FIRST TIME IN HIS LIFE...

LORD GOD, PLEASE DO NOT FORGET ME! WEAK AND BLIND, I CAN SEE THINGS CLEARLY AT LAST!

I AM SAMSON, THE NAZARITE, AND I HAVE BEEN A FOOL!

I HAVE NOT FOLLOWED YOUR LAWS, I HAVE BROKEN MY VOWS, AND NOW YOUR PEOPLE ARE LEADERLESS. HELP ME!

AND SO THE GUARDS CAME FOR SAMSON, AND HAULED HIM OUT FOR ALL THE PHILISTINES TO SEE.

AND HE *'ENTERTAINED'* THEM.

NOT SO BRAVE NOW, EH?

NOT SO STRONG NOW! LOOK AT HIM, HE'S CRYING!

CRYING LIKE A BABY! DID WE HURT HIM, POOR LITTLE THING!

KICK HIM! *HURT HIM!!*

ARRRGGH!!!

ALL RIGHT, THAT'S ENOUGH FOR NOW. WE DON'T WANT HIM DEAD. NOT *YET* ANYWAY. WE WANT TO HAVE A LOT MORE 'FUN' WITH HIM YET!

I CAN'T WALK. PLEASE, LET ME LEAN AGAINST ONE OF THE TEMPLE PILLARS!

SO IT WAS THERE, IN THE TEMPLE OF DAGON, SURROUNDED BY HIS BITTEREST ENEMIES, THAT HE PRAYED HIS LAST PRAYER –

REMEMBER ME, MY GOD! STRENGTHEN ME JUST ONE LAST TIME, AND LET ME GET REVENGE ON THE PHILISTINES!

AND, STILL PRAYING, HE PUT HIS HANDS AGAINST THE PILLARS –

WHAT DOES HE THINK HE'S DOING?

HIS MIND'S GONE AS SOFT AS HIS MUSCLES!

AND HE PUSHED WITH ALL HIS MIGHT, CRYING OUT –

GIVE ME ONE LAST BLOW AGAINST THE PHILISTINES! AS REVENGE FOR MY EYES!!

SAMSON'S FAITH HAD RETURNED, AND WITH IT, HIS GREAT STRENGTH!

THE TEMPLE WAS PACKED: GENERALS, LEADERS, KINGS, THE MOST IMPORTANT PEOPLE IN THE LAND, ALL COME TO LAUGH AT SAMSON!

UH?!

LET ME DIE WITH THE PHILISTINES!!

AS HE PUSHED WITH ALL HIS MIGHT, THE ROOF CAVED IN, KILLING EVERYONE INSIDE!

AND WITH THAT ONE BLOW, SAMSON THE MIGHTY WARRIOR KILLED MORE THAN HE HAD IN HIS ENTIRE LIFE!

AND HE DIED?

YEAH, BUT HE TOOK THE PHILISTINES WITH HIM. DON'T YOU LISTEN?

EXCELLENT!

NOW GET TO BED THE LOT OF YOU!

IN THOSE DAYS THERE WAS NO KING IN ISRAEL, AND EACH MAN DID AS HE SAW FIT.

BUT AMIDST THE BLOODSHED AND CHAOS, LIFE WENT ON AS IT HAD ALWAYS DONE. FOR EXAMPLE...

... THE STORY OF —

RUTH

OH! YOU LOOK BEAUTIFUL! LIKE A PRINCESS! LIKE RACHEL HERSELF! THE MOST BEAUTIFUL BRIDE IN THE WORLD!

I FEEL STUPID. I LOOK FAT, MY SKIN'S GONE FUNNY AND THE DRESS DOESN'T FIT ME ANY MORE!

YOU'LL HAVE TO TELL THEM THE WEDDING'S CANCELLED!

TELL EVERYONE I'VE CHANGED MY MIND.

TELL THEM I'VE FALLEN OUT OF A WINDOW AND HAVE BEEN SAT ON BY A FAT, LAME CAMEL AND YOU CAN'T MOVE IT, OR TELL WHICH OF US IS WHICH!

HUSH, HUSH, CHILD. DON'T SPEAK LIKE THAT. YOU'RE NERVOUS, THAT'S ALL. EVERYONE GETS NERVOUS BEFORE THEIR WEDDING.

LISTEN, MY LOVE, AND I'LL TELL YOU A STORY, AS IT WAS TOLD TO ME BY MY MOTHER AND HERS BEFORE HER.

LONG AGO, WHEN ISRAEL WAS RULED BY THE JUDGES, THERE WERE THREE WOMEN, NAOMI, ORPAH AND RUTH.

NAOMI WAS ONE OF US — AN ISRAELITE. ORPAH AND RUTH WERE MOABITE GIRLS, HER DAUGHTERS-IN-LAW. ALL THREE WOMEN WERE WIDOWS...

I'VE LOVED YOU TWO AS IF YOU WERE MY OWN DAUGHTERS, BUT I THINK NOW WE SHOULD SAY GOODBYE FOR GOOD. WE'RE ALL WIDOWS NOW, BUT YOU AT LEAST ARE STILL YOUNG.

FIND NEW HUSBANDS. MAKE THEM AS HAPPY AS YOU DID MY TWO SONS.

GO BACK TO YOUR FAMILIES, FOR I'VE LOST MINE. BELIEVE ME, IT'S BEST THIS WAY.

BUT WHAT ABOUT YOU?

ME? EVEN IF IT WERE POSSIBLE FOR ME TO FIND ANOTHER HUSBAND, I'M TOO OLD TO HAVE ANY MORE CHILDREN FOR YOU TO MARRY!

THAT'S NOT WHAT I MEANT.

GO ON. BE HAPPY. YOU HAVE THE REST OF YOUR LIVES AHEAD OF YOU.

ARE YOU STILL HERE, RUTH? I TOLD YOU TO GO!

GOD HAS TAKEN MY FAMILY FROM ME! I HAVE NOTHING LEFT! NOTHING TO LIVE FOR! GO WITH ORPAH!

BUT I DON'T WANT TO LEAVE YOU!

WHY?!! I HAVE NO HUSBAND, YOU HAVE NO HUSBAND, WE HAVE NO CHILDREN, NOTHING!

IT'S NO USE TELLING ME TO GO, BECAUSE I **WON'T**! WHERE YOU GO, I GO AND THAT'S ALL THERE IS TO IT! FROM NOW ON **YOUR** PEOPLE WILL BE MY PEOPLE, YOUR GOD MY GOD. WHERE YOU DIE I'LL DIE, AND THERE I'LL BE BURIED! MAY GOD DO SOMETHING DREADFUL TO ME, IF ANYTHING EXCEPT DEATH SEPARATES THE TWO OF US!

AND SO THEY STAYED TOGETHER. WITH ONLY EACH OTHER IN THE WHOLE WORLD FOR COMPANY, THE TWO WIDOWS SET OFF FOR THE HOME THAT NAOMI HAD LEFT SOME YEARS BEFORE — A SMALL, UNIMPORTANT TOWN TO THE SOUTH OF JERUSALEM.

A PLACE CALLED BETHLEHEM.

THEY ARRIVED IN APRIL, AT THE BEGINNING OF THE HARVEST. THEY WERE DESPERATELY POOR, BUT THE LAW OF MOSES PROVIDES FOR WIDOWS.

THEY WERE ALLOWED BY LAW TO COLLECT THE **GLEANINGS**, THE LEFTOVERS FROM THE HARVEST, AND IN THIS WAY RUTH GATHERED ENOUGH FOR THEM BOTH TO EAT.

HOWEVER, GOD WAS AT WORK IN THEIR LIVES FOR IT TURNED OUT THE FIELD BELONGED TO A MAN CALLED **BOAZ**...

FOREMAN, WHO'S THAT WOMAN OVER THERE?

A MOABITE WIDOW, SHE CAME BACK WITH YOUR COUSIN, NAOMI. SHE'S BEEN OUT THERE ALL DAY WITHOUT A BREAK.

TELL THE MEN THEY AREN'T TO TROUBLE HER IN ANY WAY, OR THEY'LL ANSWER TO ME. UNDERSTAND?

THERE ARE ALL SORTS OF STRANGE MEN AROUND AT HARVEST TIME, SO FOLLOW MY SERVANTS AS THEY WORK. I'VE TOLD THE MEN TO LEAVE YOU WELL ALONE, SO YOU'LL BE QUITE SAFE HERE.

HELLO! I HOPE YOU DON'T MIND SOME ADVICE?

I'VE ALSO HAD THEM BRING UP ENOUGH WATER TO DRINK WHILE THEY WORK, AND ONE MORE WON'T MAKE ANY DIFFERENCE! SO PLEASE HELP YOURSELF.

I... I DON'T KNOW WHAT TO SAY. YOU'RE VERY KIND, SIR.

NOT EVEN IF SHE PICKS THE BEST CORN IN THE FIELD. IN FACT, TELL THEM TO LEAVE THE BEST OF THE HARVEST WHERE SHE CAN FIND IT.

IF YOU SAY SO — IT'S YOUR FIELD.

NO! YOU'RE THE ONE WHO'S BEEN KIND. I HEARD HOW YOU DECIDED TO STAY AND LOOK AFTER NAOMI, EVEN THOUGH SHE HAS NO CLAIM ON YOU.

WE'RE ABOUT TO EAT — WHY NOT JOIN US?

AND THAT WAS THAT. BOAZ TOOK PITY ON RUTH, WAS MOVED BY HER KINDNESS, AND HELPED HER OUT.

OF COURSE HE COULDN'T **HELP** BUT NOTICE THAT SHE WAS ALSO YOUNG AND ATTRACTIVE, AND FREE.

HE'S NOT TAKEN HIS EYES OFF HER ONCE ALL DAY!

SSSHH! THEY'LL **HEAR** YOU! YOU HEARD WHAT HE SAID; TAKE SOME OF THE BEST CORN AND DROP IT WHERE SHE CAN 'FIND' IT... AND STOP GIGGLING.

RUTH, HOW EVER DID YOU GET SO MUCH CORN?

I MET A MAN CALLED BOAZ, HE TOLD ME TO GLEAN HIS FIELD AND —

BOAZ? YOU FOUND **BOAZ**? BUT HE'S A RELATIVE OF MINE! MAYBE GOD HASN'T ABANDONED US AFTER ALL!

NAOMI'S HEART HAD BEEN ALMOST DESTROYED BY GRIEF, AND SHE HAD BEEN FULL OF BITTERNESS. BUT GOD CAN HEAL WHAT TIME CAN'T.

AS RUTH AND BOAZ STARTED TO FALL IN LOVE, SO GOD HEALED NAOMI'S BROKEN HEART.

WHY NOT WEAR THIS COLOUR TONIGHT, RUTH. YOU KNOW, YOU ALWAYS LOOKED SO PRETTY IN IT. WHERE'S THAT PERFUME I GAVE YOU? YOU CAN'T STAY IN MOURNING FOR EVER. LIFE GOES ON, YOU KNOW!

I'M GLAD I STAYED WITH YOU. YOU'RE LIKE YOUR OLD SELF AGAIN.

LESS OF THE 'OLD' THANK YOU.

AND SO, WEARING HER NICEST CLOTHES, MOST EXPENSIVE PERFUME, AND GENERALLY LOOKING *BEAUTIFUL*, RUTH WENT TO SEE BOAZ...

IT LOOKS AS IF YOU'VE SETTLED IN NICELY, RUTH. EVERYONE SPEAKS VERY HIGHLY OF YOU. ER... HAVE YOU GIVEN ANY THOUGHT TO FINDING A... HUSBAND? I MEAN, THERE ARE ENOUGH YOUNG MEN AROUND.

I DON'T *WANT* A YOUNG MAN.

UNDER THE LAW A WIDOW WITHOUT CHILDREN HAS THE RIGHT TO MARRY ONE OF HER HUSBAND'S FAMILY.

I SEE... THERE *IS* A MAN IN THIS TOWN, A MUCH CLOSER RELATIVE THAN... WELL, THAN *I*, FOR EXAMPLE. BY LAW HE SHOULD BE ASKED FIRST.

AND IF HE SAYS NO..?

DON'T GO AWAY, I'LL BE RIGHT BACK!

AND SO HE WENT TO THE TOWN GATE, WHERE THE ELDERS GATHER, AND FOUND THE RELATIVE IN QUESTION.

IF A MAN DIES CHILDLESS, HIS WIFE MAY MARRY ONE OF HIS FAMILY SO THE NAME LIVES ON. BUT THAT'S NOT ALL...

THE NEW HUSBAND MUST BUY ALL THE DEAD MAN'S PROPERTY, BUT IT ISN'T HIS TO KEEP...

NAOMI WANTS TO SE[LL] THE LAND THAT BELONGED TO HER DEAD SON. YOU'VE TH[E] RIGHT TO IT, IF YOU WANT.

MMM. THEN I WILL – IT WAS GOOD LAND HE OWNED.

THIS MEANS YOU'LL HAVE TO MARRY HIS WIDOW, AND IT WILL ALL GO TO HER CHILDREN.

IN THAT CASE I CAN'T. IT WOULD BE TOO MUCH OF A BURDEN, AND MY OWN ESTATE WOULD SUFFER. YOU MARRY HER!

AND SO THEY WERE MARRIED, BOAZ AND RUTH, AND VERY HAPPY THEY WERE TOO!

YOU SEE, GOD IS AT WORK IN THE LIVES OF EVEN THE MOST ORDINARY PEOPLE. THESE WEREN'T KINGS OR JUDGES, AND YET GOD USED THEM IN AN INCREDIBLE WAY...

RUTH HAD A BABY BOY, AND SHE CALLED HIM OBED, WHO BECAME THE FATHER OF JESSE, WHO GREW UP TO BE THE FATHER OF THE MOST FAMOUS PERSON IN ALL ISRAEL —

RUTH WAS THE GREAT-GRANDMOTHER OF KING DAVID HIMSELF!

BUT RUTH WAS NO ONE SPECIAL! SH[E] WASN'T EVEN AN ISRAELITE!

– AND WHO KNOWS *WHERE* THE STORY OF HIS CHILDREN WILL E[ND] NOW HURRY UP – ST[ILL] WANT TO GET MARRI[ED]

OF COURSE I DO, BUT WHAT HAPPENED TO –

I'LL TELL YOU WHEN YOU'RE MARRIED; NOW *HURRY!*

THE STORY OF JOB

ONCE, LONG AGO, THERE LIVED A MAN WHO FEARED GOD, LOVED HIS NEIGHBOUR AND WORKED HARD.

AS GOOD A MAN AS YOU'D EVER MEET.

'HIS NAME WAS **JOB**. THERE WAS NO ONE LIKE HIM ON THE WHOLE EARTH AND GOD **KNEW** IT — HE WAS BLAMELESS, LOVED WHAT WAS GOOD AND SHUNNED EVIL IN ALL ITS FORMS.'

'BUT GOD WAS NOT THE **ONLY** ONE TO NOTICE.'

THE **DEVIL** CAME TO GOD SAYING:

'YOU'VE MADE JOB'S LIFE SO EASY HIS DEVOTION TO YOU IS MEANINGLESS.'

'TAKE AWAY ALL HE HAS, AND HE WILL **CURSE** YOU TO YOUR **FACE**!'

'BUT GOD HAD CONFIDENCE IN JOB, SO GOD **ALLOWED** THE DEVIL TO TEST HIM.'

'FIRST HIS **WEALTH** WENT — IN ONE **DAY** SOLDIERS STOLE HIS DONKEYS AND OXEN, FIRE FELL FROM THE **SKY** ON HIS SHEEP, AND ENEMY RAIDERS TOOK ALL HIS **CAMELS**.'

'HE LOST EVERYTHING.'

'WHILE JOB WAS STILL STUNNED, A MESSENGER ARRIVED, BRINGING EVEN **WORSE** TIDINGS.'

'A FREAK WIND HAD STRUCK HIS ELDEST SON'S HOUSE, KILLING **ALL** HIS CHILDREN.'

'TO JOB IT WAS AS IF HIS WORLD HAD ENDED.'

I CAME INTO THIS LIFE WITH NOTHING, AND I'LL **LEAVE** WITH NOTHING. GOD GIVES AND GOD TAKES **AWAY**.

'DESPITE ALL THAT HAPPENED, JOB DIDN'T BLAME GOD.'

SO GOD SAID TO THE DEVIL, 'SEE? ALTHOUGH YOU **PROVOKE** HIM, JOB REMAINS **FAITHFUL**.'

'SKIN FOR SKIN!' SAID THE DEVIL. 'A MAN WILL GIVE **EVERYTHING** HE OWNS TO SAVE HIS OWN LIFE. HE WILL SACRIFICE HIS OWN **FAMILY** IF IT'LL SAVE HIM! IF YOU AFFECT HIS HEALTH **THEN** HE WILL CURSE YOU!'

'SO JOB'S OWN **BODY** TURNED ON HIM, BREAKING OUT IN AGONIZING **SORES**.'

GOD HAS **RUINED** US. WHY DON'T YOU JUST **CURSE** HIM AND **DIE**?

DON'T **SPEAK** LIKE THAT!

GOD SENT US GOOD THINGS AND WE ACCEPTED THEM **GLADLY**. SHOULD WE FORGET THE GOOD TIMES AND TURN ON HIM WHEN THINGS GO **BAD** FOR US?

'PEOPLE WANTED NOTHING MORE TO DO WITH JOB IN CASE HIS BAD LUCK WAS SOMEHOW CONTAGIOUS, BUT HE HAD THREE FRIENDS WHO REMAINED LOYAL.'

'FOR SEVEN DAYS THEY SAT WITH HIM, NOT SAYING A WORD, SHARING HIS GRIEF. THIS WAS JOB! THE FINEST MAN THERE WAS. HOW COULD THIS HAPPEN?'

JOB, I CAN'T THINK OF ANYONE WHO WAS EVER PUNISHED WITHOUT A REASON. PEOPLE WHO DO EVIL ARE REPAID WITH EVIL. LIFE IS FULL OF TROUBLE JUST AS SMOKE FLIES UPWARDS. YOU MUST HAVE DONE SOMETHING WRONG. MY ADVICE IS TO TURN TO GOD AND AWAIT HIS ANSWER.

DO YOU THINK I HAVEN'T DONE THAT?

YOU THINK I CAN'T TELL WRONG FROM RIGHT? I'VE DONE NOTHING WRONG. I ONLY WISH I COULD SPEAK TO GOD AND ARGUE MY CASE.

JOB WAS DEVASTATED. THERE HE WAS, IN PAIN, NO MONEY, NO FAMILY, WITH INSECTS STARTING TO LAY EGGS IN HIS OPEN SORES –

UGH!

– AND HIS FRIENDS TELL HIM THIS IS SOMEHOW ALL HIS FAULT! EVENTUALLY A YOUNG MAN NEARBY, ANGRY AT THEIR ARGUMENTS, DECIDES TO ADD HIS VOICE TO THE COMMOTION...

I THOUGHT OLD PEOPLE WERE MEANT TO BE WISE! YOU SAY YOU'RE INNOCENT – YET GOD HAS PUNISHED YOU. IT'S UNTHINKABLE THAT GOD WOULD MAKE A MISTAKE, OR THAT HE WOULD BE UNJUST! HOW CAN YOU EVEN THINK SUCH THINGS?!

I ONLY WANT GOD TO TELL ME WHY THIS HAS HAPPENED...

HE HAS NO TIME FOR THE ARROGANT, FOR PEOPLE WHO ATTEMPT TO PATHETICALLY JUSTIFY THEMSELVES BEFORE SUCH A MIGHTY, POWERFUL, NOBLE GOD!

AND THAT WAS IT.

TO THE YOUNG MAN, GOD WAS UNREACHABLE, DISTANT AND NOT ALL THAT INTERESTED IN THE LIVES OF THE WEAK AND INSIGNIFICANT.

'IT WAS AT THIS POINT THAT GOD HIMSELF DECIDED TO PUT IN AN APPEARANCE!'

JOB! YOU HAVE MANY QUESTIONS, BUT ANSWER ME THIS:

WHERE WERE YOU WHEN I MADE THE WORLD?

THE STORY OF SAMUEL

WHEN JOSHUA LED THE PEOPLE INTO THE PROMISED LAND, HE SENT THE ARK OF THE COVENANT TO A PLACE CALLED **SHILOH**, AND THERE IT STAYED FOR ALMOST TWO HUNDRED YEARS.

ISRAEL HAD NO TEMPLES, BUT THE ARK WAS KEPT IN A LARGE TENT, TENDED BY A FAMILY OF PRIESTS, RESPONSIBILITY PASSING FROM FATHER TO SON. EVEN WHEN PEOPLE TREATED GOD WITH CONTEMPT, SHILOH STAYED AS THE FOCUS OF RELIGIOUS LIFE.

EVENTUALLY THE FESTIVALS BECAME MERE SOCIAL EVENTS, DEVOID OF ANY REAL MEANING.

EVERY YEAR PEOPLE WOULD TRAVEL UP TO SHILOH TO WORSHIP GOD AND MAKE SACRIFICES. AMONG THEM, AT THIS TIME, CAME A MAN NAMED ELKANAH, WITH HIS TWO WIVES, PENINNAH AND HANNAH.

AND IT IS WITH **HANNAH** THAT OUR STORY STARTS. ALTHOUGH ELKANAH'S OTHER WIFE HAD CHILDREN, HANNAH HAD NONE...

HAA-HAA!

AND PENINNAH WAS CRUEL, AND TEASED HANNAH MERCILESSLY.

YOU SHOULDN'T LET HER UPSET YOU HANNAH.

I'M NOT UPSET.

THEN WHY ARE YOU CRYING? SHE'S JUST JEALOUS. SHE KNOWS THAT I LOVE YOU MORE THAN HER, AND IT'S **TRUE**, I DO! WHAT DOES IT MATTER IF SHE HAS **TEN** SONS, I —

HANNAH? HAVE I SAID SOMETHING WRONG?

IT ALWAYS COMES BACK TO THAT, DOESN'T IT? I'M GOING TO THE TEMPLE! I'LL TALK TO YOU LATER!

OH, LORD GOD! IF ONLY YOU WOULD SEE MY MISERY AND GIVE ME JUST ONE SON, THEN I WOULD GIVE HIM BACK TO YOU FOR THE REST OF HIS LIFE!

WHAT'S THIS? ANOTHER DRUNK?!

HOW MANY TIMES MUST I **TELL** YOU PEOPLE! THIS IS THE HOUSE OF **GOD**! YOU CAN'T COME IN **HERE** TO SLEEP OFF YOUR HANGOVER!

NO SIR! I WAS PRAYING!

PRAYING?! FORGIVE ME. IT'S... WELL, IT'S BEEN A GOOD MANY YEARS SINCE I SAW SOMEONE DO **THAT** IN HERE. PRAYING, EH?

NOW THERE'S A THING...

WELL, MAY GOD BLESS YOU, CHILD. GO IN PEACE, AND MAY GOD **GIVE** YOU WHATEVER IT IS YOU WERE ASKING FOR!

AND AS ELI THE PRIEST SAID THESE WORDS, HANNAH FELT A GREAT SENSE OF **GLADNESS**. SHE SOMEHOW KNEW THAT GOD HAD HEARD HER PRAYERS, AND THAT THEY HAD BEEN ANSWERED!

SURE ENOUGH, SOON HANNAH BECAME PREGNANT AND GAVE BIRTH TO A SON, CALLED **SAMUEL**.

THOUGH SHE HAD WAITED SO MANY YEARS FOR A BABY, SHE KNEW THAT SHE MUST KEEP HER PROMISE TO GOD. HER TIME WITH SAMUEL WOULD BE VERY SHORT...

WHEN HE WAS OLD ENOUGH, SHE BROUGHT THE CHILD TO **ELI**, THE PRIEST...

I ASKED GOD FOR THIS CHILD, AND GOD GAVE HIM TO ME. NOW I GIVE HIM BACK— TO SERVE GOD FOR HIS WHOLE LIFE.

I SEE. AND WHAT DOES YOUR HUSBAND THINK OF THIS?

I SAY SHE SHOULD DO AS SHE THINKS BEST.

I MADE GOD A PROMISE, AND NOW I MUST KEEP IT. TAKE CARE OF HIM, FOR I LOVE HIM SO MUCH!

AND SO THE BOY SAMUEL SERVED THE LORD GOD.

HE GREW UP IN THE SHADOW OF THE ALTAR, MINISTERING WITH ELI, AND GROWING IN FAVOUR WITH GOD AND THE PEOPLE.

SADLY THE SAME COULD HARDLY BE SAID OF ELI'S **OWN** SONS...

ALTHOUGH THEY WOULD BE THE SPIRITUAL LEADERS OF THE NATION AFTER HIS DEATH, THEY DIDN'T CARE ABOUT GOD, THEIR DUTIES, OR ANYTHING BUT THEMSELVES!

LOOK IT'S (BURP) SAMM-UEL! SHUCH A NICE LAD!

I'LL DRINK TO THAT!

EVERY NIGHT, SAMUEL SLEPT IN THE TENT OF MEETING, NEAR THE ARK ITSELF. ONE NIGHT, AS HE LAY SLEEPING, SOMETHING **STRANGE** HAPPENED. HE HEARD A **VOICE**, CALLING HIM...

SAMUEL!

SAMUEL!

YOU CALLED ME, ELI! WHAT'S WRONG?

YOU'RE HAVING BAD DREAMS, BOY. NOW GO BACK TO BED, I DIDN'T CALL FOR YOU, AND YOU'VE A BUSY DAY TOMORROW.

SAMUEL DID AS HE WAS TOLD, BUT TEN MINUTES LATER...

ELI, YOU CALLED ME! I HEARD IT!

WELL IT WASN'T ME. THERE'S NO ONE HERE EXCEPT YOU AND I, AND IT CERTAINLY WASN'T **ME**.

GO BACK TO SLEEP, LAD.

A THIRD TIME, SAMUEL HEARD THE VOICE, AND AGAIN HE RAN TO ELI.

BUT I'M TELLING YOU, I WAS LYING BY THE ALTAR AND I HEARD A VOICE!

YOU KNOW, IF IT WERE ANYONE OTHER THAN YOU SAYING THIS I WOULD SAY THEY WERE LYING. BUT YOU...

SAMUEL, I THINK I KNOW WHAT'S HAPPENING.

GO BACK TO BED. IF YOU HEAR THE VOICE CALLING YOU AGAIN, SAY 'SPEAK, LORD, YOUR SERVANT IS LISTENING.'

BUT WHO IS IT?

IF IT'S WHO I THINK IT IS, YOU'LL KNOW SOON ENOUGH.

SO SAMUEL WENT BACK TO BED ONCE MORE, AND SOON FELL ASLEEP.

SAMUEL.

YES LORD, YOUR SERVANT IS LISTENING.

I AM ABOUT TO DO SOMETHING IN ISRAEL THAT WILL MAKE THE EARS OF ALL WHO HEAR TINGLE! I AM GOING TO JUDGE ELI AND HIS FAMILY, FOR HIS SONS WERE MEANT TO BE MY PRIESTS, BUT THEY HAVE COMMITTED BLASPHEMY AFTER BLASPHEMY IN MY NAME!

ELI KNEW, AND YET HE DID NOTHING TO STOP THEM. NO SACRIFICES WILL EVER MAKE UP FOR WHAT HE HAS ALLOWED TO HAPPEN.

AFTER GOD HAD SPOKEN, SAMUEL LAY AWAKE UNTIL MORNING, TOO SCARED TO FACE ELI WITH THE AWFUL NEWS.

SAMUEL? PLEASE ANSWER ME! WHAT HAPPENED LAST NIGHT? IT WAS HIM, WASN'T IT? THE LORD OUR GOD SPOKE TO YOU, DIDN'T HE? YOU DON'T KNOW HOW LONG IT IS SINCE ANYONE HEARD HIS VOICE. I NEVER THOUGHT WE WOULD HEAR IT IN MY LIFETIME.

WHATEVER HE SAID, WHATEVER HE TOLD YOU, YOU MUST TELL ME!

IT WAS GOD. HE SAID HE IS GOING TO JUDGE YOU AND YOUR FAMILY. YOUR SONS HAVE BLASPHEMED AND ACTED CORRUPTLY, AND YOU KNEW, BUT DID NOTHING ABOUT THEM.

I'M SORRY.

NO. DON'T BE.

HE IS GOD — LET HIM DO WHAT IS GOOD IN HIS SIGHT.

SOON AFTERWARDS, ELI'S SONS DIED IN BATTLE. THE NEWS BROKE ELI'S HEART AND HE TOO DIED.

THE YEARS PASSED BY.

SAMUEL WAS THE LAST OF THE GREAT JUDGES, AND HE LED HIS PEOPLE OUT FROM THE CHAOS OF THOSE DAYS.

HE URGED THEM TO ABANDON THE FOREIGN GODS, AND TO SEEK FORGIVENESS FOR THEIR UNHOLY PRACTICES.

THERE WAS PEACE IN ISRAEL AS THE HOSTILE PHILISTINES WERE SUBDUED, AND ISRAEL MADE PEACE WITH THE NEIGHBOURING AMORITES.

AND THROUGHOUT IT ALL THERE WAS SAMUEL, PRAYING DAY AND NIGHT, AND ADMINISTERING JUSTICE.

YEAR IN, YEAR OUT, HE TRAVELLED THE COUNTRY, SETTLING DISPUTES WITH HONESTY AND FAIRNESS. BUT ALWAYS HE RETURNED TO THE TOWN OF **RAMAH**, WHICH HE HAD MADE HIS HOME.

THE YEARS WENT BY. SAMUEL GREW OLD.

AND IT WAS TO RAMAH, THAT THE ELDERS OF ALL ISRAEL GATHERED, TO BRING SAMUEL UNBELIEVABLE NEWS...

SAMUEL, YOU HAVE LED US WELL THESE LAST YEARS, NO ONE CAN DENY IT. BUT YOU WON'T BE WITH US FOREVER, AND FRANKLY, WE WORRY ABOUT THE FUTURE.

WE HAVE DECIDED WE WANT TO BE LIKE OTHER COUNTRIES. WE WANT A **KING**!

IF YOU DO, YOU'LL CRY OUT TO GOD, BUT HE WON'T ANSWER YOU, BECAUSE YOU'VE REJECTED HIM AS YOUR RIGHTFUL KING!

WE'VE ALREADY DECIDED, SAMUEL. WE ARE UNITED ON THIS, AND YOU WON'T MAKE US CHANGE OUR MINDS.

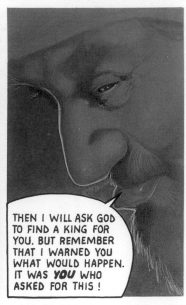

THEN I WILL ASK GOD TO FIND A KING FOR YOU. BUT REMEMBER THAT I WARNED YOU WHAT WOULD HAPPEN. IT WAS *YOU* WHO ASKED FOR THIS!

THE STORY OF SAUL

AND SO SAMUEL PRAYED, AND WAITED FOR THE MAN GOD WOULD CHOOSE AS KING.

NOW, THERE WAS A MAN CALLED KISH, FROM THE TRIBE OF BENJAMIN, WHO HAD LOST SOME DONKEYS. ANXIOUS TO RECOVER THEM, HE SENT HIS SON AND A SERVANT TO FIND THEM.

THEY WERE GONE FOR SO LONG, THAT SOON PEOPLE FORGOT ABOUT THE DONKEYS, AND STARTED WORRYING ABOUT *THEM*...

THIS IS *HOPELESS.* THEY'RE EITHER DEAD NOW, OR SOMEONE HAS FOUND THEM AND TAKEN THEM HIMSELF.

IN THE NEXT TOWN THERE'S A FAMOUS PROPHET. PERHAPS HE COULD ASK GOD WHERE THEY ARE?

IT'S WORTH A TRY. AT LEAST WE CAN TELL MY FATHER WE ASKED *EVERYONE* – WE EVEN ASKED *GOD*!

THE YOUNG MAN'S NAME WAS SAUL, AND AS HE MADE HIS WAY TOWARDS WHERE SAMUEL WAS CAMPED HE HAD NO IDEA OF THE DESTINY THAT AWAITED HIM..!

EXCUSE ME SIR, BUT WE'RE LOOKING FOR THE *SEER*, THE HOLY MAN.

ARE YOU INDEED? WELL, YOU'VE FOUND HIM, SAUL, SON OF KISH.

HOW DID YOU KNOW MY NAME? I'M ONLY A BENJAMITE, NO ONE IMPORTANT.

REALLY? ALL OF ISRAEL IS LOOKING EXPECTANTLY AT YOUR FAMILY RIGHT NOW. TONIGHT YOU WILL STAY WITH ME AND EAT. WE HAVE MUCH TO DISCUSS, YOU AND I.

AND BY THE WAY – DON'T WORRY ABOUT THE DONKEYS. THEY FOUND THEM THREE DAYS AGO!

THAT NIGHT SAUL ATE WITH SAMUEL, AS GUEST OF HONOUR AT THE HEAD OF A TABLE OF THIRTY ELDERS AND LEADERS.

SAUL AND SAMUEL TALKED LONG INTO THE NIGHT. AND WHILE THE TOWNSFOLK SLEPT AROUND THEM, SAMUEL AND SAUL CHANGED THE COURSE OF THE ENTIRE NATION...

SAUL! WAKE UP, IT'S TIME WE WERE ON OUR WAY!

WHAT TIME IS IT? I'VE ONLY JUST GOT OFF TO SLEEP!

WE'VE A LOT TO GET THROUGH TODAY. SEND YOUR SERVANT ON AHEAD, AND WE'LL CATCH HIM UP LATER.

WHAT IS IT THAT'S SO IMPORTANT THAT MY SERVANT MAY NOT HEAR?

I HAVE A MESSAGE FOR YOU. A MESSAGE FROM **GOD**, FOR YOUR EARS ALONE.

GOD ANOINTS YOU AS RULER OF ALL ISRAEL. KNEEL, SAUL, SON OF KISH!

THE SPIRIT OF GOD WILL COME UPON YOU, AND YOU WILL BECOME LIKE THE PROPHETS. YOU WILL BE CHANGED BY IT, AND WILL BE A DIFFERENT PERSON. YOU HAVE BEEN CHOSEN NOT BY MEN, BUT BY **GOD**. THE PEOPLE HAVE ASKED FOR A KING, AND SO GOD SENDS THEM **YOU**.

AND SO SAMUEL SUMMONED THE ELDERS AND LEADERS, TO BREAK THE NEWS —

HEAR ME, ISRAEL! GOD HAS ANSWERED YOU! LISTEN TO WHAT HE SAYS: 'I RESCUED YOU FROM EGYPT, I SAVED YOU FROM SLAVERY. BUT NOW YOU HAVE REJECTED YOUR GOD WHO SAVES YOU, AND HAVE ASKED FOR A KING!'

HE IS OF THE TRIBE OF BENJAMIN, OF THE CLAN OF MATRI, AND THE FAMILY OF KISH!

BUT KISH'S FAMILY ARE ALL HERE WITH US. ALL EXCEPT...

HIS NAME IS **SAUL**!

THIS IS THE MAN GOD HAS CHOSEN! THERE IS NO ONE LIKE HIM IN ALL ISRAEL!

THIS IS YOUR KING!

LONG LIVE THE KING! LONG LIVE THE KING!

IT WAS JUST WHAT THE PEOPLE HAD WANTED.

ANY CRITICS OF THE NEW RULER WERE SILENCED BY SAUL'S SUCCESS AS A MILITARY LEADER.

BEFORE HE WAS EVEN CONFIRMED AS KING, SAUL LIBERATED THE CITY OF JABESH, CAPTURED BY THE AMMONITES.

THE NATION UNITED BEHIND SAUL.

SAUL LED THE PEOPLE TO VICTORY AFTER VICTORY. ENEMIES THAT HAD THREATENED ISRAEL FOR YEARS WERE SWIFTLY DEALT WITH.

SAUL MUSTERED THE ARMY AGAINST THE PHILISTINES, BUT SAMUEL SENT WORD TO WAIT SEVEN DAYS BEFORE ATTACKING, SO THAT HE MIGHT COME AND OFFER THE REQUIRED SACRIFICES TO GOD.

BUT SAUL WOULD NOT WAIT...

SIR! WE'VE BEEN HERE SIX DAYS NOW AND STILL NO WORD! LET US ATTACK NOW OR LEAVE!

SOMETHING MUST HAVE HAPPENED TO SAMUEL TO DELAY HIM. I DON'T LIKE THIS AT ALL.

SAUL WAS THEIR KING AND ALL THE WHILE IN THE BACKGROUND THERE WAS **SAMUEL** – EVER FAITHFUL, WATCHING AND GUIDING.

BUT THERE WAS A PRICE. GOD HAD CHOSEN SAUL AS A HUMBLE MAN, BUT SOON HE WAS CONSUMED WITH ARROGANCE...

PREPARE THE OFFERINGS. THERE'S NOTHING FOR IT: I MUST DO THE SACRIFICES MYSELF!

BUT SIR, SAMUEL HAS ALWAYS –

GOD SPEAKS TO SAMUEL, SAMUEL SPEAKS TO ME, IT'S ALL THE SAME THING. NOW HURRY! LET'S GET THE SACRIFICES OVER WITH SO WE CAN GET ON WITH THE BATTLE!

SAUL!

AH, SAMUEL! THERE YOU ARE! I WAS STARTING TO WORRY ABOUT YOU.

I THOUGHT YOU WEREN'T COMING SO I'VE DONE THE OFFERINGS MYSELF!

YOU WERE TOLD TO WAIT! THE INSTRUCTION CAME FROM **GOD**, NOT ME!

IF YOU HAD ONLY DONE AS YOU WERE TOLD, YOUR KINGDOM WOULD HAVE LASTED FOR EVER!

AND NOW?

GOD WILL FIND ANOTHER. SOMEONE AFTER HIS OWN HEART.

AND FROM THAT MOMENT, SAUL STARTED TO CHANGE...

SAUL AND HIS SON, **JONATHAN**, DEFEATED THE PHILISTINES THAT DAY. DESPITE SAMUEL'S WORDS, THE VICTORIES STILL CAME THICK AND FAST.

THEN SAUL RECEIVED WORD FROM SAMUEL THAT THEY WERE TO ATTACK THE AMALEKITES. GOD HAD HIS OWN REASONS, AND SAUL WAS TO OBEY.

THE AMALEKITES WERE TO BE COMPLETELY WIPED OUT, EVEN THEIR CATTLE AND SHEEP MUST DIE.

AND SO SAUL DID ALL THAT GOD HAD SAID.

WITH ONE OR TWO EXCEPTIONS...

AGAG, KING OF THE AMALEKITES! I'VE DECIDED TO LET YOU LIVE. AFTER ALL, THERE ARE NO AMALEKITES LEFT TO RULE, ARE THERE?

WHAT WILL SAMUEL SAY?

I'M SURE HE'LL BE **DELIGHTED**!

ANOTHER VICTORY, SAMUEL. MAY GOD BLESS YOU, FOR I HAVE CARRIED OUT YOUR INSTRUCTIONS TO THE LETTER.

TO THE LETTER, EH? THEN WHY DO I HEAR THE BLEATING OF SHEEP? WHY CAN I HEAR COWS MOOING? WHY IS YOUR CAMP FULL OF HERDS OF ANIMALS?!

IT SEEMED A WASTE TO KILL THEM. SO WE SAVED THE BEST SHEEP AND CATTLE, AND I'M GOING TO SACRIFICE THEM ALL TO YOUR GOD!

STOP! I DON'T WANT TO **HEAR** ANY OF THIS!

ONCE, BY YOUR OWN ADMISSION, YOU WERE NO ONE SPECIAL. YET GOD ANOINTED YOU AS KING OF ISRAEL! WHY DIDN'T YOU JUST OBEY HIM?

LOOK, WE **WON** DIDN'T WE? I KEPT THE SHEEP AS A SACRIFICE!

SAUL, YOU POOR FOOL. DO YOU THINK GOD TAKES DELIGHT IN SACRIFICES MORE THAN SIMPLE OBEDIENCE?

TO HEAR GOD'S VOICE AND HEED IT IS BETTER THAN A WHOLE HERD OF SACRIFICES!

IF IT'S SO BAD, HOW COME WE WON?

YOU HAD A CHOICE. YOU CHOSE TO DISOBEY GOD, AND REBELLION IS AS EVIL AS WITCHCRAFT!

THERE IS NOTHING MORE THAT I CAN DO FOR YOU.

WAIT! I AM STILL THE KING! YOU CAN'T JUST LEAVE ME LIKE THIS!

RRRRiiiiP!

THIS... THIS IS A SYMBOL, SAUL. JUST AS YOU'VE TORN THIS ROBE, SO GOD HAS TORN THE KINGDOM AWAY FROM YOU, AND GIVEN IT TO SOMEONE ELSE.

ALL RIGHT, I WAS WRONG! BUT PLEASE, SAMUEL. ALL THE ELDERS OF ISRAEL ARE HERE TODAY TO CELEBRATE THE VICTORY. THEY ARE EXPECTING YOU TO LEAD US IN WORSHIP.

IF YOU AREN'T WITH ME, I WILL BE HUMILIATED! PLEASE DON'T DO THIS TO ME!

VERY WELL FOR WHAT YOU **WERE** NOT FOR WHAT YOU **ARE**, I WILL COME WITH YOU THIS ONE LAST TIME...

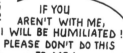

AFTER THE SACRIFICES WERE MADE, SAMUEL LEFT. HE MOURNED FOR SAUL THE REST OF HIS LIFE, BUT NEVER SAW HIM AGAIN.

ISRAEL NEEDED ANOTHER KING, AND SO AT GOD'S PROMPTING SAMUEL SET OFF TO A SMALL TOWN OVERLOOKED UP TO NOW IN THE SCHEMES OF THE STRONG AND THE POWERFUL.

HE WENT TO SEEK A MAN CALLED **JESSE**, TO BRING HIM STRANGE AND WONDERFUL NEWS.

WITH A **HEART FULL OF HOPE**, SAMUEL MADE HIS WAY TOWARDS THE TOWN OF **BETHLEHEM**.

THE STORY OF DAVID

IT'S NO USE, I CAN'T SLEEP!

MY BONES ARE TOO OLD AND MY EYES ARE TOO TIRED.

YOUR MAJESTY?

OH. THERE YOU ARE, ABISHAG. I WAS THINKING YOU'D RUN OFF WITH A YOUNGER MAN!

MY LORD! HOW COULD YOU EVER SAY SUCH A THING?

DEAR WOMAN, I WAS JOKING. I CAN STILL JOKE, YOU KNOW. IT'S ABOUT ALL I CAN DO THESE DAYS.

FORGIVE ME, SIR.

FOR PITY'S SAKE, STOP YOUR BOWING AND SCRAPING. I'VE BEEN KING FOR TOO LONG TO BE IMPRESSED BY ALL THAT. NOW THEN, WHERE WAS I?

YOU WERE ABOUT TO TELL ME HOW YOU BECAME KING.

HOW I BECAME KING. YES.

WE LIVED IN BETHLEHEM. MY FATHER WAS A SHEPHERD CALLED JESSE, THE SON OF OBED, THE SON OF BOAZ. AN UNIMPORTANT FAMILY IN AN INSIGNIFICANT LITTLE TOWN IN THE SOUTH. I'M OUT MINDING THE SHEEP AS USUAL WHEN MY BROTHER SHOUTS—

HEY DAVID! COME QUICKLY!

AND THAT'S IT. THAT'S HOW IT STARTS.

I SUPPOSE I COULD HAVE IGNORED HIM. I COULD HAVE STAYED UP ON THE HILL. BUT THEN NONE OF THIS WOULD HAVE HAPPENED, WOULD IT?

OOMPH!

WHAT IS IT? WHAT'S HAPPENED?

DAVID! BE CAREFUL BOY!

WELL, SAMUEL. YOU'VE SEEN ALL MY SONS BUT THIS ONE. AND HE'S THE YOUNGEST— ARE YOU SURE ABOUT THIS?

IT'S HIM. THIS IS THE ONE I'VE BEEN LOOKING FOR, THERE'S NO DOUBT.

DAVID. SO, THAT'S YOUR NAME, EH?

SIR?

MY NAME IS SAMUEL, AND I'VE TRAVELLED A LONG WAY JUST TO SEE YOU WITH MY OWN EYES. KNEEL BEFORE ME, DAVID.

GOD ANOINTS YOU, DAVID SON OF JESSE. FROM TODAY THE SPIRIT OF GOD WILL COME UPON YOU IN GREAT POWER. YOU WILL BE CHANGED BY IT.

IT WAS ONLY LATER I FOUND OUT THAT SAMUEL HAD RISKED HIS LIFE TO COME AND SEE ME. THAT IF SAUL HAD FOUND OUT WHAT HE WAS UP TO, HE COULD WELL HAVE HAD HIM MURDERED!

SAUL WAS HAVING TROUBLE WITH PHILISTINES AGAIN, BUT THINGS QUICKLY SETTLED INTO A STALEMATE, WITH NEITHER SIDE GAINING GROUND.

MY BROTHERS WENT OFF TO FIGHT. SOON MY FATHER SENT ME TO BRING THEM FOOD AND FIND OUT HOW THEY WERE DOING...

DAVID! WHAT ON EARTH ARE YOU DOING HERE?!

IDIOT! YOU'VE LEFT THE SHEEP ALONE, SO YOU COULD COME AND WATCH THE BATTLE!

FATHER **TOLD** ME TO COME, AND WHAT'S MORE I — **LOOK AT THE SIZE OF HIM!**

WELL? WHAT ARE YOU WAITING FOR? I'M A PHILISTINE, AREN'T I? AND WE'RE AT WAR, AREN'T WE? SO WHY DON'T YOU SEND SOMEONE DOWN TO FIGHT ME? IF YOU THINK YOU'RE UP TO IT, THAT IS.

I COULDN'T UNDERSTAND IT. THE ARMY OF THE LIVING GOD COULDN'T BE STOPPED BY ANY ONE MAN, NO MATTER **HOW** BIG HE MIGHT BE! I STARTED COMPLAINING. **LOUDLY!**

IT DOESN'T MATTER **HOW** BIG HE IS! HE'S ONLY ONE MAN!

IT WAS THEN I SAW THE REASON FOR THE STAND-OFF! HIS NAME WAS **GOLIATH**, AND HE WAS THE BIGGEST MAN I'D EVER SEEN.

OVER NINE FEET TALL, WEARING A HUNDRED AND TWENTY-FIVE POUNDS OF ARMOUR, HE'D HELD OUR ARMY OFF FOR DAYS.

THERE'S NO WAY THE ARMY CAN ADVANCE UNTIL WE GET RID OF HIM.

HAVE YOU THOUGHT ABOUT SENDING SOMEONE TO GO AND **FIGHT** HIM? I MEAN, ISN'T IT **OBVIOUS**?

I ENDED UP CAUSING SUCH A FUSS THAT I WAS TAKEN TO THE MAN WHO COULD GIVE ME THE ANSWER I WAS AFTER...

THE KING HIMSELF!

THIS IS **ABSURD**, YOUR MAJESTY! IF THE MEN ARE ALL TOO SCARED, **I'LL** GO AND FIGHT HIM FOR YOU!

SIR! WITH **RESPECT**, I'VE LOOKED AFTER MY FATHER'S SHEEP FOR YEARS. IF THEY WERE ATTACKED, I'D DEFEND THEM! I'VE FOUGHT LIONS AND BEARS. WHY SHOULD THIS PHILISTINE **DOG** BE ANY DIFFERENT?

SO I TOLD HIM, 'GOD DELIVERED ME FROM LIONS AND BEARS, HE'LL DELIVER ME FROM GOLIATH.' AND THAT SEEMED TO PERSUADE HIM. HE SUMMONED HIS ARMOURERS AND HAD ME DRESSED FOR BATTLE THERE AND THEN.

NO ONE DOUBTS YOUR BRAVERY, ER... **DAVID**, IS IT? BUT YOU MUST FACE **FACTS**. GOLIATH IS A **GIANT**, AND THERE ISN'T A MAN IN THE ARMY WHO COULD HOPE TO DEFEAT HIM IN BATTLE. I MEAN, HAVE YOU **SEEN** HOW BIG HE IS?

SAUL GAVE ME HIS OWN ARMOUR TO WEAR. IT WAS RIDICULOUS. I COULD HARDLY **MOVE** IN THE STUFF, IT WAS SO HEAVY! I COULDN'T EVEN LIFT SAUL'S **SWORD**! IN THE END I DECIDED I'D BE BETTER OFF WITHOUT IT.

WHEN GOLIATH FINALLY CLAPPED EYES ON ME, HE WENT **BERSERK**! I WASN'T WHAT HE HAD BEEN EXPECTING...

YOU'RE SENDING A **BOY**?! DO YOU THINK I'M A **DOG**, AND HAVE SENT A BOY WITH A STICK TO CHASE ME OFF? COME ANY CLOSER AND I'LL TEAR YOUR **SKIN** OFF!

'HA', I SAID. 'YOU'VE COME ARMED WITH A SPEAR, BUT I'M HERE IN THE NAME OF **GOD**'!

SO GOLIATH STARTED CHARGING DOWN THE HILL TOWARDS ME, SHOUTING AND SWEARING ALL THE WAY.

I PUT A PEBBLE IN THE SLING I USED TO SCARE AWAY WOLVES AND, WHIRLING IT HIGH IN THE AIR, I LET FLY AS HARD AS I COULD!

WHACK!

STRAIGHT BETWEEN THE EYES! THE GIANT WENT DOWN LIKE A FELLED TREE.

SO I TOOK THE GIANT'S GREAT BIG SWORD, AND HACKED HIS **HEAD** OFF! THEN I GAVE IT TO KING SAUL AS A PRESENT.

TRUST GOD — FIND OUT FOR YOURSELF HOW GOOD GOD IS, EVEN LIONS AND WOLVES GROW WEAK AND HUNGRY, BUT THIS POOR MAN CALLED AND GOD ANSWERED HIM.

AND SO I WENT TO LIVE WITH THE KING. I PLAYED THE HARP AND SANG, AND MY SONGS SEEMED TO SOOTHE HIS BLACK MOODS.

BUT RIGHT FROM THE START, SAUL WAS AFRAID OF ME.

HE TAUGHT ME TO FIGHT WITH A SWORD, AND I QUICKLY LEARNED HOW TO DEFEND MYSELF IN BATTLE.

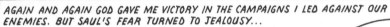

AGAIN AND AGAIN GOD GAVE ME VICTORY IN THE CAMPAIGNS I LED AGAINST OUR ENEMIES. BUT SAUL'S FEAR TURNED TO JEALOUSY...

HURRAH FOR **DAVID**! SAUL HAS KILLED **THOUSANDS**! BUT DAVID HAS KILLED **TENS** OF THOUSANDS!

DAVID!! **DAVID**!! GOD IS **WITH** YOU!!

IF THE PEOPLE ACCEPTED ME, IT WAS BECAUSE **GOD** HAD PUT HIS POWER IN ME.

SAUL'S SON **JONATHAN** AND I BECAME LIKE BROTHERS. HE GAVE ME HIS OWN WEAPONS, HIS OWN SWORD. WE FOUGHT SIDE BY SIDE AND I WOULD HAVE GLADLY **DIED** FOR HIM.

OUR FRIENDSHIP MADE SAUL ALL THE MORE JEALOUS. AND HIS JEALOUSY TURNED TO RAGE...

STAY **STILL**!! I'M THE **KING**! I COMMAND IT!

THAT NIGHT THE KING HAD HIS SERVANTS KEEP WATCH. HE WOULD KILL ME NEXT DAY.

LUCKILY HIS AIM WASN'T WHAT IT ONCE HAD BEEN!

BUT MICHAL, MY WIFE AND SAUL'S OWN **DAUGHTER**, HELPED ME ESCAPE. IN ALL ISRAEL, IT SEEMED AS IF THE KING WAS THE **ONLY** MAN WHO HATED ME!

I WAS AN OUTLAW.

BUT SAUL'S OWN FAMILY WERE ON MY SIDE. THEY WERE MY EYES AND EARS, AND SO I ESCAPED FROM HIS CLUTCHES.

AFTER MANY ADVENTURES, I FOUND MY WAY TO THE TOWN OF NOB. THIS WAS A KEY PLACE FOR WORSHIP AT THE TIME, AND I WAS CERTAIN THAT AHIMELECH THE PRIEST WOULD RECEIVE ME WARMLY.

DAVID?! WHAT ARE YOU DOING HERE? I-I MEAN, WHY ARE YOU ON YOUR OWN?

OH, YOU KNOW. THE KING SENT ME. ONLY I'VE ER... LOST MY SWORD. I DON'T SUPPOSE YOU'VE GOT ONE SPARE?

A SWORD?

HMM. I DON'T SUPPOSE YOU'VE GOT ANYTHING TO EAT? I'M STARVING!

FOOD? SORRY, WE WEREN'T EXPECTING GUESTS. THERE'S NOTHING HERE EXCEPT THE BREAD ON THE ALTAR.

OOMPH! THAT'LL DO!

ER... YOU HAVE CONSECRATED YOURSELF ACCORDING TO HOLY LAW I TAKE IT?

GOES WITHOUT SAYING. HOW HEAVY IS THIS THING?

DON'T YOU REMEMBER? THAT'S GOLIATH'S SWORD.

ARE YOU SURE THE KING SENT YOU? YOU COME HERE STARVING AND WITHOUT EVEN A SWORD!

THE TRUTH IS I'M ON A SECRET MISSION FROM KING SAUL. NO ONE EXCEPT US KNOWS ABOUT IT!

OR SO I THOUGHT. SAUL HAD BECOME INCREASINGLY PARANOID. HIS SPIES WERE EVERYWHERE.

IN HIS ANGER, SAUL SLAUGHTERED THE ENTIRE TOWN. I LIED TO THEM, AND THEY HELPED ME. AND SO SAUL KILLED THEM ALL.

EVENTUALLY I MADE MY HOME IN THE CAVES AT ADULLAM, LIVING THE LIFE OF AN OUTLAW. MEN CAME FROM ALL OVER ISRAEL TO JOIN ME.

THE ANGRY AND DISCONTENTED, THOSE IN DEBT, SURVIVORS OF SAUL'S ATTACKS, THEY FLOCKED TO ME. IN ALL ABOUT SIX HUNDRED MEN, ARMED TO THE TEETH AND READY FOR TROUBLE.

NO MATCH FOR SAUL'S ARMY, EVEN SO. BUT THANKFULLY HE WAS OFF FIGHTING THE PHILISTINES AGAIN, AND SO WE WERE LEFT ALONE FOR A WHILE. BUT NOT WITHOUT SOME NARROW ESCAPES. ONE TIME, SAUL CAME BY WITH THE ENTIRE ARMY BEHIND HIM. WE SCARCELY HAD TIME TO HIDE...

WE HID AT THE BACK OF THIS CAVE, KEEPING *QUIET.* BUT THEN -HEH- SAUL IS CAUGHT SHORT! WELL, HE'S THE *KING*, CAN'T DO IT IN FRONT OF HIS MEN! SO HE COMES INTO THE CAVE!

IMAGINE IT! HE'S GOT THE WHOLE ARMY OUT LOOKING FOR US, AND THERE WE ARE IN THE CAVE WITH HIM! I COULD HAVE KILLED HIM THERE AND THEN. I ACTUALLY REACHED OUT AND CUT A PIECE OFF HIS CLOAK. JUST TO PROVE THE POINT!

AH! YOU'VE BROUGHT MY HARP, AT LAST.

SIR.

BRING IT HERE THEN. I'VE WRITTEN A NEW SONG – A *PSALM.*

'GOD IS MY FORTRESS, MY PROTECTOR. HE IS MY *SHIELD*, TO KEEP ME SAFE. I CALL ON HIM, AND HE RESCUES ME FROM MY ENEMIES.'

'THE WAVES OF DESTRUCTION ROLLED OVER ME, DEATH WAS ALL AROUND ME. BUT I CALLED ON THE LORD, MY GOD, AND HE ANSWERED ME.'

THERE'S MORE. I'VE NOT FINISHED YET... BUT WHERE WAS I?

OH YES – SO THE KING WAS AFTER OUR BLOOD. EVERY DAY WE STAYED IN ISRAEL WE RISKED OUR NECKS.

SO WE LEFT ISRAEL, AND WENT TO JOIN THE *PHILISTINES* AS MERCENARIES.

YOU'VE DONE A WISE THING, DAVID. I DIDN'T KNOW ISRAELITES WERE SO *SHREWD.*

THANK YOU.

IDIOT.

THE PHILISTINES HIRED US TO ATTACK *ISRAEL.*

BUT INSTEAD WE ATTACKED THE *GESHURITES*, THE *GIRZITES* AND THE *AMALEKITES* — ISRAEL'S OLD ENEMIES. AND THE PHILISTINES NEVER KNEW! WE LEFT NO ONE ALIVE TO TELL TALES!

THINKING THAT WE'D WIPED OUT HALF OF *ISRAEL'S* ARMY, THE PHILISTINES GAVE US THE CITY OF ZIKLAG — ME AND SIX HUNDRED SOLDIERS.

IT WASN'T *HOME*, BUT IT WAS A HUNDRED TIMES BETTER THAN SLEEPING IN A CAVE!

DO YOU TRUST HIM, SIR?

DAVID? HE'S KILLED HIS OWN PEOPLE – THEY'LL NEVER HAVE HIM BACK NOW! HE'S OURS FOR GOOD!

EVEN SO, THE PHILISTINES SLOWLY STARTED TO DISTRUST ME.

AND THEY WOULD SOON HAVE GOOD CAUSE. EVENTS IN ISRAEL WERE TO FORCE OUR RETURN – *SAMUEL*, MY TEACHER AND FRIEND WAS DEAD AND SAUL HAD ABANDONED GOD. HE EVEN SOUGHT ADVICE FROM *WITCHES*! WE HAD TO MOVE, AND *SOON*! BUT WHILE WE WERE AWAY, GETTING READY FOR BATTLE...

THE AMALEKITES COUNTER-ATTACKED. ZIKLAG WAS BURNED TO THE GROUND.

OUR WIVES.

OUR CHILDREN.

EVERYTHING WE HAD, THEY **TOOK** WITH THEM.

I THOUGHT MY MEN WERE GOING TO **STONE** ME! BUT IN MY DESPAIR I ASKED GOD'S HELP, AND HE TOLD ME 'GO AND **RESCUE** THEM'!

WE FOUND THE AMALEKITES IN THE PLAINS, DRINKING THEMSELVES STUPID ON **OUR** WINE. AND EXHAUSTED THOUGH WE WERE, WE UTTERLY DEFEATED THEM.

WE GOT EVERYONE BACK SAFELY, WIVES, CHILDREN, THE LOT. JUST ME AND FOUR HUNDRED MEN.

BUT YOU SAID YOU HAD **SIX** HUNDRED MEN. WHERE WERE THE OTHERS?

TOO EXHAUSTED TO COMPLETE THE JOURNEY. BUT EVERYTHING THEY OWNED WAS RETURNED TO THEM WHETHER THEY FOUGHT THAT DAY OR NOT!

WE DIDN'T WIN THE BATTLE THAT DAY. **GOD** DID IT FOR US. WE WERE SO TIRED. SO... VERY TIRED...

SSHH. LET HIM SLEEP.

PLEASE!

KILL ME.

KILL ME, YOU DOG! I **COMMAND** IT! I, THE KING! KILL ME!!

NO!

MY LORD?

NOTHING. JUST A DREAM. AN OLD MAN'S MEMORIES, THAT'S ALL. SAUL AND HIS MEN ATTACKED THE PHILISTINES. JONATHAN AND HIS BROTHERS WERE KILLED, AND SAUL WOUNDED.

RATHER THAN FACE CAPTURE, IN THE END HE THREW HIMSELF ON HIS OWN SWORD...

GOD'S CHOSEN ONE, LYING IN THE MUD AND **BEGGING** FOR DEATH. EVEN NOW I STILL GRIEVE FOR THEM. EVEN NOW.

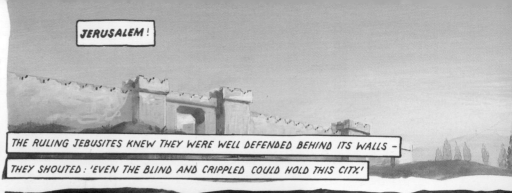

JERUSALEM!

I WAS THIRTY YEARS OLD WHEN I BECAME KING. I UNITED THE WARRING TRIBES, AND TOGETHER WE LAID SIEGE TO THE CITY THAT WOULD BEAR MY NAME:

DAVID'S CITY —

THE RULING JEBUSITES KNEW THEY WERE WELL DEFENDED BEHIND ITS WALLS —

THEY SHOUTED: 'EVEN THE BLIND AND CRIPPLED COULD HOLD THIS CITY.'

OUCH! MY HEAD! COULDN'T WE JUST STORM THE WALLS LIKE LAST TIME?

SHUT UP AND KEEP CRAWLING!

AND THAT'S EXACTLY HOW WE **CONQUERED** IT. CRAWLING ALONG THE TUNNELS BENEATH THE CITY ON OUR HANDS AND KNEES IN THE DARKNESS, WE LEAPT OUT TO TAKE THEM BY SURPRISE!

WAS IT A HARD BATTLE?

HARD? THERE ARE NO EASY BATTLES. PEOPLE FIGHT, PEOPLE DIE. IF IT'S GOD'S WILL, WE WIN. IF NOT... WELL, **THIS** BATTLE WAS GOD'S WILL ANYWAY.

THE CITY WAS OURS!

I HAD THE **ARK** BROUGHT UP TO THE CITY. ALL ISRAEL TURNED OUT TO GREET IT, SINGING AND DANCING, AND SHOUTING..!

IT WAS **WONDERFUL**! FROM NOW ONWARDS, JERUSALEM WOULD BE OUR **HOME**, THE PLACE WHERE WE WOULD BUILD THE TEMPLE OF OUR GOD.

I DANCED IN FRONT OF THE PEOPLE, STRIPPED DOWN TO A LOINCLOTH. I WAS **WITH** THE PEOPLE, ONE OF THEM! LEAPING AND DANCING BEFORE OUR GOD, BECAUSE WE WERE SO HAPPY! HE **LIVED** WITH US! NOT A GOD OF WOOD OR STONE, BUT **ALIVE**!

OF COURSE, MY **WIFE** DIDN'T LIKE IT. SAID IT WAS **UNDIGNIFIED**, ALL THAT PRANCING ABOUT AND SHOUTING - NOT FIT BEHAVIOUR FOR A KING. BAH! I WASN'T DOING IT FOR **HER**!

IT WAS THEN THAT GOD TOLD ME THE NEWS THAT ONE OF **MY** HEIRS WOULD BUILD A KINGDOM THAT WOULD LAST **FOREVER**. AND ALTHOUGH PUNISHED BY THE **WHIPS** OF MEN, GOD WOULD BE HIS FATHER, AND HE WOULD BE HIS SON, AND HIS KINGDOM WOULD HAVE **NO END**...

ALL THIS, FROM AN HEIR TO **MY** THRONE, DESPITE THE SINS I COMMITTED. OH AND I **KNOW** THE WRONG I'VE DONE TO OTHERS. I HAVE BEEN SINFUL FROM THE TIME MY MOTHER CONCEIVED ME, EVEN BEFORE I WAS BORN.

AND MY SINS WERE THE MOST **UNORIGINAL**.

IT WAS SPRING, THE TIME WHEN KINGS GO OFF TO WAR. I WAS LOOKING DOWN FROM THE PALACE ROOF WHEN I **SAW** HER.

OH, I HAD WIVES ENOUGH ALREADY. I HAD SONS AND DAUGHTERS, ALL THAT A MAN COULD WANT.

EVERYTHING EXCEPT **HER**.

SHE WAS CALLED **BATHSHEBA**.

SHE WAS BEAUTIFUL.

SHE WAS ENCHANTING.

SHE WAS ENOUGH TO MAKE ME LOSE MY MIND WITH DESIRE.

SHE WAS ANOTHER MAN'S WIFE.

AND I DIDN'T **CARE**.

URIAH, HER HUSBAND WAS A **HITTITE**, ONE OF MY SPECIAL GUARD, AND AWAY FIGHTING MY WARS. UNDER LAW, SOLDIERS WERE NOT ALLOWED TO RETURN TO THEIR WIVES WHILE ON ACTIVE DUTY, AND HE WAS A MAN OF GREAT PRINCIPLE. WHILE HE SLEPT IN TENTS BENEATH THE CITY WALLS OF RABBAH I MADE LOVE TO HIS WIFE IN MY PALACE.

BATHSHEBA BECAME PREGNANT. **FOOL** THAT I WAS, I COVERED ONE EVIL WITH **ANOTHER** - I SENT URIAH ON A DANGEROUS MISSION, AND GAVE ORDERS FOR HIM TO BE LEFT **STRANDED** WHERE THE FIGHTING WAS THE THICKEST.

IT WAS AS IF I'D MURDERED HIM **MYSELF**.

AND SO, AS I SAT THERE THINKING I'D GOT AWAY WITH THINGS, I WAS VISITED BY NATHAN, A HIGHLY RESPECTED PROPHET...

WHOEVER IT WAS, HE DESERVES TO DIE!

I SWEAR BY GOD, THAT WHOEVER DID THIS SHOULD PAY BACK FOUR TIMES AS MUCH, BECAUSE OF HIS CRUELTY!

OF COURSE, NATHAN WAS REALLY TALKING ABOUT ME. GOD MADE ME KING OVER ISRAEL, HE GAVE ME MY KINGDOM, MY WIVES, EVERYTHING. IF I'D SAID IT WASN'T ENOUGH, THEN HE'D HAVE GIVEN ME EVEN MORE!

THERE ARE TWO MEN IN YOUR KINGDOM. ONE IS RICH AND OWNS WHOLE HERDS OF SHEEP, WHILE THE OTHER OWNS NOTHING BUT ONE SMALL LAMB, WHICH HE HAS RAISED SINCE BIRTH. IT'S ALL HE HAS IN THE WORLD, YET THE RICH MAN TOOK IT FROM HIM TO SERVE TO A GUEST, RATHER THAN SLAUGHTER ONE OF HIS OWN FLOCK.

INSTEAD I STOLE FROM SOMEONE ELSE, AND MURDERED TO COVER MY CRIME.

I WAS A FOOL TO THINK I COULD HIDE FROM GOD, OR THAT MY SIN WOULD GO UNPUNISHED. THE CHILD BATHSHEBA WAS BEARING DIED. EVEN SO, GOD HONOURED HIS PROMISE OF A DESCENDANT WHO WOULD RULE FOR EVER. SOON BATHSHEBA GAVE BIRTH TO ANOTHER SON. I NAMED HIM SOLOMON AND THANKED GOD THAT I HAD BEEN FORGIVEN...

I HAD OTHER SONS BY OTHER WIVES. MY ELDEST SON, ABSALOM HATED HIS HALF-BROTHER AMNON WITH A VENGEANCE.

IT WAS TERRIBLE! AMNON HAD FALLEN IN LOVE WITH HIS HALF-SISTER TAMAR, AND IN HIS LUST HE RAPED HER. AFTER THE ATTACK, HE WANTED NOTHING MORE TO DO WITH HER, AND HAD HER THROWN FROM HIS HOUSE.

ABSALOM SOUGHT ONLY REVENGE FROM THAT MOMENT ON...

FATHER, I'M HAVING MY ENTIRE HERD SHEARED. COME AND JOIN ME IN THE CELEBRATIONS — BRING ALL MY BROTHERS, ALL YOUR COURTIERS! BE MY GUESTS.

NOT NOW ABSALOM — WE'RE BUSY. MAYBE NEXT YEAR, MM?

NO! YOU MUST ALL COME NOW!

'MUST'?

THIS IS IMPORTANT TO ME!

I DON'T UNDERSTAND, ABSALOM. WHY ALL THIS FUSS NOW? YOU'VE NEVER BOTHERED WITH PARTIES BEFORE?

IF YOU'RE DETERMINED TO MAKE ME LOOK STUPID, THEN FINE. BUT AT LEAST LET MY HALF-BROTHER AMNON COME!

ABSALOM, MY OWN SON, KILLED HIS HALF-BROTHER AND THEN FLED TO THE LAND OF A FOREIGN KING. EVEN SO, I MISSED HIM TERRIBLY. IN THE END I HAD TO FORGIVE HIM AND HE RETURNED TO ME, ALTHOUGH I REFUSED EVEN TO BE IN THE SAME ROOM AS HIM FOR THE FIRST TWO YEARS.

HE WAS WITHOUT DOUBT, THE MOST HANDSOME MAN IN ALL OF ISRAEL. PEOPLE WOULD DO ANYTHING FOR HIM.

I WAS BLIND TO HIS AMBITIONS, EVEN THEN. I NEVER LOOKED PROPERLY, OR LISTENED PROPERLY, NEVER KNEW HOW FAR HE WAS WILLING TO GO...

IF IT WILL SHUT YOU UP, CERTAINLY!

THE PARTY WENT EXACTLY AS ABSALOM HAD PLANNED IT — HE WAITED UNTIL AMNON WAS DULLED WITH WINE, AND HAD HIS SERVANTS MURDER HIM.

ABSALOM HAD HIS OWN AGENDA.

HE ASKED PERMISSION TO GO TO HEBRON TO WORSHIP GOD. OF COURSE I CONSENTED. BUT AS SOON AS HE WAS OUT OF MY SIGHT, HE HAD HIS TRUMPETS SOUND, GATHERING MEN FROM ALL OVER THE COUNTRY.

AT HEBRON, ABSALOM DECLARED HIMSELF *KING*.

HE SET HIMSELF UP AS A *JUDGE*, OFFERING ADVICE LACED WITH FLATTERY, WINNING FAVOURS FROM THOSE HE HELPED, AND ALWAYS MAKING SURE THEY KNEW THEY OWED HIM.

IT WAS DEBT HE INTENDED THEM TO REPAY *IN FULL*.

HE FORCED ME TO RETREAT UNTIL I COULD GATHER MY FORCES. THEN I SPLIT MY MEN INTO THREE GROUPS AND FACED HIM.

JOAB, MY MILITARY CHIEF TOOK ONE; HIS BROTHER ABISHAI ANOTHER, AND ITTAI, A FOREIGNER WHO OWED ME NOTHING YET REMAINED FAITHFUL, THE THIRD. I GAVE EXPRESS ORDERS THAT ABSALOM WAS TO BE BROUGHT TO ME *UNHARMED*. YOU ASKED IF SOME BATTLES WERE HARD? IN TRUTH, THEN: THIS WAS THE *HARDEST* OF THEM ALL.

THE BATTLE TOOK PLACE IN THE FOREST OF EPHRAIM.

THE FIGHTING WAS CLOSE AND BRUTAL, SWORD AGAINST SWORD, AS EACH MAN STRUGGLED THROUGH THE FOREST.

AND ALL THE WHILE JOAB PUSHED ON, RELENTLESSLY HACKING HIS WAY TOWARDS THE TARGET OF HIS ANGER —

ABSALOM.

I AM THE *KING* NOW! DO YOU HEAR ME?! *THE KING! YOU WILL DO AS I COMMAND!*

SURRENDER, IN THE NAME OF KING DAVID! SURRENDER OR DIE!

FOOL! MY FATHER WOULD NEVER HARM ME!

AND SO WITH HIS MEN IN DEFEAT, ABSALOM FLED THE BATTLE, PERHAPS HOPING TO REGROUP AND ATTACK AT A LATER DATE.

WITH JOAB'S TROOPS AT HIS HEELS, HE FLED INTO THE DARKEST PART OF THE FOREST...

WAARGG!! NO! **NO!**

HELP ME..! PLEASE, SOMEBODY **HELP ME!**

THERE, SIR! AS I SAID!

WHY DIDN'T YOU **KILL** HIM WHEN YOU FOUND HIM?

SIR, STANDING ORDERS SAY HE'S TO BE CAUGHT **UNHARMED**!

AND **I** SAY TEN PIECES OF SILVER TO THE MAN WHO —

AARRGG!!

— FOLLOWS ME WITH HIS SPEAR!

AAAARRRGG->hhk!<

TEN MEN FOLLOWED JOAB'S LEAD.

ABSALOM WAS DEAD. MY OWN SON... ORDER RESTORED, THE KINGDOM SAFE, MESSENGERS RAN TO BRING THE NEWS. THEY EVEN CALLED IT 'GOOD' NEWS — BUT MY EARS WERE DEAF TO THEM.

ALL I CARED ABOUT WAS ABSALOM.

ABSALOM... IF I COULD HAVE DIED IN YOUR PLACE I WOULD HAVE!

MY SOLDIERS RETURNED TO JERUSALEM, NOT AS VICTORS, BUT LIKE COWARDS, CREEPING INTO THE CITY ASHAMED OF THEMSELVES.

ALL EXCEPT **JOAB**.

YOU HAVE **HUMILIATED** YOUR OWN MEN! THE PEOPLE WHO'VE SAVED YOUR LIFE! THE MEN WHO RISKED THEIR NECKS FOR YOURS!

YOU'VE MADE IT **QUITE** CLEAR THAT YOU'D BE HAPPIER IF WE WERE ALL **DEAD**, IF IT MEANT ABSALOM WERE ALIVE! NOW GET **UP** AND GO SPEAK TO THEM AND **THANK** THEM, BECAUSE IF YOU DON'T, THEY'LL ALL BE **GONE** BY MORNING!

I WAS STILL **KING**. I HAD A DUTY TO THE PEOPLE. THERE WOULD BE OTHER BATTLES, OTHER FAILURES, OTHER VICTORIES.

GOD HAS BEEN WITH ME FROM THE DAY HE TOOK ME FROM THE FIELDS, TENDING MY FATHER'S **SHEEP**, AND SET ME UP AS RULER OVER HIS PEOPLE, ISRAEL.

AND AS IF THAT WASN'T ENOUGH, GOD HAS TOLD ME THAT MY ROYAL LINE WILL ENDURE **FOR EVER**.

BELIEVE ME, **I** HAVE DONE NOTHING TO DESERVE THIS HONOUR. THE KING WHO RULES WITH **JUSTICE** IS LIKE A GREAT LIGHT SHINING AFTER THE STORMS. AND **THIS** IS HOW GOD WILL BLESS MY DESCENDANTS – BECAUSE GOD HAS MADE AN **EVERLASTING** AGREEMENT WITH ME.

SOON I WILL GO THE WAY OF ALL THE EARTH. **SOLOMON** WILL SUCCEED ME.

THE LORD GOD IS MY SHEPHERD, I SHALL NEVER WANT. IN GREEN PASTURES HE GIVES ME REST, HE LEADS ME TO THE STILL, FRESH WATERS. HE WILL REVIVE MY SPIRIT AND MY STRENGTH. HE GUIDES ME IN THE PATHS OF RIGHTEOUSNESS.

ALTHOUGH I WALK THROUGH THE VALLEY OF THE SHADOW OF DEATH, I WILL FEAR NO EVIL, FOR HE IS WITH ME. HIS SHEPHERD'S CROOK AND STAFF, THEY COMFORT ME.

SURELY GOODNESS AND LOVE SHALL FOLLOW ME ALL THE DAYS OF MY LIFE, AND I SHALL DWELL IN THE HOUSE OF THE LORD... FOR EVER.

116

THE STORY OF SOLOMON

SOLOMON WAS THE SON OF DAVID AND **BATHSHEBA**, URIAH'S WIFE. ALTHOUGH NOT THE ELDEST OF DAVID'S SONS, HE WAS CHOSEN TO SUCCEED HIM AS KING.

IN THOSE DAYS THERE WAS NO TEMPLE IN ISRAEL, AND THE ARK OF THE COVENANT STILL RESIDED IN A TENT AS IT HAD DONE FOR HUNDREDS OF YEARS.

ONE NIGHT, AS SOLOMON SLEPT NEAR THE PLACE WHERE SACRIFICES WERE OFFERED, HE HAD A DREAM IN WHICH **GOD** SPOKE TO HIM...

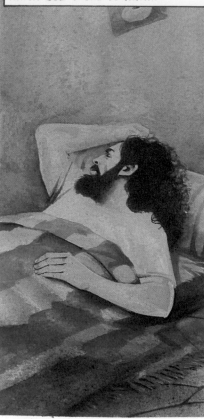

SOLOMON, ASK FOR WHATEVER YOU WANT ME TO GIVE YOU.

YOU SHOWED MY FATHER, DAVID, GREAT KINDNESS ALL HIS LIFE. YOU MADE ME HIS HEIR, BUT I DON'T KNOW HOW TO **RULE** THIS COUNTRY. I FEEL LIKE A CHILD WITH THE WHOLE NATION **WATCHING** ME. GIVE ME AN UNDERSTANDING HEART, TO JUDGE YOUR PEOPLE; GIVE ME THE **WISDOM** TO RULE WITH JUSTICE AND FAIRNESS.

I WILL MAKE YOU THE **WISEST** MAN ON EARTH! I WILL ALSO GIVE YOU THE THINGS YOU DID **NOT** ASK FOR! YOU WILL **HAVE** WEALTH AND POWER AND, IF YOU OBEY ME, YOU WILL LIVE A LONG LIFE TOO!

YOU COULD HAVE ASKED FOR ANYTHING - POWER; WEALTH; A LONG **LIFE** - BUT INSTEAD YOU ASK FOR **WISDOM**.

THEN SOLOMON AWOKE - AND HE REALIZED IT HAD BEEN A DREAM.

AND SO SOLOMON BECAME KING.

THE WISEST, RICHEST, AND MOST REGAL OF ALL THE KINGS OF ISRAEL. IT WAS TO BE A RARE TIME OF **PEACE** AND PROSPERITY IN ISRAEL'S HISTORY.

THIS WAS THE **GOLDEN AGE**.

117

ONE OF SOLOMON'S FIRST JUDGMENTS INVOLVED TWO *PROSTITUTES*.

THIS WOMAN AND I LIVE IN THE SAME HOUSE, AND WE BOTH HAD A *BABY* AT THE SAME TIME. BUT ONE NIGHT SHE ROLLED OVER IN HER SLEEP AND SMOTHERED HERS TO DEATH, SO SHE SWAPPED IT WITH MINE WHILE I SLEPT!

LIAR! YOUR BABY DIED AND YOU STOLE MINE! SHE'S *LYING!*

I KNOW MY OWN BABY!

ONE OF THEM IS TELLING THE TRUTH, BUT WHICH ONE...?

GUARD, BRING ME A SWORD.

MY LORD!

CUT THE CHILD IN TWO AND GIVE HALF TO ONE AND HALF TO THE OTHER.

NO!! GIVE HER THE BABY. DON'T KILL HIM.

NEITHER OF US WILL HAVE HIM. CUT HIM IN TWO.

GUARD! GIVE *HER* THE CHILD. SHE'S THE TRUE MOTHER. SHE WOULD DO ANYTHING TO SAVE HIS LIFE.

WHEN THE PEOPLE OF ISRAEL HEARD THE VERDICT SOLOMON HAD GIVEN THEY WERE IN AWE.

GOD HAD SURELY GIVEN THEM A MAN OF *WISDOM*.

SOLOMON SOON ESTABLISHED TRADING LINKS WITH HIS NEIGHBOURS, AND WITH HIS FATHER'S OLD ALLIES, BRINGING GREAT PROSPERITY TO ISRAEL.

KING HIRAM OF TYRE SENDS YOU THESE GIFTS, MY LORD, WITH HIS EVERY BLESSING.

BECAUSE OF THE WARS WAGED AGAINST MY FATHER FROM ALL SIDES HE COULD NOT BUILD A TEMPLE. BUT GOD HAS GIVEN US PEACE. LET'S USE IT TO HIS GLORY!

FOUR HUNDRED AND EIGHTY YEARS AFTER THE PEOPLE OF ISRAEL ESCAPED FROM EGYPT, THE CONSTRUCTION OF THE GREAT TEMPLE BEGAN.

THE LAND HAD BEEN SET ASIDE IN DAVID'S REIGN, ON ONE OF THE HILLS OF JERUSALEM – THE SAME PLACE WHERE **ABRAHAM** HAD MET GOD CENTURIES BEFORE.

THE MIGHTIEST TREES IN THE GREAT FORESTS OF LEBANON WERE FELLED FOR THEIR TIMBER, AND HAULED OVER LAND AND SEA TO JERUSALEM.

THE MEN WORKED IN NEAR SILENCE. THE STONE WAS CUT WHILE STILL IN THE QUARRIES, THE WOOD PLANED WHILE STILL IN THE FORESTS. A QUIET REVERENCE HUNG IN THE AIR.

IT WAS AS IF THE GROUND WAS HOLY FROM THE START.

A BUILDING NOT MEANT FOR PRIESTS OR KINGS, BUT A HOUSE FOR **GOD**.

AND SO, ALMOST 500 YEARS AFTER ITS MAKING, THE ARK WAS BROUGHT INTO THE TEMPLE.

... AND WAS FINALLY LAID TO REST.

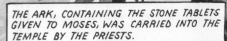

THE ARK, CONTAINING THE STONE TABLETS GIVEN TO MOSES, WAS CARRIED INTO THE TEMPLE BY THE PRIESTS.

119

THERE, TO THE SOUND OF TRUMPETS, THE ISRAELITES SHOUTED AS IF WITH ONE VOICE: *GOD IS GOOD! HIS LOVE LASTS FOR EVER!*

AND STILL SHOUTING AND WORSHIPPING GOD, THEY SACRIFICED SO MANY ANIMALS THAT IT WAS IMPOSSIBLE TO COUNT THEM ALL.

THE CEREMONY FINISHED, THE PRIESTS STARTED TO FILE OUT OF THE TEMPLE; BUT AS THEY DID SO, SOMETHING *WONDERFUL* HAPPENED...

THE TEMPLE BECAME FILLED WITH A *CLOUD*, BRIGHT AND *SHINING*, SO FULL OF *LIGHT* THAT IT HURT THEIR EYES TO LOOK AT IT!

LORD, GOD OF ISRAEL, THERE IS *NO ONE* LIKE YOU IN HEAVEN OR EARTH!

YOUR LOVE LASTS *FOR EVER!*

BUT WILL YOU *REALLY* LIVE WITH US? IF THE WHOLE OF HEAVEN IS TOO *SMALL* TO CONTAIN YOU, HOW WILL THIS ONE SMALL *HOUSE* BE ENOUGH?

PLEASE KEEP THE PROMISES YOU MADE TO MY FATHER, DAVID - MAY THERE *ALWAYS* BE A KING DESCENDED FROM THE HOUSE OF DAVID ON THE THRONE OF ISRAEL BEFORE YOU!

LISTEN TO ME, ISRAEL, AND WORSHIP YOUR *GOD*! HE HAS GIVEN US PEACE, AND FULFILLED *ALL* THE PROMISES HE MADE TO *MOSES*!

MAY OUR GOD *NEVER* LEAVE US OR ABANDON US, AND MAY OUR HEARTS AND MINDS ALWAYS LOOK TO HIM! GOD IS GOOD, AND HIS LOVE LASTS -

FOR EVER!

120

WORD OF SOLOMON'S FAME QUICKLY SPREAD THROUGHOUT THE KNOWN WORLD.

THE QUEEN OF **SHEBA**, A COUNTRY FAR TO THE SOUTH, HEARD OF SOLOMON, OF HIS FABULOUS PALACE AND INCREDIBLE WISDOM.

AND SO, BEARING WONDERFUL GIFTS, SHE MOUNTED A VAST EXPEDITION TO SEE THIS KING WITH HER OWN EYES.

PLEASE, ACCEPT THESE SPICES AS A TOKEN OF OUR GOODWILL.

YOUR COUNTRY MUST BE A **WONDERFUL** PLACE, SHEBA. I WOULD BE MORE THAN INTERESTED IN TRADE LINKS WITH YOU.

YOU DESIRE TO BE EVEN RICHER, THEN?

MORE **WEALTH**? NO - IT'S **FAR** BETTER TO BE POOR AND FEAR GOD THAN TO BE RICH AND LIVE A LIFE OF CONSTANT TROUBLE. IT'S **BETTER** TO ENJOY A SIMPLE BOWL OF COLD VEGETABLES WITH PEOPLE YOU LOVE, THAN TO GO TO A **BANQUET** WITH PEOPLE WHO COULDN'T CARE IF YOU LIVED OR DIED!

BUT YOU HAVE EVERYTHING YOU COULD EVER WANT.

EATING TOO MUCH HONEY WILL MAKE YOU **SICK**. IT'S THE SAME WITH MONEY. BUT IF YOU **HELP** OTHERS WITH WHAT YOU HAVE, THEN YOU'LL BE HELPED IN RETURN.

SOME WOULD SAY IT'S A SIGN OF WEAKNESS TO SHOW KINDNESS.

LET THEM. INSULTS CAN NEVER HURT YOU, UNLESS THEY'RE **TRUE**, OF COURSE.

IN THE END IT'S WHAT **YOU** SAY AND WHAT **YOU** DO THAT WILL AFFECT YOUR LIFE. IN THE END WE'LL ALL GET WHAT WE DESERVE, SO WHY NOT ALTER THE OUTCOME NOW?

YOU KNOW, EVERYTHING I HEARD ABOUT YOU IS TRUE. BUT I NEVER WOULD HAVE BELIEVED IT IF I HADN'T SEEN WITH MY OWN EYES.

YOUR GOD IS GOOD TO YOU! HE'S SHOWN HIS LOVE TO HIS PEOPLE BY MAKING YOU THEIR KING.

ISRAEL IS THE MOST BLESSED NATION IN THE WORLD.

SOLOMON WAS GREATER IN WISDOM AND WEALTH THAN ANY RULER ON EARTH. EVERY KING IN THE WORLD MADE HIS WAY TO ISRAEL TO ASK SOLOMON'S ADVICE.

120

SOLOMON WAS CERTAINLY RICH AND UNDOUBTEDLY WISE, BUT HE WAS NOT PERFECT. HE SPENT MORE THAN HE EARNED, MAKING HIS PEOPLE PAY HEAVY TAXES TO MEET THE DEBTS.

YOU CAN SEE IT THERE IN BLACK AND WHITE.

ALL RIGHT, WE'LL LEVY HIGHER TAXES, BUT THE BUILDING WORK CONTINUES.

WHEN SOLOMON NEEDED WORKERS TO BUILD HIS PALACES, HE SENT OFFICIALS TO FORCE MEN TO WORK AND PAID THEM NOTHING. GOD WAS NOT PLEASED WITH SOLOMON FOR ILL-TREATING HIS PEOPLE.

AND THEN THERE WERE THE **WOMEN**...

IT WAS COMMON FOR A RICH MAN TO HAVE SEVERAL WIVES, AND SOLOMON WAS **VERY** RICH, AFTER ALL. THE MAJORITY WERE **POLITICAL** UNIONS.

THEY CAME FROM MANY DIFFERENT CULTURES, BRINGING THEIR OWN CUSTOMS AND PRACTICES...

AND THEIR OWN GODS. INSTEAD OF TEACHING HIS WIVES TO FOLLOW THE TRUE GOD, SOLOMON BUILT TEMPLES FOR THEIR IDOLS.

AND SO AS SOLOMON COMPROMISED HIS RELATIONSHIP WITH GOD, IT WAS AS IF ALL THE COLOUR WAS BEING DRAINED OUT OF THE LAND.

THE GOLDEN AGE WAS NEARING ITS END.

THROUGHOUT HIS REIGN, SOLOMON HAD HELD THE TWELVE TRIBES OF ISRAEL TOGETHER AS ONE NATION UNDER ONE GOD.

BUT THE UNITY OF ISRAEL BEGAN TO TEAR AT THE SEAMS.

IT ALL STARTED WITH A **BUILDER** ON THE WALLS OF THE CITY, A MAN CALLED **JEROBOAM**...

JEROBOAM HAD WORKED HARD BUILDING THE EASTERN CITY WALLS, AND HAD BEEN MADE MANAGER OF FORCED LABOUR IN TWO OF THE TWELVE TRIBES AS A REWARD.

I DON'T KNOW WHY WE NEED THE TEMPLE *HERE* IN THE SOUTH THOUGH. WOULDN'T IT HAVE BEEN SENSIBLE TO PUT IT SOMEWHERE *CENTRAL*?

WELL, IT'S NOT *PERFECT*, BUT IT'LL DO. THERE'S NOT A CITY *BUILT* THAT CAN LAST FOR EVER AGAINST AN ARMY.

NO ONE ASKS *US*, OF COURSE. WE JUST BUILT IT, THAT'S ALL!

I KNOW YOU, AHIJAH. YOU'RE THE *PROPHET* WHO LIVES IN SHILOH. IF YOU'RE LOOKING FOR THE *KING*, HE'S PROBABLY BUSY.

GREETINGS, JEROBOAM OF THE TRIBE OF EPHRAIM!

MY NAME IS *AHIJAH*, AND I HAVE –

IS THIS A MAGIC TRICK OR SOMETHING? I MEAN, I'M BUSY RIGHT NOW, AND –

BE QUIET AND *WATCH*!

I DON'T WANT THE *KING*, I WANT *YOU*. I HAVE BROUGHT WITH ME A BRAND NEW *CLOAK*. SEE? NEVER WORN BEFORE TODAY...

'BECAUSE HE WORSHIPPED IDOLS, I WILL TAKE TEN OF THE TWELVE TRIBES OF ISRAEL AND GIVE THEM TO *YOU*.'

AS NEWS OF THIS PROPHECY SPREAD, AND FACED WITH OPEN REVOLT, SOLOMON ACTED AS *ANY* KING MIGHT –

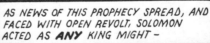

WISELY, JEROBOAM FLED TO EGYPT.

THE MESSAGE HAD BEEN FROM *GOD* – ALL HE HAD TO DO NOW WAS *WAIT*...

KILL HIM!!

– ON SIGHT.

I'M GOING TO TEAR THIS CLOAK INTO *TWELVE PIECES*! LISTEN TO WHAT GOD SAYS: 'TEN PIECES ARE FOR *YOU* – THE OTHER TWO ARE FOR *SOLOMON*.'

'BUT BECAUSE OF THE PROMISE I MADE TO HIS FATHER, I WILL LET HIM KEEP *TWO* TRIBES, SO THERE WILL BE A DESCENDANT OF DAVID ON THE THRONE IN JERUSALEM.

IF YOU OBEY GOD AND KEEP HIS COMMANDS, AS DAVID DID, THEN *YOU* WILL BE KING OF ISRAEL AS *HE* WAS.'

THE STORY OF ELIJAH

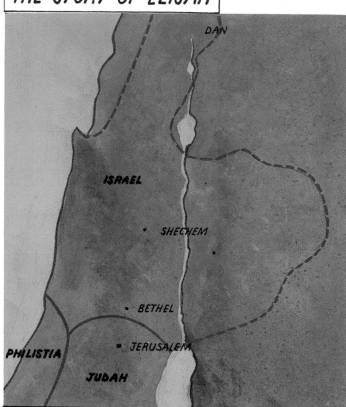

DAN

ISRAEL

SHECHEM

BETHEL

PHILISTIA

JERUSALEM

JUDAH

JEROBOAM DIDN'T HAVE TO WAIT LONG TO BE A KING. SOLOMON DIED AND A BLOODY CIVIL WAR FOLLOWED. THE COUNTRY WAS TORN IN TWO, AS THE PROPHET HAD SAID.

REHOBOAM, SOLOMON'S SON HELD THE TWO SOUTHERN TRIBES, FORMING THE KINGDOM OF JUDAH. JEROBOAM WAS CROWNED KING OF ISRAEL, MADE UP OF THE TEN NORTHERN TRIBES.

WITH A SUCCESSION OF EVIL RULERS, THE TWIN KINGDOMS SANK INTO DEGENERACY.

THE WORST WAS KING AHAB, AND HIS WIFE, JEZEBEL.

AND SO IT WAS TO THEM THAT GOD FINALLY SENT THE GREATEST OF ALL THE PROPHETS.

ELIJAH, ISN'T IT? WHY AREN'T YOU DEAD?

I BRING YOU A MESSAGE FROM GOD! FROM THIS DAY ONWARDS THERE WILL BE NO RAIN IN THE LAND, UNLESS I, ELIJAH, SAY SO! THE COUNTRY WILL DIE OF THIRST UNLESS YOU RENOUNCE EVIL AND TURN BACK TO GOD!

FASCINATING.

DELIGHTFUL.

SHALL WE HAVE HIM SKINNED ALIVE?

I'M BORED WITH SKINNINGS. FEED HIM TO THE LIONS INSTEAD?

YOUR THREATS DON'T SCARE ME. HAVE IT YOUR WAY - IT'S YOUR LIVES THAT ARE IN DANGER.

BAAL WAS A FERTILITY IDOL - A RAIN GOD. BUT HE WAS JUST A STATUE, AN IDOL MADE BY HUMAN HANDS.

ELIJAH KNEW HIS GOD TO BE ALIVE, AND IN CONTROL. WHEN GOD SPOKE, THE WHOLE EARTH OBEYED.

AND SO BECAUSE THE KING REFUSED TO LISTEN, A TERRIBLE DROUGHT CAME TO THE LAND.

ELIJAH HAD OBEYED GOD COMPLETELY IN GOING TO SEE THE KING, EVEN AT THE RISK OF HIS OWN LIFE.

BUT ELIJAH DIDN'T REJOICE. INSTEAD HE HID HIMSELF IN A RAVINE IN THE HILLS, AND FELL INTO A BLACK MOOD.

WHAT **NOW**, MY GOD?

I AM GOD. I WILL FEED YOU, ELIJAH.

GOD SENT **RAVENS** TO ELIJAH, AND THEY CARED FOR HIM.

EVERY MORNING AND EVERY EVENING THEY FLEW DOWN TO ELIJAH, AND BROUGHT HIM BREAD AND MEAT.

THERE WAS A TINY STREAM IN THE RAVINE, AND SO HE HAD WATER TO DRINK AS WELL AS THE FOOD THE BIRDS BROUGHT HIM.

AND SO ELIJAH SURVIVED, FED BY THE RAVENS AND DRINKING FROM THE SMALL STREAM, WHILE DROUGHT SAVAGED THE LAND AROUND HIM.

BUT EVENTUALLY THE STREAM DRIED UP.

SO GOD SENT ELIJAH NORTH, TO SEEK OUT A WIDOW AND HER SON.

GOOD DAY TO YOU! I WAS WONDERING IF YOU COULD SPARE ME SOME BREAD?

DON'T BE AFRAID. GO HOME AND MAKE YOUR MEAL, BUT BEFORE YOU DO, MAKE A SMALL LOAF FOR ME.

GOD SAYS IF YOU DO THIS, THE FLOUR AND OIL WILL NOT RUN OUT UNTIL HE SENDS **RAIN** AGAIN.

THE WOMAN DID AS ELIJAH SAID. EVERY TIME SHE EMPTIED THE JAR OF FLOUR, IT FILLED AGAIN, AND WHEN SHE USED UP THE LAST OF THE OIL, IT WAS REPLENISHED.

THE THREE OF THEM LIVED TOGETHER IN THE WIDOW'S HOUSE, PROTECTED AGAINST THE WORST OF THE FAMINE.

BREAD? WE HAVEN'T HAD BREAD FOR **WEEKS**! ALL I HAVE IS A TINY BIT OF FLOUR AND A DROP OF OIL.

I WAS GOING TO USE IT TO MAKE A CAKE. IT'S ALL WE HAVE LEFT, AND WHEN IT'S GONE WE'LL DIE!

ONE DAY ELIJAH MET **OBADIAH**, THE GOVERNOR OF KING AHAB'S PALACE, WHO HAD BEEN SENT IN SEARCH OF WATER. OBADIAH STILL LOVED AND SERVED GOD.

MY LORD ELIJAH, IS IT REALLY **YOU**?

YES, IT'S ME.

GO AND TELL THE KING WHERE I AM.

BUT ELIJAH, IF KING AHAB FINDS YOU, HE'LL MURDER YOU!

TRUST ME, OBADIAH. IT'S TIME TO STOP HIDING. GO AND TELL THE KING WHERE HE CAN FIND ME.

OBADIAH TRUSTED ELIJAH ENOUGH TO DO AS HE SAID, EVEN AT THE RISK OF HIS OWN LIFE; AND SO HE WENT STRAIGHT TO THE KING.

AND THE KING WENT STRAIGHT TO ELIJAH!

IS THAT REALLY *YOU*?! I'D HOPED YOU WERE DEAD, THE TROUBLE YOU'VE CAUSED ME.

MIND YOU, WE CAN FIX THAT!

GIVE ME A SWORD! A BLUNT ONE!

NONE OF THIS IS *MY* FAULT! THE BLAME LIES WITH *YOU*, AHAB!

IF YOU HAD TURNED TO GOD AND FOLLOWED HIS COMMANDS, THEN *NONE* OF THIS WOULD HAVE HAPPENED! INSTEAD YOU FOLLOW FALSE IDOLS – MAN-MADE GODS OF WOOD AND STONE, YOU FOOL!

THERE CAN ONLY BE ONE TRUE GOD – LET'S PROVE WHICH GOD IS SUPREME.

YOU PRAY TO YOUR BAAL AND I'LL PRAY TO GOD. WHICHEVER ONE ANSWERS WITH *FIRE* IS THE *TRUE* GOD!

AND SO THE 450 PROPHETS OF BAAL, TOGETHER WITH THE 400 PROPHETS OF ASHTAROTH, STARTED TO PRAY TO THEIR GODS.

WITH THEIR VOICES RAISED, THEY PRAYED AND PRAYED.

PLEADED.

DEMANDED.

SUMMONED.

BARGAINED.

BESEECHED.

BEGGED.

HOUR AFTER HOUR AFTER HOUR...

BAAL! ANSWER US!

THIS IS GOING TO TAKE *FOR EVER*! CAN'T WE GET SOME BETTER PROPHETS?

I'M SORRY YOUR MAJESTY, BUT WE'VE GOT A *THOUSAND* OF THEM OUT THERE. I DON'T THINK THERE *ARE* ANY MORE!

NOT VERY GOOD, ARE THEY?

WHY DON'T YOU *SHOUT* LOUDER? PERHAPS BAAL IS *DEAF* AND CAN'T HEAR YOU!

IN THE END, THE PROPHETS FELL TO THE GROUND, DEFEATED AND EXHAUSTED.

ONCE ISRAEL WAS FULL OF PROPHETS, MEN WHO LIVED FOR GOD.

NOW THEY'RE GONE. I AM THE LAST OF THE PROPHETS, JUST *ONE* MAN PRAYING TO THE TRUE GOD.

I'VE MADE AN ALTAR OF TWELVE STONES, FOR THE TWELVE *TRIBES* OF THE SONS OF JACOB, BECAUSE IT WAS *GOD* WHO SAID 'YOUR NAME SHALL BE *ISRAEL*.'

I HAVE DRENCHED THE ALTAR IN *WATER*, EVEN THOUGH WE ARE LOOKING FOR *FIRE*!

LORD OF ALL, GOD OF *ABRAHAM*, *ISAAC*, AND *JACOB*, LET IT BE KNOWN THAT YOU ARE *GOD* IN *ISRAEL*!

I HAVE DONE EVERYTHING YOU ASKED OF ME. ANSWER ME NOW, SO THESE PEOPLE WILL *KNOW* YOU AGAIN!

TURN THEIR HEARTS BACK TO *YOU*!

AND GOD ANSWERED.

THE **LORD**! **HE** IS GOD!

THE GOD OF **ISRAEL**!

THE FALSE PROPHETS BROUGHT US NOTHING BUT **EVIL**!

KILL THEM ALL!

GO NOW, KING AHAB, GO AND EAT. THERE IS A GREAT STORM COMING, AND YOU SHOULD BE PREPARED FOR THE WORST.

IT HADN'T RAINED FOR **YEARS**, AND NOW THE HEAVENS OPENED. IT POURED AND POURED.

TAKING ADVANTAGE OF THE CONFUSION, ELIJAH FLED FOR HIS LIFE...

AND WITH GOOD REASON.

...AND THAT'S HOW IT HAPPENED, MY QUEEN. ELIJAH PRAYED, FIRE CAME DOWN, THE RAIN STARTED AND THE PEOPLE KILLED THE PROPHETS!

THEN MAY THE GODS STRIKE ME DEAD IF I DON'T MAKE ELIJAH AS **DEAD** AS **THEY** ARE!

BY THIS TIME TOMORROW, I WANT ELIJAH'S **HEAD** STUCK ON THE PALACE GATES!!

AS BEFORE, ELIJAH'S TRIUMPH WAS FOLLOWED BY FEELINGS OF UTTER **DESPAIR**.

LEAVING EVERYONE HE KNEW, ELIJAH HEADED OUT INTO THE DESERT, ALONE.

I HAVE HAD **ENOUGH**, LORD.

ALL MY LIFE HAS BEEN SPENT HIDING, ALWAYS ON THE RUN.

TAKE MY LIFE NOW. TAKE ME WITH YOU AND HAVE DONE WITH IT.

...?

WHERE DID THAT COME FROM?

I'M **SURE** IT WASN'T THERE A SECOND AGO.

EAT AND DRINK, ELIJAH. THINGS ALWAYS SEEM WORSE WHEN YOU'RE HUNGRY.

THERE'S A LONG JOURNEY AHEAD OF YOU, AND YOU'LL NEED YOUR STRENGTH.

ENCOURAGED BY THE ANGEL, ELIJAH SET OUT ACROSS THE DESERT TO THE PLACE WHERE GOD HAD SPOKEN TO **MOSES** MANY CENTURIES BEFORE.

AND THERE HE FOUND A CAVE, WHERE HE WAITED FOR **GOD**.

IN A CAVE ON **MOUNT SINAI** ELIJAH WAITED FOR GOD.

AND THEN GOD **SPOKE** TO ELIJAH, SAYING:

ELIJAH, WHAT ARE YOU DOING HERE, ALL BY YOURSELF, ALONE IN THE DESERT?

MY LORD GOD, I HAVE ALWAYS SERVED YOU - AND **ONLY** YOU. THE ISRAELITES HAVE TURNED THEIR BACKS ON YOU, TORN DOWN YOUR ALTARS AND MURDERED YOUR PROPHETS -

I AM THE ONLY ONE LEFT.

GET UP, ELIJAH. GET UP ON YOUR FEET, BECAUSE YOUR GOD IS ABOUT TO PASS BY, RIGHT IN FRONT OF YOU!

AND SUDDENLY THERE WAS A TERRIBLE **STORM**, A **HURRICANE** THAT CAME FROM NOWHERE, SENDING ROCKS AND TREES FLYING IN ITS WAKE, TEARING THE BREATH FROM ELIJAH'S LUNGS.

BUT GOD WAS NOT IN THE WIND.

AND THEN THE EARTH **BUCKLED** BENEATH ELIJAH'S FEET, AS A MIGHTY **EARTHQUAKE** SHOOK THE MOUNTAIN DOWN TO ITS ROOTS, TEARING THE GROUND IN TWO AND BREAKING THE CLIFFS AS IF THEY WERE NO MORE THAN **GLASS**.

BUT GOD WAS NOT IN THE EARTHQUAKE.

AND THEN THERE CAME A **FIRE**, AN INFERNO THAT SCORCHED THE EARTH, BLACKENING THE ROCKS IN ITS PATH.

BUT GOD WAS NOT IN THE FIRE.

BUT **AFTER** THE FIRE, THERE CAME A SMALL, STILL VOICE - THE GENTLEST OF **WHISPERS**...

ELIJAH...?

AND AT LAST ELIJAH KNEW THAT WAS GOD.

ELIJAH. WHAT ARE YOU DOING HERE, HALFWAY UP A MOUNTAIN IN THE MIDDLE OF NOWHERE?

GO BACK DOWN. YOUR GOD WILL LOOK AFTER YOU.

AND SO ENCOURAGED, ELIJAH SET OFF TO SEEK THE MAN GOD HAD CHOSEN TO SUCCEED HIM.

HIS NAME WAS *ELISHA.*

ELIJAH FOUND HIM AS HE WORKED THE FIELDS, PLOUGHING WITH HIS TEAM OF OXEN. ELIJAH TOOK OFF HIS CLOAK AND, VERY DELIBERATELY, PLACED IT ON ELISHA'S SHOULDERS...

YOU UNDERSTAND WHAT THIS MEANS, ELISHA? YOU KNOW WHAT IT IS I'M DOING?

I THINK SO, THAT IS... *YES.* YES, I UNDERSTAND.

GOOD. YOU MUST FOLLOW ME.

BUT I CAN'T JUST DROP EVERYTHING! AT LEAST LET ME GO AND SAY GOODBYE TO MY PARENTS!

I DIDN'T ACTUALLY MEAN THIS *INSTANT.* BUT WE WILL NEED TO LEAVE SOON. WE'VE MUCH WORK TO DO.

SO ELISHA FOLLOWED ELIJAH, LEARNING THE LIFE OF A PROPHET.

AND BY FOLLOWING ELIJAH, HE TOO MADE HIS WAY INTO THE COURT OF THE TYRANT, KING AHAB...

ELIJAH! WHAT ARE YOU *DOING?* IF THE KING SEES YOU HE'LL KILL YOU!

GOD HAS A MESSAGE FOR AHAB WHICH I MUST DELIVER.

ENJOYING THE APPLES, ARE WE?

SO, MY OLD ENEMY, WE MEET AGAIN. WHAT IS IT *THIS* TIME?

EVERYTHING YOU DO, EVERYTHING YOU'VE *EVER* DONE, HAS BEEN *EVIL!*

EVEN THE FRUIT YOU EAT IS STOLEN FROM A MAN YOU *MURDERED!* YOU KILLED A MAN JUST FOR SOME APPLES!

YOU WILL *DIE!* EVERY MALE IN YOUR FAMILY WILL *DIE!* YOUR WIFE WILL *DIE!* THIS IS NOT ME SPEAKING, BUT *GOD!* YOU WILL *DIE* AND *DOGS* WILL DRINK YOUR *BLOOD!!*

HEARD IT ALL BEFORE.

YES, BUT THE *RAIN*, REMEMBER THE TIME WHEN THE *DROUGHT* CAME..?

WHAT IF... WHAT IF HE'S *RIGHT*?

OH DON'T BE RIDICULOUS. HE'S JUST TRYING TO SCARE YOU, THAT'S ALL.

BUT WHAT IF HE'S RIGHT!?

WHAT DO YOU MEAN, 'IF'? COME ON ELISHA, WE MUST LEAVE.

GOD HAS SEEN WHAT WE'VE DONE! WE'RE *DOOMED*!

PLEASE MY LORD, EAT SOMETHING.

WOE TO ME! WOE TO US! WE'RE DOOMED!

REALLY, DARLING. DON'T GO ON! WE'VE NOTHING TO FEAR.

YOU DON'T *SEE* IT, DO YOU?

BECAUSE OF THE THINGS WE'VE DONE, THINGS YOU *MADE* ME DO, GOD WILL STICK TO HIS WORD!

I *KNOW* HE WILL!

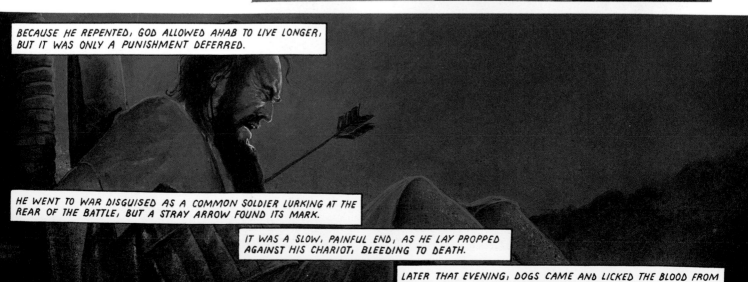

BECAUSE HE REPENTED, GOD ALLOWED AHAB TO LIVE LONGER, BUT IT WAS ONLY A PUNISHMENT DEFERRED.

HE WENT TO WAR DISGUISED AS A COMMON SOLDIER LURKING AT THE REAR OF THE BATTLE, BUT A STRAY ARROW FOUND ITS MARK.

IT WAS A SLOW, PAINFUL END, AS HE LAY PROPPED AGAINST HIS CHARIOT, BLEEDING TO DEATH.

LATER THAT EVENING, DOGS CAME AND LICKED THE BLOOD FROM THE CHARIOT, AS ELIJAH HAD SAID THEY WOULD.

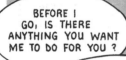

LOOK OUT!

ELIJAH, WHAT'S HAPPENING?

DON'T LEAVE ME! DON'T GO!

ELIJAH WAS TAKEN TO BE WITH THE GOD HE HAD SERVED ALL HIS LIFE.

ELISHA WATCHED, HARDLY BELIEVING WHAT WAS HAPPENING.

THROUGH TEAR-FILLED EYES ELISHA SAW HIS MASTER'S CLOAK FALL FROM THE SKY.

AS THE CLOAK FELL, ELISHA CALLED OUT ONE LAST TIME...

BUT AS ELISHA PICKED UP THE CLOAK HE KNEW THAT HE WOULD NEVER SEE HIS MUCH-LOVED MASTER AGAIN.

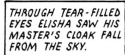

GREAT PROPHET OF ISRAEL – DON'T LEAVE ME!

AND HE KNEW THAT HIS WORK WAS JUST BEGINNING...

HOW CAN I CARRY ON YOUR WORK? I THOUGHT I'D BE BETTER PREPARED THAN THIS.

THERE'S ONE WAY TO FIND OUT, I SUPPOSE.

IT WAS THEN THAT ELISHA KNEW GOD WAS WITH HIM.

AND SO ELISHA STRUCK THE WATER'S EDGE WITH HIS CLOAK, AND AS HE DID SO, THE WATERS PARTED AS THEY HAD FOR ELIJAH.

ELIJAH HAD SPOKEN FOR GOD IN THE COURTS OF KINGS AND NOBLES; ELISHA SPOKE FOR GOD IN THE LIVES OF ORDINARY PEOPLE.

UTTERLY REFUSING TO ACCEPT PAYMENT OF ANY KIND, ELISHA CUR NAAMAN, GENERAL OF THE ARAMEAN ARMY, OF LEPROSY.

AS HE OBEYED ELISHA AND BATHED IN THE WATER OF THE RIVER JORDAN, NAAMAN KNEW FOR HIMSE WHAT THE PROPHETS HAD SAID WAS TRUE:

THE POWER OF GOD SO FILLED ELISHA THAT HE WAS ABLE TO RAISE A YOUNG BOY FROM DEATH.

THERE IS NO GOD IN THE WHOLE WORLD EXCEPT IN *ISRAEL*.

DO NOT FEAR. TOMORROW THERE WILL BE FOOD IN ABUNDANCE. GOD HAS TOLD ME.

WHEN THE ARAMEANS ATTACKED ISRAEL, IT WAS ELISHA WHO PRAYED THAT THE INVADERS WOULD BE BLINDED AND UNABLE TO FIGHT.

IT WAS ELISHA WHO LED THEM TO THE ISRAELITES, AND HE WHO SPARED THEIR LIVES.

WHEN THE CITY OF SAMARIA, THE CAPITAL CITY OF ISRAEL, WAS BESIEGED, AND THE PEOPLE GREW SO DESPERATE THAT THEY WERE REDUCED TO *CANNIBALISM*, ELISHA WAS ABLE TO SEE BEYOND THE MISERY AROUND THEM, EVEN RISKING THE ANGER OF THE KING...

BUT IF THE ISRAELITES THOUGHT THAT THEIR TROUBLES WERE OVER THEY WERE VERY MUCH MISTAKEN.

AND THE MORE THEY TURNED AWAY FROM GOD, THE GREATER THEIR PROBLEMS BECAME.

A GREAT DARKNESS WAS ABOUT TO FALL ON *JERUSALEM*, THE HOLY CITY, ITSELF...

THE FALL OF ISRAEL AND JUDAH

THE ENEMY HAS BREACHED THE SOUTH GATE! IT WON'T BE LONG NOW. IT'S HARD ENOUGH TRYING TO GET THIS ALL DOWN CORRECTLY, WITHOUT A *WAR* GOING ON!

AS THE NATIONS OF JUDAH AND ISRAEL SANK FURTHER INTO DEGENERACY SO GOD WITHDREW HIS PROTECTION. JERUSALEM WAS ATTACKED AGAIN AND AGAIN.

THROUGHOUT THESE TROUBLED TIMES THE EVENTS WERE RECORDED BY THOSE WHO REMAINED FAITHFUL TO GOD.

ASSUMING I LIVE LONG ENOUGH TO FINISH IT; ASSUMING THERE'S ANYONE LEFT ALIVE TO *READ* IT! WHERE WAS I? OH YES, KING *AHAB* AND HIS REVOLTING WIFE, *JEZEBEL*! BAD TO THE BONE, THE PAIR OF THEM.

AS ELIJAH HAD PREDICTED, JEZEBEL DIED A VIOLENT DEATH. HURLED OUT OF A CASTLE WINDOW, HER BODY WAS TRAMPLED BY HORSES AND EATEN BY DOGS UNTIL THERE WASN'T ENOUGH LEFT TO BURY.

ALTHOUGH AHAB AND JEZEBEL HAD BEEN EVIL TO THE CORE, NONE OF THEIR SUCCESSORS WAS ANY BETTER: THE WORSHIP OF BAAL CAME TO A TEMPORARY HALT IN BLOODY AND VIOLENT SLAUGHTER, BUT THE PEOPLE STILL BOWED DOWN TO GOLDEN CALVES.

YOUNG JOASH REMAINED HIDDEN AWAY WITHIN THE TEMPLE ITSELF FOR SIX YEARS, PROTECTED BY THE FAITHFUL PRIEST JEHOIADA.

GOD HAD PROMISED DAVID THAT ONE OF HIS DESCENDANTS WOULD RULE THE KINGDOM THAT HAS *NO END*, AND THAT GOD HIMSELF WOULD BE A FATHER TO HIM.

IN JUDAH, IN A VICIOUS ATTEMPT TO WIN POWER, QUEEN ATHALIAH DESTROYED THE ENTIRE ROYAL FAMILY. THE HOUSE OF DAVID WAS ALL BUT WIPED OUT: THE ONLY SURVIVOR WAS A BABY BOY, THE YOUNG PRINCE *JOASH* RESCUED BY THE WIFE OF ONE OF THE PRIESTS.

IN ANY EVENT, JEHOIADA KNEW HIS POLITICS AS WELL AS HIS SCRIPTURES, AND SAW HE HAD AN OPPORTUNITY TO SEIZE POWER BACK FROM THE EVIL QUEEN.

WHEN JOASH WAS SEVEN YEARS OLD JEHOIADA SUMMONED THE GENERALS AND COMMANDERS OF THE ARMY TO THE TEMPLE, AND THEN AS THEY WAITED IN WONDER, HE PRODUCED HIS SURPRISE GUEST!

LISTEN TO ME! TODAY I HAVE ARMED YOU WITH THE WEAPONS KEPT IN THE TEMPLE — THE WEAPONS THAT BELONGED TO KING DAVID! TODAY WE RESTORE HIS *HEIR* TO THE THRONE!

SURROUND THE NEW KING AND THE TEMPLE! SUMMON THE GUARDS WHO ARE OFF DUTY AND HAVE THEM JOIN US! TODAY WE CROWN THE KING OURSELVES!

LONG LIVE KING JOASH! LONG LIVE KING JOASH!

GOD PROTECT THE NEW KING!

AS A PLAN, IT WAS *BRILLIANT!* JOASH WAS PUT ON THE THRONE OF JUDAH WITH SCARCELY A DROP OF BLOOD SPILLED!

CROWNED BY THE PRIEST JEHOIADA, SURROUNDED BY ARMED GUARDS, THERE WAS NOTHING THE QUEEN COULD DO TO PREVENT IT!

NO! THIS IS *TREASON*!

GUARDS! *GUARDS*! I WANT HIM *DEAD*!!

BUT THE ENTIRE ARMY BACKED THE NEW KING. WHEN THE GUARDS FINALLY ANSWERED THE QUEEN'S CALL, IT WAS ONLY TO TAKE HER TO A PLACE OF *EXECUTION*.

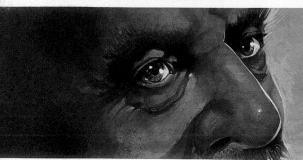

JOASH WAS A RARITY. A GOOD KING, HE TORE DOWN THE ALTARS TO BAAL, AND RESTORED THE OLD WAYS, BRINGING THE PEOPLE BACK TO GOD.

HE REBUILT THE TEMPLE, AND ENDED CORRUPTION IN THE PRIESTHOOD. BUT AFTER JEHOIADA'S DEATH JOASH ALSO TURNED HIS BACK ON GOD, EVEN ORDERING THAT JEHOIADA'S SON, A PROPHET, BE STONED TO DEATH IN THE VERY TEMPLE JOASH HAD HELPED TO REBUILD.

THE KINGS OF ISRAEL COULD NOT TURN FROM THE DARKNESS, AND SO GOD WITHDREW HIS PROTECTION ALTOGETHER.

THE PEOPLE OF THE NORTHERN KINGDOM OF ISRAEL WERE MADE SLAVES BY THE KING OF ASSYRIA, AND WERE TAKEN AWAY IN EXILE.

KING HOSHEA WAS THE LAST KING OF ISRAEL, THE LAST OF THE NORTHERN KINGS.

HE HAD REIGNED AS A PUPPET OF HIS ASSYRIAN MASTERS, AND WAS FINALLY CAUGHT OUT ATTEMPTING TO BETRAY THEM TO THE EGYPTIANS.

NOW ONLY THE SOUTHERN KINGDOM OF *JUDAH* SURVIVED. OF THE TWELVE TRIBES OF JACOB, ONLY *TWO* NOW REMAINED FREE, AND WITH THEM THE HOPE FOR ALL ISRAEL.

HAVING SUCCESSFULLY PLUNDERED THE LARGER KINGDOM OF ISRAEL, IT WAS ONLY A MATTER OF TIME BEFORE THE ASSYRIAN CONQUERORS TURNED THEIR ATTENTION TOWARDS JUDAH.

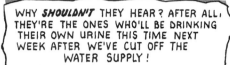

EIGHT YEARS AFTER THE FALL OF SAMARIA AND THE END OF THE KINGDOM OF ISRAEL, THE SIEGE OF JERUSALEM **BEGAN**...

LISTEN TO ME, MEN OF SYRIA! THIS IS NO WAY TO CONDUCT AFFAIRS OF WAR!

WE'RE WILLING TO LISTEN TO YOUR DEMANDS, BUT YOU MUST SPEAK TO US IN ARAMAIC! IF YOU CONTINUE TO SPEAK HEBREW, THEN OUR OWN TROOPS WILL **HEAR** US!

WHY **SHOULDN'T** THEY HEAR? AFTER ALL, THEY'RE THE ONES WHO'LL BE DRINKING THEIR OWN URINE THIS TIME NEXT WEEK AFTER WE'VE CUT OFF THE WATER SUPPLY!

AND SINCE WHEN HAS A **GOD** EVER SAVED A PEOPLE FROM AN ARMY SUCH AS OURS? IF YOU SURRENDER, THEN WE WILL BE MERCIFUL!

WE HAVE CONQUERED ALL THE NATIONS AROUND YOU, AND WHEN DID ONE OF **THEIR** GODS SAVE THEM? IF YOUR KING TELLS YOU THAT YOUR GOD WILL SAVE YOU, HE IS **LYING**!

KING **HEZEKIAH** OF JUDAH TRUSTED GOD LIKE NONE OF THE KINGS OF JUDAH BEFORE OR AFTER HIM. WHEN THE ASSYRIANS DEMANDED HIS SURRENDER, HE WENT UP TO THE TEMPLE, LAID THE LETTER OF DEMAND ON THE GROUND BEFORE GOD, AND **PRAYED**:

LORD, GOD OF ISRAEL, YOU ALONE ARE GOD OVER ALL THE KINGDOMS OF EARTH, FOR YOU **MADE** THE EARTH!

AND SOON AN ANSWER CAME; A MESSENGER FROM THE PROPHET **ISAIAH** BROUGHT HEZEKIAH GOD'S RESPONSE:

GOD HAS TOLD ISAIAH THAT THE KING WILL NOT ENTER JERUSALEM, OR SHOOT ONE ARROW AGAINST YOU. HE WILL DEFEND THIS CITY FOR THE SAKE OF HIS SERVANT, DAVID.

OUR GOD WILL FIGHT FOR US, YOUR HIGHNESS.

THAT NIGHT, SOMETHING **TERRIBLE** PASSED IN THE AIR ABOVE THE ASSYRIAN CAMP.

THE ASSYRIANS HAVE DESTROYED ALL THE NATIONS AROUND THEM, AND THROWN THEIR GODS INTO THE FIRE; BUT THEY WERE NOT **REAL** GODS, ONLY STATUES MADE OF WOOD AND STONE!

DELIVER US, MY GOD. SAVE US SO THAT ALL THE KINGDOMS OF THE WORLD MAY KNOW THAT YOU, AND **ONLY** YOU, ARE GOD!

THE ASSYRIANS THOUGHT THAT THEIR BATTLE WAS WITH **MEN** ARMED WITH SWORDS AND SHIELDS, BUT THEY WERE WRONG.

THAT NIGHT THE ANGEL OF **DEATH** PASSED OVER THE ASSYRIAN ARMY.

TERROR-STRUCK, THE ASSYRIAN KING BROKE OFF THE SIEGE. HE RETURNED TO NINEVEH, HIS CAPITAL, AND STAYED THERE UNTIL HE WAS MURDERED BY HIS OWN SONS.

STILL, IT WASN'T **ALL** WARS AND BATTLES! SOME PEOPLE STILL LOOKED TO GOD FOR THE FIRST SOLUTION TO TROUBLE INSTEAD OF THE SWORD. FOR EXAMPLE, THE PROPHET CALLED **ISAIAH**.

IN THE YEAR THAT KING UZZIAH DIED, ISAIAH SAW GOD WITH HIS OWN EYES.

GOD WAS ON A BIG THRONE, AND HIS ROBE FILLED THE TEMPLE.

ANGELS COVERED THEIR FACES WITH THEIR WINGS BECAUSE GOD WAS SO **HOLY** THAT THEY COULD NOT EVEN LOOK AT HIM, AND THEY CALLED TO EACH OTHER:

HOLY, HOLY, HOLY IS THE LORD GOD ALMIGHTY: THE WHOLE EARTH IS FULL OF HIS GLORY.

AT THE SOUND OF THEIR VOICES, THE TEMPLE **SHOOK** AND FILLED WITH SMOKE!

ISAIAH FULLY EXPECTED TO **DIE** AT THIS POINT. AFTER ALL, HOW COULD HE, A SINFUL MAN, LOOK UPON THE HOLY FACE OF GOD AND **LIVE** WHEN EVEN **ANGELS** HID THEIR FACES?

BUT AN ANGEL TOUCHED HIS LIPS WITH A BURNING COAL, TAKEN FROM THE ALTAR, SAYING: 'YOUR GUILT IS TAKEN AWAY, YOUR SIN **PAID** FOR.'

I AM DEAD! I AM A MAN OF UNCLEAN LIPS AND LIVE AMONG A PEOPLE OF UNCLEAN LIPS, AND YET MY EYES HAVE SEEN THE LORD GOD, KING OF ALL!!

AND **GOD** SAID:

WHO WILL I SEND? WHO WILL SPEAK FOR US?

HERE I AM LORD! SEND ME!

THE MESSAGE GOD GAVE ISAIAH CONCERNED THE HOUSE OF **DAVID**, AND THE FUTURE **KING** THAT GOD HAD PROMISED TO SEND. ISAIAH WENT TO THE ROYAL COURT WITH THE MOST AMAZING PROPHECY...

GOD WILL GIVE US A **SIGN**! A **VIRGIN** WILL GIVE BIRTH TO A **SON**. AND WE WILL CALL HIM **IMMANUEL** – 'GOD WITH US'!

IN **GALILEE**, THE PEOPLE LIVING IN DARKNESS WILL SEE A **LIGHT**! FOR TO US A CHILD IS BORN, AND THE GOVERNMENT WILL REST ON **HIS** SHOULDERS! **HE WILL REIGN ON DAVID'S THRONE FOR EVER!**

DISASTER SEEMS INEVITABLE NOW. WARNING AFTER WARNING, PROPHET AFTER PROPHET, THE FOOLS DEAFENED THEIR EARS AND HID THEIR EYES FROM THE TRUTH.

WE WERE NEVER MEANT TO BE A NATION OF **WARRIORS**, AS WE IMAGINED IN OUR VANITY, BUT A HOLY NATION! GOD WAS OUR **ONLY** PROTECTION!

NOW LOOK AT US! RUNNING FROM THE ENEMY WITH WHATEVER WE CAN SAVE CLUTCHED IN OUR ARMS — **ME**, I'M NO DIFFERENT FROM **THEM** IN THAT RESPECT!

IDIOTS! WEAK, ARROGANT **FOOLS**. THEY BOWED DOWN AND WORSHIPPED METAL AND WOOD, HURLED THEMSELVES DOWN IN FRONT OF **ANYTHING** THEY COULD FIND TO PRAY TO — STARS, PLANTS, CALVES, ANYTHING! AND THEIR 'WORSHIP' BECAME MORE AND MORE **OBSCENE** AS THE YEARS WENT BY.

NOW IT'S ALL CAUGHT UP WITH US AND THERE'S NOT A THING ANY OF US CAN DO TO ESCAPE.

JERUSALEM IS FALLING...

I ONLY HOPE THERE WILL STILL BE PEOPLE LEFT TO **READ** THIS WHEN IT'S ALL OVER.

THE WORLD MAY CHANGE, BUT PEOPLE STAY THE SAME. PERHAPS OUR CHILDREN'S CHILDREN'S CHILDREN WILL LEARN FROM OUR DISASTER: IT IS **GOD** ALONE WHO TRULY KEEPS US SAFE.

THEY SHOULD HAVE LISTENED TO THE PROPHETS. THEY **SHOULD** HAVE LISTENED TO **JEREMIAH**. HE WAS THEIR LAST WARNING. EVEN **THEN** THERE WOULD HAVE BEEN TIME ENOUGH TO UNDO THE HARM!

JEREMIAH WAS STILL A YOUNG MAN WHEN GOD SPOKE TO HIM:

GO TO THE PEOPLE, JEREMIAH, AND SPEAK TO THEM FOR ME! TELL THEM EVERYTHING I TELL **YOU**!

BUT THEY WON'T LISTEN TO ME! THEY ARE OLDER AND WISER. THEY'LL JUST LAUGH!

THEN I WILL GIVE YOU THE WORDS TO SAY. **LOOK** AND TELL ME WHAT YOU SEE.

THIS? BUT IT'S JUST A POT OF STEW.

WATCH. IN THE SAME WAY AS THE STEW IS SPILLED FROM THIS POT, SO WILL DISASTER COME TO JERUSALEM.

AN ARMY WILL COME FROM THE NORTH, AND YOU WILL BE **HELPLESS** BEFORE THEM!

LISTEN TO ME! YOUR LIVES ARE IN DANGER! YOU HAVE WORSHIPPED ROCKS AND PLANTS INSTEAD OF **GOD**, AND HE IS ABOUT TO REMOVE HIS PROTECTION FROM US!

SO? WE'LL CHANGE OUR GODS IF WE HAVE TO.

BUT DON'T YOU SEE? IT'LL BE TOO LATE THEN! YOU WILL BE LIKE A LEOPARD TRYING TO CHANGE ITS SPOTS! IF YOU VALUE YOUR LIVES, THEN GET ON YOUR KNEES AND REPENT **TODAY**!!

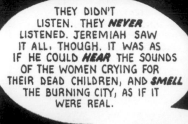

THEY DIDN'T LISTEN. THEY *NEVER* LISTENED. JEREMIAH SAW IT ALL, THOUGH. IT WAS AS IF HE COULD *HEAR* THE SOUNDS OF THE WOMEN CRYING FOR THEIR DEAD CHILDREN, AND *SMELL* THE BURNING CITY, AS IF IT WERE REAL.

HE WAS TORTURED BY THE VISIONS OF JERUSALEM, THE HOLY CITY OF GOD, TORN TO PIECES BY ITS OWN EVIL.

IN THE PLACES WHERE THEY HAD ONCE WORSHIPPED GOD, AND THE AIR HAD BEEN FULL OF SINGING AND LAUGHTER, THE PEOPLE *BURNED* THEIR OWN CHILDREN AS *SACRIFICES* TO STONES AND STARS AND TREES.

JEREMIAH WAS THROWN DOWN A WELL FOR HIS TROUBLE AND LEFT TO DIE.

HIS CONSTANT PREACHING WAS CONSIDERED BAD FOR MORALE.

LISTEN TO ME! IF WE STAY IN THE CITY WE WILL ALL *DIE*!

SURRENDER TO THE BABYLONIANS. GOD WILL BE MERCIFUL! WHY WON'T YOU *LISTEN*?!

YOUR MAJESTY, JEREMIAH WILL SURELY DIE IN THE WELL. THERE'S LITTLE ENOUGH FOOD IN THE CITY, LET ALONE WHERE HE IS. HE IS STILL A MAN OF GOD, AND DESERVES BETTER THAN THIS.

VERY WELL. BRING HIM UP TO THE COURTYARD, BUT HE'S NOT TO BE RELEASED. I DON'T WANT TO ANGER THE PEOPLE ANY FURTHER.

IT'S YOUR LUCKY DAY, TRAITOR. THE KING WANTS YOUR ADVICE, AND ASKS YOU TO TELL THE TRUTH.

IF I TELL THE TRUTH HE'LL HAVE ME KILLED, AND IF I GIVE HIM ADVICE HE WON'T LISTEN!

EVEN SO, JEREMIAH WAS SPARED. BUT HIS FATE WAS STILL TIED TO THE FATE OF THE PEOPLE BESIEGED IN THE CITY OF JERUSALEM AND...

WHAT'S THAT NOISE?

NO! NOT NOW! NOT WHEN I'VE ALMOST FINISHED!

EVEN IF MOSES AND SAMUEL STOOD HERE AND PLEADED, GOD WOULDN'T CHANGE HIS MIND NOW.

HEAR MY PRAYER, OH GOD, AND SHOW US MERCY.

DO NOT ABANDON YOUR PEOPLE FOR EVER, LORD MY GOD.

MASTER! THE KING'S BEEN TAKEN ALIVE HE'S SURRENDERED! IT'S ALL OVER!

NO! MAY GOD FORGIVE ME, I SHOULD HAVE BEEN HERE WITH YOU!

AFTER ALL HE'D LIVED THROUGH, TO BE KILLED IN THE LAST HOUR OF THE BATTLE IS THE CRUELLEST BLOW OF ALL.

WHO IS THERE LEFT TO FINISH THE STORY?

MM. YOU KNOW, IT DOESN'T QUITE FLOW HERE, A TOUCH MELODRAMATIC I FEEL. TOO WORDY.

OH! AND LOOK AT THIS SPEECH! JEREMIAH NEVER SPOKE LIKE THAT...!

IN THE TENTH MONTH OF THE NINTH YEAR THAT ZEDEKIAH WAS KING IN JUDAH, KING NEBUCHADNEZZAR OF BABYLON CAME WITH HIS ENTIRE ARMY, AND LAID SIEGE TO THE CITY OF JERUSALEM.

EVERY HOUSE IN THE CITY WAS BURNED TO THE GROUND, EVEN THE ROYAL PALACE. THE CITY WALLS THEMSELVES WERE TORN DOWN.

JERUSALEM WAS UTTERLY DESTROYED.

THE KING WAS CAUGHT TRYING TO ESCAPE THROUGH THE PALACE GARDEN AT NIGHT. THE INVADERS KILLED HIS SONS IN FRONT OF HIM, AND THEN PUT OUT HIS EYES WITH THEIR SWORDS.

HE WAS TAKEN IN CHAINS TO BABYLON.

MOST OF THE PEOPLE OF JERUSALEM WERE TAKEN AWAY IN CHAINS, LIKE SLAVES, TO THE FAR-OFF KINGDOM OF BABYLON.

ISRAEL HAD FALLEN, JUDAH HAD FALLEN, JERUSALEM WAS REDUCED TO RUBBLE.

AS FOR JEREMIAH, THE BABYLONIAN KING OFFERED HIM A PLACE AT HIS COURT, PERHAPS A REWARD FOR ADVOCATING SURRENDER. INSTEAD JEREMIAH CHOSE TO REMAIN WITH THE SCARCE FEW WHO AVOIDED CAPTURE, PREACHING RIGHT TO THE END TO A PEOPLE WHO REFUSED TO LISTEN.

GOD'S ANGER WILL NOT LAST FOR EVER, A TIME WILL COME WHEN HE WILL CHOOSE A KING, A RIGHTEOUS DESCENDANT OF DAVID.

HE WILL RULE WITH WISDOM; HIS NAME WILL MEAN SALVATION. THROUGH HIM GOD WILL SAVE US ALL! HEAR ME AND KNOW THE TRUTH: AN HEIR OF DAVID WILL RULE AGAIN!

142

THE STORY OF JONAH

GOD SPOKE TO **JONAH**, A PROPHET OF ISRAEL, TELLING HIM TO GO TO THE CITY OF **NINEVEH**, AND TELL THE PEOPLE THERE TO SEEK FORGIVENESS FOR THEIR EVIL WAYS.

NINEVEH WAS ISRAEL'S HATED **ENEMY**, AND JONAH DIDN'T SEE **WHY** GOD SHOULD FORGIVE THEM. WHY COULDN'T HE JUST **DESTROY** THEM?

AND EVEN **THEN** HE DIDN'T STOP, BOARDING THE FIRST AVAILABLE SHIP BOUND FOR WHO-KNOWS-WHERE, JUST AS LONG AS IT WAS FAR, FAR AWAY FROM THE DOOMED CITY OF **NINEVEH**.

AND SO JONAH SET OFF AT ONCE, AS FAST AS HIS LEGS WOULD CARRY HIM - IN THE **OPPOSITE** DIRECTION!

IN FACT, JONAH KEPT ON RUNNING UNTIL HE REACHED THE **SEA**, AS FAR AWAY FROM NINEVEH AS HE COULD POSSIBLY GET.

OF COURSE, RUNNING AWAY FROM **PEOPLE** IS ONE THING - RUNNING AWAY FROM **GOD** IS A DIFFERENT MATTER ALTOGETHER.

THE SHIP WAS ONLY A FEW DAYS OUT OF PORT WHEN A TERRIBLE **STORM** TOOK HOLD, WORSE THAN ANYTHING THE CREW HAD EVER SEEN!

WE'RE TAKING IN WATER! ABANDON THE CARGO BEFORE WE GO UNDER!

IT'S NOT ENOUGH! WE'RE STILL OVERLADEN! WE'LL HAVE TO DRAW STRAWS AND THROW SOMEONE OVERBOARD!

IT'S ALL MY FAULT! **GOD** TOLD ME TO GO TO THE CITY OF MY ENEMIES, BUT I RAN AWAY INSTEAD!

BUT WE'RE ONLY GOING TO **SPAIN**! YOU CAN HIDE FROM GOD IN **SPAIN**!

I CAN SEE THAT **NOW**, OBVIOUSLY! **LISTEN**, IF YOU THROW ME OVERBOARD, THE STORM WILL STOP, I JUST **KNOW** IT WILL!

THIS ISN'T **YOUR** FAULT!

COME ON. LET'S GET IT OVER WITH.

I'VE JUST REMEMBERED! I CAN'T SWI-!

143

JONAH SANK LIKE LEAD, BUT BEFORE HE COULD REACH THE BOTTOM HE WAS SWALLOWED BY A MASSIVE **FISH**.

OR **WHALE**.

SOMETHING LIKE THAT, ANYWAY. IT WAS PRETTY DARK DOWN THERE AND JONAH DIDN'T GET TOO GOOD A LOOK AT IT.

WHATEVER IT WAS, JONAH WAS STUCK INSIDE ITS BELLY FOR THREE DAYS AND THREE NIGHTS.

ON THE THIRD DAY THE FISH SPEWED JONAH ONTO THE BEACH IN A MOST **UNDIGNIFIED** FASHION.

AND SO, SMELLING OF ROTTEN FISH AND SEAWEED, JONAH SET OFF TO DELIVER THE MESSAGE GOD HAD GIVEN HIM TO THE PEOPLE OF THE CITY OF NINEVEH...

WHO IMMEDIATELY **FELL** ON THEIR KNEES, AND **BEGGED** GOD'S FORGIVENESS FOR THEIR WICKED WAYS AND TURNED THEIR BACKS ON EVIL FOR THE REST OF THEIR LIVES.

I DON'T **UNDERSTAND**! I MEAN, I REALLY DON'T GET IT! THE PEOPLE IN NINEVEH ARE AMONGST THE WICKEDEST ON EARTH, AND YET YOU LET THEM OFF, AS IF IT WERE NOTHING!

LOOK AT THEM! DESPITE THEIR ATROCITIES, ONE WORD FROM GOD AND THEY'RE FREE FROM GUILT!

I GIVE UP. DO YOU **HEAR** ME GOD? I **GIVE UP**! I DON'T WANT TO LIVE ANY MORE!

AND SO JONAH SAT AND WAITED TO DIE, RESTING FROM THE BURNING SUN IN THE SHADE OF A TINY TREE.

AFTER A COUPLE OF DAYS GOD CAUSED THE **TREE** TO SHRIVEL AND DIE.

OH **THANK** YOU GOD! SENT OFF ON MAD QUESTS, SWALLOWED BY SEA MONSTERS... NOW I HAVEN'T EVEN GOT A **TREE** LEFT!

IT WASN'T AS IF IT WAS DOING ANY **HARM**!

JONAH? WHY ARE YOU ANGRY WITH ME?

DID **YOU** PLANT THE TREE OR WATER IT? DID YOU MAKE IT GROW? IT CAME FROM NOTHING IN ONE DAY, AND WAS GONE THE NEXT, AND YET YOU FEEL SORRY FOR IT?

THERE ARE THOUSANDS UPON THOUSANDS OF **INNOCENT** PEOPLE IN NINEVEH ALONG WITH THE GUILTY, AND YET YOU ARE ANGRY WITH ME FOR SPARING THEIR LIVES, WHILE YOU MOURN THE LOSS OF ONE SMALL SHRUB!

BUT... BUT THEY WEREN'T EVEN **JEWISH**!!

NOR WAS THE TREE!

THE STORY OF EZEKIEL

EZEKIEL HAD TRAINED FOR THE PRIESTHOOD, TO SERVE GOD IN THE TEMPLE IN JERUSALEM. ON HIS THIRTIETH BIRTHDAY HE WAS TO HAVE TAKEN OFFICE, AS HIS FATHERS HAD BEFORE HIM. INSTEAD, BEFORE THE FINAL SIEGE OF JERUSALEM HAD EVEN BEGUN, HE WAS AMONG THE EXILES TAKEN AWAY TO BABYLON, FAR FROM HOME IN A STRANGE LAND WITH A STRANGE PEOPLE.

AND FOR THE LAST 430 DAYS HE HAS BEEN LYING ON HIS SIDE IN THE DIRT IN THE MIDDLE OF THE MARKET SQUARE...

GOD HAS TOLD ME TO LIE HERE, THE DAYS... >OUCH I'M STIFF <... THE DAYS REPRESENTING THE *YEARS* ISRAEL AND JUDAH HAVE SINNED AGAINST GOD !

I THOUGHT HE WAS GOING TO BE THERE *FOR EVER* !

EZEKIEL'S GOT UP! TELL *EVERYONE*! EZEKIEL'S GETTING UP AGAIN !

WHO KNOWS *WHAT* IT MEANS? HURRY TO THE MARKET SQUARE !

ARE WE GOING HOME? HAS THE EXILE BEEN LIFTED ?

EZEKIEL IS STANDING UP ! *GOD* MUST HAVE TOLD HIM SOMETHING ! PERHAPS WE ARE GOING HOME !

OR HAS SOMETHING *DREADFUL* HAPPENED ? PERHAPS WE'RE ALL GOING TO DIE !

JERUSALEM WILL SOON FALL TO ENEMIES AND BE DESTROYED ! WE HAVE DONE TERRIBLE THINGS ! IN OUR *STUPIDITY* AND *GREED* WE HAVE BEHAVED EVEN WORSE THAN THE EVIL PEOPLE AROUND US !

IT'S NOT ENOUGH THAT WE DISOBEYED GOD; WE ACTUALLY PUT ALTARS TO *DEVILS* IN THE TEMPLE AND BURNED OUR *CHILDREN* ALIVE AS SACRIFICES TO THEM !

GOD'S JUDGMENT IS UPON US !

WATCH ME, AND LISTEN !

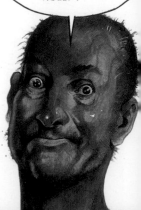

LOOK AT ME, BY CUTTING MY HAIR I HAVE UTTERLY *DISGRACED* MYSELF IN FRONT OF YOU !

I HAVE BECOME AN OBJECT OF HORROR AND A RUIN, LIKE JERUSALEM ITSELF !

HAS HE LOST HIS **MIND**?

HE LOOKS SANE ENOUGH TO ME, IF A BIT BALD... WHY NOT LISTEN TO HIM?

LOOK AS I WEIGH MY HAIR. IN THE SAME WAY, **GOD** HAS WEIGHED OUR SINS AND FOUND US GUILTY! THE HAIR REPRESENTS **US**, THE PEOPLE OF ISRAEL.

ONE THIRD OF THE PEOPLE WILL **BURN** WHEN JERUSALEM FALLS. AS SURELY AS THIS HAIR BURNS, JERUSALEM WILL BURN. AND ONE THIRD OF THE NATION ALONG WITH IT!

ONE THIRD WILL FALL TO THE **SWORD**! AS SURELY AS I'M CUTTING THIS HAIR NOW IN FRONT OF YOU, ONE THIRD WILL DIE AT THE HANDS OF OUR ENEMIES.

THE FINAL THIRD WILL BE SCATTERED TO THE FAR REACHES OF THE EARTH! JUST AS THE WIND CARRIES THIS HAIR, SO THE REMAINING PEOPLE WILL BE SCATTERED ACROSS THE EARTH!

BUT **LOOK**! HERE HIDDEN IN THE FOLDS OF MY CLOAK, THERE STILL REMAIN A FEW STRANDS OF HAIR!

ONLY THOSE IN **EXILE**, THOSE HIDDEN AWAY, WILL SURVIVE. ALTHOUGH IT WAS OUR SIN THAT CAUSED US TO BE TAKEN AWAY TO **BABYLON**, GOD WILL SAVE US!

BUT WHAT IS THERE TO GO **BACK** TO? GOD HAS **LEFT** THE TEMPLE: THE PLACE WHERE OUR GOD LIVED WITH US IS NOW EMPTY EXCEPT FOR STATUES AND FOOLS.

ONCE THE HOLIEST OF HOLIES, NOW IT'S JUST ANOTHER BUILDING.

IN THE TWELFTH YEAR OF THE EXILE, NEWS CAME THAT JERUSALEM HAD FINALLY FALLEN TO ITS ENEMIES.

ISRAEL, AS A COUNTRY, NO LONGER EXISTED. THE SOUTHERN KINGDOM OF JUDAH WAS NO MORE, ITS PEOPLE DEAD OR SCATTERED ACROSS THE EARTH.

BUT STILL EZEKIEL REMAINED HOPEFUL. LIKE A WATCHMAN IN THE DARKEST HOUR BEFORE DAWN, EZEKIEL WAITED FOR NEWS OF THE RESTORATION OF GOD'S PEOPLE.

AND AS EZEKIEL WAITED, GOD SPOKE TO HIM AGAIN, GIVING HIM A STRANGE VISION OF A VALLEY, WHERE THE AIR WAS STILL AND SILENT, AND NOT EVEN THE WIND MOVED THROUGH THE BONES OF THE DEAD WHICH WERE PILED HIGH...

EZEKIEL! THESE BONES YOU SEE BEFORE YOU, CAN THEY **LIVE**? CAN DEAD BONES GET UP AND TALK AND SING LIKE THE LIVING?

MY LORD AND GOD, ONLY YOU KNOW THE ANSWER TO THAT!

WATCH WHAT I AM DOING, EZEKIEL. I AM GOING TO BREATHE LIFE BACK INTO THE DRY BONES BEFORE YOU.

AND AS EZEKIEL WATCHED, THE BONES JOINED THEMSELVES TOGETHER, FORMING WHOLE SKELETONS.

AND THEN MUSCLES AND SINEWS, NERVES AND VEINS, GREW OVER THE BONES, SPREADING LIKE THE ROOTS OF A TREE.

FINALLY, SKIN STRETCHED OVER THE BODIES, AND THEY LAY ON THE GROUND LIFELIKE, BUT UNMOVING, FOR THERE WAS NO LIFE IN THEM.

THEN GOD BREATHED HIS SPIRIT INTO THEM, AND THEY ROSE BEFORE EZEKIEL'S EYES.

EZEKIEL, THESE BONES ARE THE ENTIRE HOUSE OF **ISRAEL**. THEY SEEM DEAD, THEIR LIFE AND HOPE GONE, BUT I AM THEIR **GOD**!

I WILL RESTORE THEM, I WILL BRING THEM BACK TO ISRAEL AND BREATHE MY SPIRIT INTO THEM, AND THEN THEY SHALL **KNOW** THAT I AM THE **LORD**!

NOT AS TWO DIVIDED KINGDOMS, BUT AS **ONE** NATION. AND THEY WILL BE RULED BY A KING LIKE **DAVID**, AND WILL NEVER AGAIN TURN AWAY AND FALL INTO EVIL!

I WILL MAKE AN EVERLASTING AGREEMENT WITH THEM. I WILL LIVE WITH THEM FOR EVER. I WILL BE THEIR GOD AND THEY WILL BE MY PEOPLE.

I WILL MAKE MY NEW TEMPLE AMONG THEM AND IT SHALL NEVER BE DESTROYED - AND THEN ALL THE NATIONS ON EARTH WILL KNOW THAT I HAVE MADE ISRAEL **HOLY**, AND CHOSEN THEM ABOVE ALL OTHERS TO BE MINE FOR EVER!

THE STORY OF DANIEL

NEBUCHADNEZZAR, THE KING OF BABYLONIA, TOOK A GREAT MANY ISRAELITES - OR JEWS AS THEY WERE ALSO KNOWN - AS PRISONERS, HAULING THEM OFF IN CHAINS TO HIS PALACE IN BABYLON.

HE WAS KING OF THE GREATEST NATION ON EARTH AND THERE WAS NO ONE WHO COULD RESIST HIM.

HE LOOTED THE TEMPLE AND TOOK THE GOLD AND SILVER TREASURES AS SPOILS OF WAR.

AMONG THE EXILES LIVING IN BABYLON WERE FOUR YOUNG MEN — SHADRACH, MESHACH AND ABEDNEGO, AND THEIR FRIEND **DANIEL** — WHO WERE SPECIALLY CHOSEN TO BE TRAINED TO BE ADVISORS AT THE ROYAL COURT. THE FOUR ISRAELITE STUDENTS RESISTED THE PRIVILEGES OF THE COURT AND KEPT TO THE LAWS OF THE TRUE GOD.

BUT NEBUCHADNEZZAR SOON FORGOT ABOUT DANIEL'S GOD AND BUILT A MASSIVE GOLD **STATUE**, INTENDING IT TO BE WORSHIPPED. HE CALLED THE OFFICIALS OF THE WHOLE KINGDOM TO COME TOGETHER FOR A CEREMONY OF DEDICATION.

YOU'RE THE BRIGHTEST OF THE LOT, DANIEL. YOU INTERPRET MY DREAMS BETTER THAN ALL OF MY WISE MEN. YOU SHALL BE MY CHIEF ADVISER - YOUR GOD MUST BE VERY POWERFUL.

I CAN ONLY TELL YOU WHAT MY GOD HAS TOLD ME.

JUDGES, LAWYERS, GOVERNORS, COMMISSIONERS, ALL CAME TO THE STATUE AND BOWED DOWN BEFORE IT. EVERYONE, THAT IS, EXCEPT THE **ISRAELITES** —

WHY DO YOU NOT **KNEEL**?! HAVE I NOT ISSUED A **COMMAND**?

YOUR MAJESTY WE ARE **ISRAELITES**. WE ARE FORBIDDEN TO WORSHIP STATUES. WE CAN WORSHIP NO ONE BUT THE ONE TRUE GOD.

THEN LET **HIM** SAVE YOU, IF HE CAN!

GUARDS! TAKE THESE TRAITORS AND HAVE THEM THROWN INTO THE FURNACE! **BURN THEM ALIVE!**

DANIEL'S THREE FRIENDS WERE TIED UP AND THROWN **ALIVE** INTO THE FURNACE; THE HEAT WAS SO FIERCE THAT THE GUARDS THEMSELVES WERE BADLY BURNED.

SEE? THERE ARE NO GODS WHO CAN **SAVE** YOU NOW!

YOU WERE WARNED BUT YOU WOULDN'T **LISTEN**! THERE ARE NO...

...! WHAT **IS** THIS? WHY ARE THERE **FOUR** MEN IN THERE?!

YOUR MAJESTY, WE ONLY THREW **THREE** MEN IN, I **SWEAR IT**!

THE FOURTH MAN IS DIFFERENT— HE LOOKS LIKE AN ANGEL OF GOD!

PRAISE THE GOD OF YOUR PEOPLE! YOU RISKED YOUR LIVES BY REFUSING TO WORSHIP ANY GOD BUT YOUR OWN! AND LOOK! THE ROPES HAVE BURNED AWAY, BUT YOU ARE UNHARMED! YOUR GOD HAS **SAVED** YOU!

FROM THIS DAY ON, IF **ANY** MAN SPEAKS ILL OF YOUR GOD, THEN I, THE **KING**, DECREE THAT HE BE TORN LIMB FROM LIMB!

HE ALONE IS GOD!

KING NEBUCHADNEZZAR DIED BELIEVING IN THE GOD OF ISRAEL, BUT HIS SON BELSHAZZAR NEITHER KNEW NOR CARED.

ONE NIGHT KING BELSHAZZAR THREW A PARTY FOR ALL THE NOBLES AND LORDS IN BABYLON.

THEY DRANK FROM THE VERY SAME GOLD CUPS THAT ONCE SAT IN THE TEMPLE IN **JERUSALEM**, NOW NO MORE THAN A **RUIN**. A FORGOTTEN, DEAD CITY IN A COUNTRY ON THE FAR SIDE OF THE CONTINENT.

A TOAST! A TOAST TO BABYLON, THE GREATEST EMPIRE THE WORLD HAS EVER KNOWN! WE HAVE CONQUERED ALL THAT WE'VE SEEN! WE HAVE TAKEN WHATEVER WE WANTED! *NOTHING* CAN COME AGAINST US! *NOTHING*!

AS SOON AS BELSHAZZAR FINISHED SPEAKING, A STRANGE *HAND* APPEARED FROM OUT OF THIN AIR, AND BEGAN TO *WRITE* ON THE PALACE WALL!

GUARDS! SAVE ME!

QUICKLY, SEND FOR MY WISE MEN. I WANT THE MAGICIANS, THE ASTROLOGERS AND MEDIUMS HERE WITHIN THE *HOUR*! *NOTHING* LIKE THIS HAS HAPPENED IN ALL OUR HISTORY! WELL, WHAT ARE YOU *WAITING* FOR?! *GO*!

AND SO IT HAPPENED THAT FINALLY *DANIEL* WAS BROUGHT FACE TO FACE WITH THE KING...

YOUR MAJESTY?

THE *OLD* QUEEN, NEBUCHADNEZZAR'S WIDOW, SHE SPEAKS VERY *HIGHLY* OF YOU, DANIEL. *EXPLAIN* THE WRITING AND ANYTHING YOU ASK FOR IS YOURS.

KEEP YOUR GIFTS. I ONLY TELL WHAT MY GOD TELLS ME. HE SAYS TO YOU: 'NUMBERS, WEIGHTS, DIVISIONS' AND THIS IS WHY: 'NUMBERS', BECAUSE GOD HAS NUMBERED THE DAYS OF YOUR EMPIRE AND HAS CALLED IT TO AN END. 'WEIGHTS' BECAUSE YOU HAVE BEEN WEIGHED ON GOD'S SCALES AND FOUND WANTING, AND 'DIVISIONS' BECAUSE YOUR EMPIRE WILL BE DIVIDED.

YOUR FATHER, NEBUCHADNEZZAR, WAS THE MOST POWERFUL MAN ON EARTH, AND YET HE FINALLY HUMBLED HIMSELF BEFORE GOD. YOU HAVE *NOT*. YOU DRANK FROM CUPS STOLEN FROM THE *TEMPLE*, AND WORSHIPPED GODS OF WOOD AND METAL INSTEAD OF THE *LIVING* GOD. THE WORDS SPELL THE *END* OF BABYLON AS *YOU* KNOW IT.

AS HE HEARD DANIEL'S WORDS, KING BELSHAZZAR *KNEW* THEM TO BE THE TRUTH. LATER THAT NIGHT *DARIUS*, KING OF THE MEDES, SEIZED POWER IN THE CAPITAL. BELSHAZZAR DIED BEFORE DAWN.

DARIUS WAS NO FOOL, AND WAS QUICK TO ENSURE THAT BELSHAZZAR'S GOVERNMENT BECAME LOYAL TO HIM.

I HAVE HEARD GOOD THINGS ABOUT YOU *DANIEL*. I WILL MAKE YOU ONE OF MY CHIEF SUPERVISORS.

IT'S NO USE! THE NEW KING FAWNS OVER DANIEL AS MUCH AS THE OLD ONES DID! IF WE HAVE *ANY* CHANCE OF PROMOTION, WE NEED TO GET DANIEL OUT OF OUR WAY FOR GOOD!

HIS ONLY WEAKNESS IS HIS *RELIGION*! SURELY WE CAN USE IT TO SNARE HIM.

I'LL SUGGEST THE KING ISSUES A *DECREE* – NO ONE MAY ASK ANYTHING OF *ANY* GOD FOR A WHOLE MONTH! INSTEAD THEY SHOULD TAKE THEIR REQUESTS TO THE *KING*!

AND SO THE ORDER WAS PASSED. AS SOON AS DANIEL HEARD THE NEWS, HE WENT STRAIGHT TO HIS ROOM, STOOD IN FRONT OF HIS OPEN WINDOW –

AND *PRAYED*.

LOUDLY.

THE RESPONSE WAS IMMEDIATE. THE KING HAD GIVEN AN ORDER THAT COULD NOT BE REVOKED. DANIEL WOULD BE THROWN TO THE LIONS.

DANIEL! WHATEVER WERE YOU *THINKING*? PLEASE TELL ME YOU WERE SIMPLY *FORGETFUL*...

YOUR MAJESTY, I PRAYED AS I ALWAYS HAVE DONE. DELIBERATELY.

THEN MAY YOUR GOD SHOW YOU MERCY.

AND SO DANIEL WAS PUT IN A PIT WITH THE LIONS AND A HEAVY STONE WAS PUT OVER THE TOP.

THAT NIGHT, THE KING COULD NOT SLEEP. HE SENT HIS SERVANTS AWAY WHEN THEY BROUGHT FOOD AND ENTERTAINMENT.

GOVERNING THE KINGDOM WOULD BE ALL THE MORE DAUNTING WITHOUT DANIEL'S WISDOM AND COURAGE.

AT FIRST LIGHT, THE KING *RAN* TO THE LION PIT AND ORDERED THE GUARDS –

ROLL THE STONE AWAY AND BREAK THE SEALS ON THE CAGE! I NEED TO SEE FOR MYSELF!

DANIEL! WAS THE GOD YOU SERVE ABLE TO *SAVE* YOU?

THE STORY OF ESTHER

THROUGHOUT THE EXILE, THE JEWS CLUNG TO THE HOPE THAT ONE DAY THEY WOULD BE RETURNED TO ISRAEL.

IN THE LAND OF **PERSIA**, THE ISRAELITE EXILES FACED TERRIBLE DANGER, BUT ONE WOMAN'S COURAGE SAVED THE ENTIRE NATION FROM EXTERMINATION.

ESTHER WAS THE MOST BEAUTIFUL WOMAN IN THE PERSIAN KINGDOM. A JEWISH EXILE, SHE WAS MADE **QUEEN** OF PERSIA BY THE KING, XERXES.

NOW, ESTHER HAD A **COUSIN**, CALLED MORDECAI, WHO HAD CAUSE TO ARGUE WITH HAMAN, THE KING'S GOVERNOR.

MORDECAI, WHY DO YOU REFUSE TO KNEEL BEFORE ME? WHY DON'T YOU THANK OUR GODS THAT THEY HAVE SET ME UP AS THE KING'S GOVERNOR?

I AM A **JEW**, HAMAN. MY PEOPLE KNEEL ONLY BEFORE **GOD**.

THEN I WILL MAKE YOU **REGRET** YOUR FOOLISHNESS! THIS INSULT WILL NOT GO UNAVENGED!

EVEN SO, I STAND BY WHAT I HAVE SAID.

YOUR IMPERIAL MAJESTY, SOME OF THE FOREIGNERS ARE DISOBEYING YOUR WISHES, MOST EXALTED LORD AND MASTER.

AND WHAT DO YOU SUGGEST I DO?

DESTROY THEM. UTTERLY. EVERY LAST MAN, WOMAN AND CHILD – REMOVE THE TROUBLEMAKERS FOR EVER!

THE KING DID NOT KNOW THAT ESTHER WAS A **JEW**. HE ISSUED HIS ORDERS DECREEING DEATH TO ALL HER RACE A MONTH HENCE.

ESTHER, OF ALL THE PEOPLE IN PERSIA, ONLY **YOU** CAN SAVE US!

BUT I CAN'T APPROACH THE KING. ANYONE WHO GOES TO HIM WITHOUT BEING SUMMONED CAN BE PUT TO DEATH.

BUT DON'T YOU SEE? IF WE DIE, THEN GOD'S PLAN WILL COME TO **NOTHING**! PERHAPS IT WAS FOR THIS REASON THAT **YOU**, A JEW, WERE MADE QUEEN!

AND SO, TAKING HER LIFE IN HER HANDS, ESTHER APPROACHED THE KING, INVITING HIM TO A BANQUET, ALONG WITH HAMAN THE GOVERNOR.

SUCH INDEPENDENT THOUGHT MIGHT HAVE BEEN ENOUGH TO SIGN HER DEATH WARRANT; BUT SHE WAS SO BEAUTIFUL THE KING COULD REFUSE HER NOTHING!

THAT NIGHT AT THE BANQUET ESTHER GAVE THEM AN INVITATION TO ANOTHER BANQUET THE NEXT EVENING. SHE WOULD MAKE HER REQUEST THEN.

HAMAN WAS FLATTERED BY ALL THE ATTENTION.

A PLEASANT EVENING, HAMAN?

JEWISH DOG! I WAS HAVING A FINE EVENING UNTIL I SAW YOUR DISGUSTING FACE! AT LEAST I WON'T HAVE TO LOOK AT YOU FOR MUCH LONGER!

HAMAN IMMEDIATELY BEGAN WORK ON THE GALLOWS ON WHICH HE PLANNED TO HANG MORDECAI.

IS THIS HIGH ENOUGH, MY LORD?

HIGHER. I WANT EVERYONE TO SEE WHAT HAPPENS TO MY - I MEAN, TO THE KING'S - ENEMIES.

THAT NIGHT THE KING COULDN'T SLEEP SO HE SENT FOR THE ROYAL RECORDS - READING THEM WOULD SURELY SEND HIM TO SLEEP!

BUT AS HE READ THE MORE RECENT ENTRIES HE CAME ACROSS AN INTERESTING INCIDENT.

'MORDECAI'. NEVER HEARD OF HIM, BUT IT SAYS HERE THAT HE EXPOSED A PLOT BY THE PALACE GUARDS.

THIS MAN SAVED MY LIFE. BUT HE HASN'T EVEN BEEN ACKNOWLEDGED FOR HIS BRAVERY! THIS IS TERRIBLE!

AH, HAMAN! LISTEN, I WANT YOU TO HONOUR A MAN CALLED MORDECAI! THE FELLOW SAVED MY LIFE, AND YET NO ONE'S EVER HEARD OF HIM! DO YOU KNOW HIM?

ERM... THE NAME SEEMS VAGUELY FAMILIAR YOUR MAJESTY.

HAVE HIM PARADED THROUGH THE STREETS ON MY HORSE, ALLOW HIM TO WEAR MY OWN ROBE AND HAVE THE PEOPLE CHEER HIM!

NOW, MY BEAUTIFUL QUEEN WE DINE AGAIN. HOW CAN I REWARD YOU FOR YOUR HOSPITALITY?

YOUR MAJESTY, I ASK YOU TO SPARE MY LIFE!

...YOUR LIFE? WHAT DO YOU MEAN?

YOU HAVE ISSUED A DECREE TO KILL ALL MY PEOPLE. THAT INCLUDES NOT ONLY MYSELF, BUT MORDECAI, WHOM YOU WISH TO HONOUR! WE ARE BOTH JEWS.

IT'S ALL HAMAN'S DOING! HE WANTS US SLAUGHTERED JUST BECAUSE MORDECAI WOULD NOT TREAT HIM AS A KING!

IS THIS TRUE, HAMAN? DID YOU PLAN REVENGE PURELY BECAUSE ONE MAN WOULD NOT FLATTER YOU?

MY LORD, I-I MEAN - THAT IS...

I THINK WE HAVE FOUND A BETTER USE FOR YOUR GALLOWS!

HAMAN WAS HANGED AND MORDECAI WAS MADE GOVERNOR IN HIS PLACE. HE WAS A WISE AND FAIR MAN, AND WAS LOVED BY THE PEOPLE HE GOVERNED.

THE JEWS NOT ONLY ESCAPED DESTRUCTION, BUT THE HEARTS OF THE PERSIANS SOFTENED TOWARDS THEM. THE DESCENDANTS OF THE HOUSE OF DAVID WOULD NOT ONLY SURVIVE, BUT WOULD SOON EVEN BE ALLOWED HOME...

THE STORY OF EZRA AND NEHEMIAH

THE LONG YEARS OF EXILE ARE COMING TO AN END.

THE GREAT KINGDOM OF BABYLON HAS **FALLEN**, TO CYRUS, KING OF THE PERSIANS, WHO DECIDES TO RELEASE THE JEWS FROM THEIR EXILE.

AT LAST THEY CAN RETURN TO THE COUNTRY THEIR GRANDPARENTS SPOKE OF. FOR THE **SECOND** TIME IN THEIR HISTORY, THE JEWS MAKE THEIR WAY BACK TO ISRAEL, THE PROMISED LAND.

AND EVENTUALLY THEY ARRIVE IN **JERUSALEM**.

OVERGROWN, DERELICT AND SILENT, BUT FOR THE WILD ANIMALS WHO ROAM THE ONCE-BUSY STREETS. THE BROKEN WALLS LIE LIKE DRY BONES IN THE SUN...

IT'S AGREED THEN? WE START THE REBUILDING AT FIRST LIGHT. BUT THE TEMPLE **MUST** BE FIRST ON THE LIST.

AS SOON AS THE **FOUNDATIONS** ARE LAID WE CAN START OFFERING SACRIFICES AGAIN. WE'LL BUILD THE ROOF AND WALLS **AROUND** THE ALTAR IF WE HAVE TO!

AND SO THE WORK BEGAN — THE WRECKAGE OF THE OLD TEMPLE BEING RESHAPED INTO MATERIAL FOR THE NEW.

BUT WHILE THE YOUNGER PEOPLE SHOUTED WITH **JOY** WITH EACH BRICK HIGHER THAN THE LAST, THE OLD PEOPLE, WHO COULD STILL JUST REMEMBER THE OLD JERUSALEM, COVERED THEIR HEADS AND WEPT WITH **SHAME**.

BUT ALMOST AS SOON AS THE REBUILDING STARTED, THE PROBLEMS BEGAN THAT WOULD PLAGUE THEM THROUGHOUT THEIR LABOURS.

THE NEIGHBOURING PEOPLES HAVE BEEN WATCHING US CLOSELY THESE PAST MONTHS. THEY WANT TO JOIN US IN REBUILDING THE TEMPLE. WHATEVER HAPPENS WE MUST **NEVER** ALLOW IT!

BUT WE COULD USE THEIR HELP!

WHILE WE WERE AWAY THEY'VE STARTED WORSHIPPING OTHER GODS. THEY WANT TO ADD THEIR GODS TO OURS IN THE TEMPLE, AND **THAT** WAS OUR DOWNFALL LAST TIME!

THE LOCAL PEOPLES DIDN'T TAKE KINDLY TO THE REBUTTAL, AND SOON THE BUILDERS FOUND THEMSELVES THE TARGET OF POLITICAL CONSPIRACIES, OF SLANDER, AND IN THE END, OF VIOLENCE ITSELF.

AGAINST THE ODDS THE TEMPLE WAS COMPLETED WITHIN 20 YEARS, BUT THE WALLS HAD TO WAIT...

155

NEWS OF THE QUARRELS AND DISPUTES IN JERUSALEM SOON SPREAD TO JEWS LIVING IN OTHER PARTS OF THE EMPIRE.

WORD CAME BACK TO BABYLON OF ATTACKS BY NEIGHBOURING TRIBES, OF INTERNAL DISPUTES, AND OF JERUSALEM WITH ITS WALLS STILL LITTLE MORE THAN RUINS.

ONE OF THOSE TO HEAR THE NEWS WAS THE CUPBEARER TO THE KING HIMSELF...

NEHEMIAH, YOU LOOK SO... SO *UNHAPPY*.

VERY FEW MEN HAVE THE *AUDACITY* TO APPEAR BEFORE ME IN A STATE OF MIND THAT'S LESS THAN *ECSTATIC*! ARE YOU *UNWELL*?

YOUR MAJESTY FORGIVE ME! I HAVE SERVED YOU FAITHFULLY AND FEARED YOU ALL MY LIFE. BUT NEWS OF MY COUNTRYMEN IN JERUSALEM HAS REACHED ME, AND I CANNOT SLEEP FOR WORRY.

THEN YOU ARE *RELEASED* NEHEMIAH. GO AND FIND YOUR OWN PEOPLE. YOU MAY RETURN WHEN YOUR WORK THERE IS FINISHED.

AND SO HE DID AS HIS HEART TOLD HIM. WITH THE BLESSING OF THE KING HE MADE THE JOURNEY TO JERUSALEM ALONE.

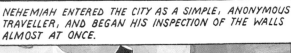

NEHEMIAH ENTERED THE CITY AS A SIMPLE, ANONYMOUS TRAVELLER, AND BEGAN HIS INSPECTION OF THE WALLS ALMOST AT ONCE.

UNLESS HE COULD UNITE THE JEWS IN FINISHING THE BUILDING WORK, THEY WOULD SOON FALL PREY TO NEARBY AGGRESSORS, AND GOD'S PLANS FOR THEM WOULD COME TO NOTHING.

WATCHMAN! IS THERE ANY WAY FOR ME TO GET BEYOND THIS POINT?

ONLY ON FOOT. THERE'S SO MUCH RUBBLE PILED OVER THIS GATE YOU'D HAVE TO SCRAMBLE ON YOUR HANDS AND KNEES. IT'S BEEN LIKE THAT AS LONG AS I CAN REMEMBER.

THEN IT'S TIME WE DID SOMETHING ABOUT IT! TAKE A MESSAGE FOR ME TO THE ELDERS OF THE CITY —

SAY THAT *NEHEMIAH*, CUPBEARER TO THE *KING* IN BABYLON, REQUIRES THEIR COMPANY. THE REBUILDING OF THE WALLS STARTS *TOMORROW*!

UNDER NEHEMIAH'S LEADERSHIP, THE WORK BEGAN AT ONCE — BUT IT WAS NOT WITHOUT SETBACKS.

HAVE YOU SEEN THE SIZE OF THAT CROWD DOWN THERE? IT'S LIKE THEY GET ANGRIER WITH EVERY STONE WE LAY!

THEN STOP STARING AT THEM AND HELP ME WITH THIS! THE SOONER IT'S DONE THE BETTER. BESIDES — WE DON'T KNOW HOW SERIOUS THEY ARE, OR HOW GOOD THEIR *AIM* IS!

ARRG!

WELL, YOU'VE GOT YOUR ANSWER!

CAREFUL, CAREFUL, CARE-OW! YOU GOT MY THUMB!

WELL I CAN'T SEE WHAT I'M DOING CAN I? AT LEAST THIS WAY WE HAVEN'T GOT PEOPLE THROWING STONES AT US!

NO. JUST YOU DROPPING GREAT BIG CHUNKS OF MASONRY ON MY FINGERS! I DON'T KNOW WHICH IS WORSE.

FROM NOW ON WE WORK NIGHT *AND* DAY. THE COVER OF DARKNESS WILL GIVE US SOME PROTECTION AGAINST THE STONE THROWERS.

EVERY WORKER IS TO CARRY A SWORD. IF WE GIVE UP NOW, WHEN THINGS SEEM THE HARDEST, THEN OUR NATION WILL VANISH FOR EVER!

WATCHMAN! ANY SIGN OF THE ENEMY?

NO SIR, NOTHING. THE PEOPLE ARE SAYING THEY'VE GIVEN UP AND GONE HOME, THAT THEY SAW OUR GOD WAS HELPING US AND THEY COULDN'T WIN.

MAYBE. BUT DON'T GET TOO COMPLACENT. UNTIL THE *DOORS* ARE IN PLACE WE'RE STILL WIDE OPEN FOR ATTACK.

IN JUST TWO MONTHS OF BACKBREAKING LABOUR, THE WALLS WERE FINISHED. NEHEMIAH'S WORK WAS NEARLY DONE...

LORD GOD, THE WALLS ARE IN PLACE. BUT THE CITY IS STILL ALL BUT EMPTY. BRING YOUR PEOPLE *BACK*, LORD, TO FILL JERUSALEM AGAIN.

YOU SAID CENTURIES AGO THAT IF WE WERE UNFAITHFUL YOU WOULD SCATTER US ACROSS THE FACE OF THE EARTH, BUT IF WE OBEYED YOUR COMMANDS YOU WOULD BRING US BACK, EVEN FROM THE FURTHEST CORNER OF THE WORLD!

LORD GOD, WE ARE STILL YOUR PEOPLE!

EZRA, A DIRECT DESCENDANT OF AARON, THE FIRST HIGH PRIEST, WAS AN EXPERT IN THE LAW OF GOD. HE WAS PART OF GOD'S RESCUE PLAN.

WE MUST ALL ATTEND TO THE WORDS OF GOD'S LAW. OUR FUTURE STRENGTH RELIES ON US STAYING PURE. WE MUST LEARN THE LESSONS OF THE PAST.

SO, AMID THE CELEBRATIONS OF THE *HOME-COMING* AND THE COMPLETION OF THE WALLS, EZRA'S MESSAGE WOULD BE VITAL FOR GOD'S PEOPLE. HIS STORY BEGINS SOME YEARS EARLIER...

SOME SIXTY YEARS AFTER THE FIRST WAVE OF EXILES RETURNED, ANOTHER GROUP SET OUT ON THE LONG AND DANGEROUS JOURNEY BACK TO JERUSALEM, LED BY *EZRA*.

BY GOD'S GRACE I HAVE WON THE FAVOUR OF THE EMPEROR AND HIS COURT; THE LORD GOD HAS GIVEN ME COURAGE AND NOW... NOW WE CAN RETURN HOME.

BUT ON ARRIVAL IN JERUSALEM IT WAS CLEAR THAT DESPITE THE COMPLETION OF THE TEMPLE ALL WAS NOT WELL.

I CAN'T BELIEVE WHAT I'M HEARING! HOW CAN PEOPLE HAVE SUCH SHORT MEMORIES?! WE MUST FOLLOW GOD'S LAW AND THAT MEANS NO MARRIAGES OUTSIDE OUR COMMUNITY.

ISN'T THIS HOW OUR TROUBLES *STARTED*?

GRIEF-STRICKEN AND FULL OF DESPAIR EZRA TORE HIS CLOTHES AND HAIR.

LORD GOD OF ISRAEL, YOU ARE JUST, BUT YOU HAVE LET US SURVIVE. WE CONFESS OUR GUILT TO YOU; WE HAVE NO RIGHT TO COME INTO YOUR PRESENCE.

THERE IS NO *EASY* WAY TO SAY THIS! AND THIS IS NO *EASY* THING TO DO. BUT THOSE OF YOU WHO HAVE MARRIED OUTSIDE OUR COMMUNITY MUST SEPARATE YOURSELVES FROM YOUR WIVES IMMEDIATELY.

GOD HAS GIVEN US A SECOND CHANCE TO REBUILD OUR NATION, BUT IF WE DISOBEY HIM IT WILL COME TO NOTHING! WE ACCEPT THIS, OR WE ALL *PERISH*!

WHILE EZRA WEPT AND PRAYED A CROWD OF ISRAELITES GATHERED. TWO MEN CAME FORWARD. ONE OF THEM SPOKE ON BEHALF OF THE CROWD.

WE HAVE BROKEN FAITH WITH GOD. SHOW US HOW TO PURIFY OURSELVES. LEAD US, EZRA. INSTRUCT US AND WE *WILL* DO WHAT GOD'S LAW DEMANDS.

SO EZRA BEGAN HIS WORK. A MESSAGE WAS SENT THROUGHOUT JERUSALEM AND JUDAH THAT ALL THOSE WHO HAD RETURNED FROM EXILE WERE TO MEET IN THREE DAYS' TIME IN THE TEMPLE SQUARE.

THE CROWD KNEW THAT EZRA WAS RIGHT: THEY MUST FOLLOW GOD'S LAW OR FACE THE CONSEQUENCES.

AND THAT'S *IT*, IS IT? WE GO TO THE TEMPLE, DAY IN, DAY OUT, YEAR AFTER YEAR, AND FOR *WHAT*?

GOD *HEARS* US, I KNOW, BUT WHY DO WE NEVER HEAR *HIM* ANYMORE, AS OUR FATHERS DID?

IN THE OLD DAYS GOD WOULD COME TO US IN *FIRE* LIKE A *STORM* OR AN *EARTHQUAKE*, BUT NOW... HAH!

I WONDER WHY WE *BOTHER*. WHY KEEP ALL THIS *RITUAL*? IF GOD IS INTENT ON KEEPING SILENT FOR EVER, WHY BOTHER?

BECAUSE YOUR GOD *LOVES* YOU.

BECAUSE YOUR GOD BELIEVES YOU'RE *WORTH IT*. YOU WHINE LIKE CHILDREN, MUMBLING YOUR PRAYERS LIKE A MAN IN HIS SLEEP.

BUT *MALACHI*, YOU KNOW AS WELL AS WE DO THAT GOD HAS DONE NOTHING FOR *CENTURIES*!

GOD WILL SORT THE GOOD FROM THE *EVIL*. GOD WILL SAVE THOSE WHO OBEY HIM, SENDING HIS MERCY LIKE THE *SUN*, AND HEALING LIKE THE SUN'S *RAYS*.

LIKE THE *SUN*...

GOD *WILL* WALK IN THIS TEMPLE AGAIN.

BUT *FIRST* HE WILL SEND HIS *MESSENGER* AHEAD OF HIM. WHEN YOU SEE *HIM*, THEN YOU'LL *KNOW* GOD IS ON HIS WAY!

MALACHI'S WORDS HUNG IN THE AIR FOR *400 YEARS*. FOUR CENTURIES OF INVASION, WARS AND STRUGGLE. BUT MALACHI SPOKE TRUTHFULLY. GOD *WOULD* WALK IN THE TEMPLE AGAIN...

IN THE BEGINNING WAS THE **WORD**, AND THE WORD WAS WITH **GOD**, AND THE WORD **WAS** GOD...

ALL THINGS CAME INTO BEING THROUGH **HIM**, AND WITHOUT HIM NOT ONE THING CAME INTO BEING.

WHAT HAS COME **INTO** BEING IN HIM WAS **LIFE**, AND THE LIFE WAS THE LIGHT OF **ALL** PEOPLE.

THE LIGHT **SHINES** IN THE DARKNESS, AND THE DARKNESS CANNOT OVERCOME IT.

THERE WAS A MAN CALLED **JOHN**. HE HIMSELF WAS NOT THE LIGHT, BUT CAME AS A **WITNESS** TO THE LIGHT, THAT ALL MIGHT BELIEVE.

THE **TRUE** LIGHT, WHICH ENLIGHTENS EVERYONE WAS COMING INTO THE **WORLD**!

AND SO GOD STARTS TO UNFOLD THE NEXT STAGE OF HIS GREAT PLAN, DRAWING TOGETHER THE THREADS SET IN PLACE SINCE THE DAWN OF TIME.

AND, AS ALWAYS WITH GOD, IT BEGINS, NOT WITH KINGS AND QUEENS AND GENERALS, BUT WITH ORDINARY MEN AND WOMEN LIVING ORDINARY LIVES...

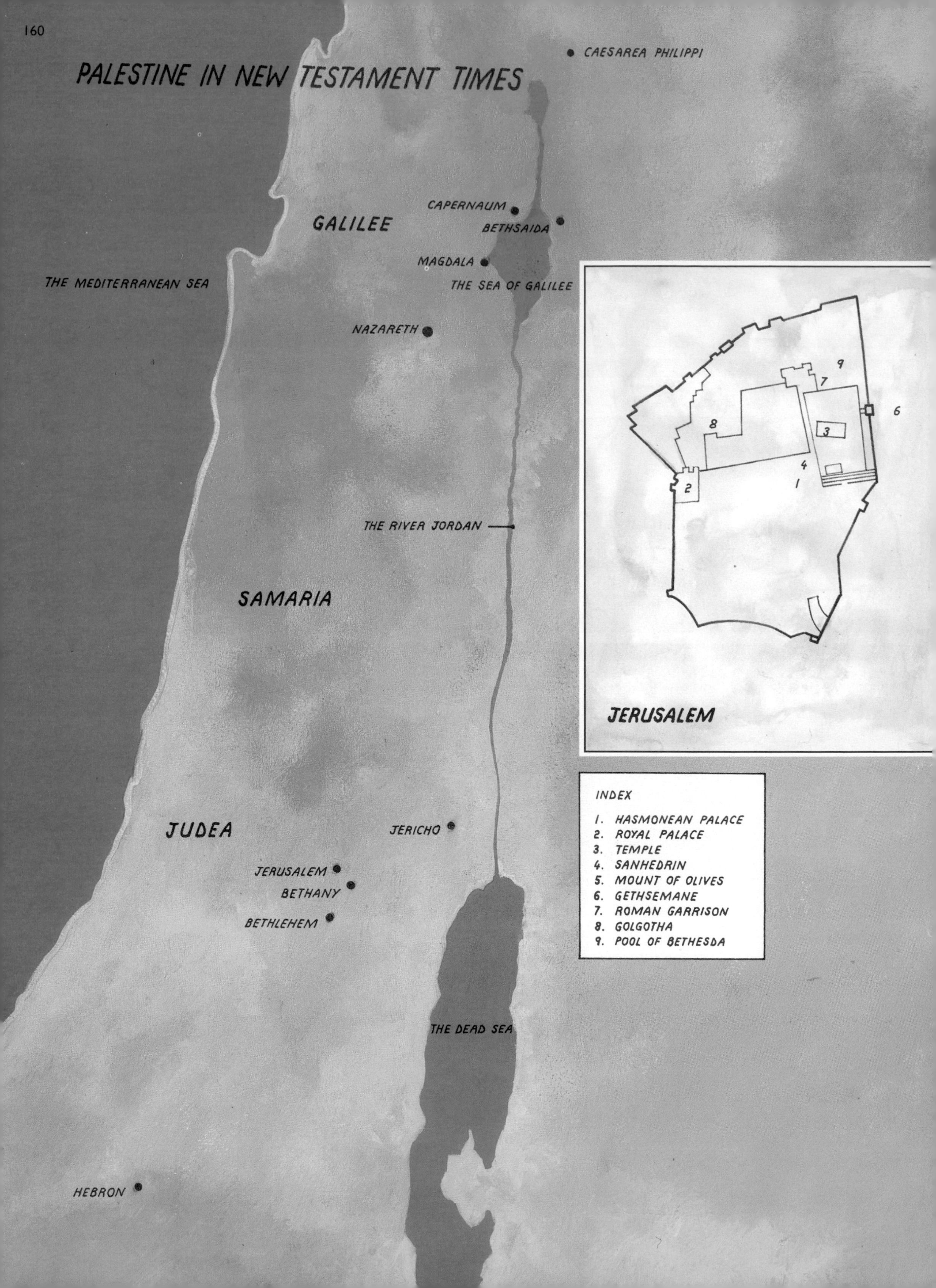

PALESTINE IN NEW TESTAMENT TIMES

CAESAREA PHILIPPI

GALILEE

CAPERNAUM

BETHSAIDA

MAGDALA

THE SEA OF GALILEE

THE MEDITERRANEAN SEA

NAZARETH

THE RIVER JORDAN

SAMARIA

JUDEA

JERICHO

JERUSALEM

BETHANY

BETHLEHEM

THE DEAD SEA

HEBRON

JERUSALEM

INDEX

1. HASMONEAN PALACE
2. ROYAL PALACE
3. TEMPLE
4. SANHEDRIN
5. MOUNT OF OLIVES
6. GETHSEMANE
7. ROMAN GARRISON
8. GOLGOTHA
9. POOL OF BETHESDA

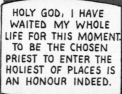

IT ALL STARTS WITH A **PRIEST**, AN OLD MAN NAMED ZECHARIAH, IN THE TEMPLE IN JERUSALEM, ON THE GREATEST DAY OF HIS LIFE...

HOLY GOD, I HAVE WAITED MY WHOLE LIFE FOR THIS MOMENT. TO BE THE CHOSEN PRIEST TO ENTER THE HOLIEST OF PLACES IS AN HONOUR INDEED.

LORD GOD, ALL ISRAEL WAITS FOR YOU TO SAVE US. IN THE SAME WAY, MY WIFE AND I HAVE WAITED ALL OUR LIVES FOR A **CHILD** - BUT IT'S TOO LATE FOR US NOW.

BUT IT'S NOT TOO LATE FOR ISRAEL, LORD GOD - SEND THE CHOSEN ONE, THE SAVIOUR, THE MESSIAH. PRAISE YOUR NAME FOR EVER.

DON'T BE AFRAID, ZECHARIAH! GOD HAS HEARD YOUR PRAYER! YOUR WIFE **WILL** HAVE A CHILD, AND YOU WILL CALL HIM JOHN.

HE WILL BE STRONG IN THE POWER OF GOD, LIKE ELIJAH HIMSELF IN THE ANCIENT DAYS!

WHO - WHO **ARE** YOU, SIR?!

I AM THE ANGEL GABRIEL. I STAND IN **GOD'S** PRESENCE, JUST AS I STAND IN **YOURS**! YOUR SON WILL BE FILLED WITH THE HOLY SPIRIT. HE WILL TURN MANY PEOPLE BACK TO GOD AND PREPARE THE WAY FOR THE GREAT KING WHO WILL **FOLLOW** HIM - THE **MESSIAH**!

BUT HOW CAN I BE **CERTAIN** OF ALL THIS? I AM AN OLD MAN, AND MY WIFE ELIZABETH ISN'T AS YOUNG AS SHE ONCE WAS!

IT WILL HAPPEN **EXACTLY** AS I HAVE SAID, ZECHARIAH. BUT I WILL GIVE YOU **ANOTHER** SIGN: YOU WILL NOT BE ABLE TO SAY **ONE WORD** UNTIL THE CHILD IS BORN!

AND WITH THAT, THE ANGEL VANISHED. ZECHARIAH OPENED HIS MOUTH TO CALL AFTER HIM-

BUT THE WORDS JUST WOULDN'T COME OUT!

WHAT'S WRONG WITH ZECHARIAH? WHY CAN'T HE SPEAK?

SOMETHING MUST HAVE **HAPPENED** TO HIM IN THERE! GOD MUST HAVE **SPOKEN** TO HIM!

HELLO DEAR. YOU'RE HOME LATE — EVERYTHING ALL RIGHT AT THE TEMPLE?

WRITING? WHY ARE YOU **WRITING**? WHY WON'T YOU **SPEAK** TO ME?

BUT WHEN ELIZABETH READ WHAT HER HUSBAND HAD WRITTEN, HER HEART FILLED WITH **JOY** AND HER EYES WITH TEARS!

THEIR PRAYERS HAD BEEN HEARD - GOD WAS AT WORK IN ISRAEL ONCE MORE.

WHICH BRINGS US TO NAZARETH, A TOWN IN THE HILL-COUNTRY OF GALILEE, IN THE NORTH OF ISRAEL.

MARY, A YOUNG WOMAN, IS ENGAGED TO BE MARRIED TO JOSEPH, A LOCAL CARPENTER.

UNDER ROMAN OCCUPATION, ISRAEL IS RULED BY A PUPPET KING, CORRUPT, AND DIVORCED FROM THE PEOPLE.

BUT JOSEPH IS A DESCENDANT OF KING DAVID, IN A LINE THAT STRETCHES BACK TO ABRAHAM.

HERE, THROUGH THE LIVES OF ORDINARY PEOPLE, AMIDST THE UNREMARKABLE AND THE MUNDANE, GOD FINALLY BRINGS HIS PLAN TO FRUITION.

SOMETHING **WONDERFUL** IS ABOUT TO HAPPEN...

REJOICE, MARY, FOR GOD IS WITH YOU! BLESSED ARE YOU AMONG WOMEN! OF ALL THE WOMEN ON EARTH, YOU HAVE FOUND FAVOUR WITH GOD!

BE AT PEACE, AND HAVE NO FEAR!

ME? BUT I DON'T UNDERSTAND — I MEAN, I'M NO ONE SPECIAL. WHAT HAVE I DONE?

YOU WILL HAVE A CHILD, AND HIS NAME WILL BE JESUS!

HE WILL BE CALLED THE SON OF THE MOST HIGH. THE LORD GOD HIMSELF WILL GIVE HIM THE THRONE OF HIS ANCESTOR, DAVID. HE WILL RULE THE DESCENDANTS OF THE HOUSE OF JACOB FOR EVER!

AND OF HIS KINGDOM, THERE WILL BE NO END!

BUT HOW? I'M NOT PREGNANT; I'M NOT EVEN MARRIED, I — I'M STILL A VIRGIN!

THE HOLY SPIRIT WILL REST UPON YOU, AND THE POWER OF GOD WILL OVERSHADOW YOU. IN THIS WAY YOUR CHILD WILL BE CALLED THE SON OF GOD.

NOTHING IS IMPOSSIBLE TO GOD! YOUR OWN RELATIVE, ELIZABETH — CHILDLESS AND PAST CHILD-BEARING — IS NOW SIX MONTHS PREGNANT. NOTHING IS IMPOSSIBLE, MARY! NOTHING!

STIRRED BY THE ANGEL'S WORDS, MARY MADE HER WAY SOUTH TO THE HILLS OF JUDEA, TO VISIT HER COUSIN ELIZABETH. PERHAPS SHE COULD ANSWER SOME OF MARY'S QUESTIONS.

BUT ELIZABETH'S GREETING TOOK HER ABACK...

MARY! GOD'S BLESSING IS ON YOU ABOVE ALL WOMEN ON EARTH, AND BLESSED IS THE CHILD YOU WILL BEAR!

AS SOON AS I HEARD YOUR VOICE, THE CHILD IN MY WOMB LEAPED FOR JOY!!

MY SPIRIT AND MY SOUL REJOICE IN GOD. FROM THIS DAY ON, ALL PEOPLE WILL COUNT ME HAPPY, BECAUSE OF WHAT GOD HAS DONE. HE HAS KEPT HIS PROMISE TO COME TO HIS PEOPLE'S AID.

MARY STAYED THREE MONTHS WITH HER COUSIN, AND THEN RETURNED HOME.

IN TIME, ELIZABETH GAVE BIRTH TO A BOY, AS THE ANGEL HAD PREDICTED.

HE'S BEAUTIFUL, ELIZABETH. YOU MUST BE SO HAPPY. YOU'LL NAME HIM ZECHARIAH, AFTER HIS FATHER?

INDEED, THAT'S TO BE EXPECTED - AND HE CERTAINLY HAS HIS FATHER'S EYES!

THE CHILD IS GOD'S SPECIAL GIFT TO US - AND WE'RE GOING TO CALL HIM JOHN.

AREN'T WE, DEAR?

JOHN.

ZECHARIAH MADE HIS AGREEMENT CLEAR - AND WITH THAT, HE BEGAN TO SPEAK AGAIN!

BUT WHILE ELIZABETH AND ZECHARIAH REJOICED IN THEIR GOOD FORTUNE, IN THE TOWN OF NAZARETH, THINGS WERE NOT GOING SO SMOOTHLY...

JOSEPH! WHY ARE YOU STILL WORKING AT THIS HOUR? COME OUT, MAN, YOU CAN'T HIDE IN HERE FOR EVER!

I'M NOT HIDING! I HAVE NOTHING **TO** HIDE!

I JUST WANTED TO GET THE JOB FINISHED ON TIME, THAT'S ALL. WHY? WHAT ARE PEOPLE SAYING?

THOUGH I CAN WORK THAT OUT FOR MYSELF. THERE'S NO HIDING IT NOW, IS THERE? SHE GETS LARGER EACH DAY.

WHAT CAN BE DONE, JOSEPH? IT'S NOT AS IF YOU'RE THE FIRST TO MARRY IN A HURRY!

TRUE. BUT I KNOW FOR A FACT THE CHILD ISN'T MINE. AND THAT KNOWLEDGE IS KILLING ME..!

UNDER JEWISH LAW AN ENGAGEMENT WAS AS BINDING AS MARRIAGE, AND JOSEPH COULD HAVE PUBLICLY HUMILIATED MARY, EVEN ACCUSING HER OF ADULTERY!

BUT JOSEPH WAS A GOOD MAN. SO INSTEAD, HE DECIDED TO BREAK THE CONTRACT PRIVATELY. A QUIET DIVORCE SEEMED BEST.

ONLY THEN, AFTER THE DECISION WHICH SHOWED HIS GENTLENESS, DID GOD LET JOSEPH IN ON HIS PLAN. AN ANGEL CAME TO JOSEPH IN HIS SLEEP...

GREETINGS JOSEPH, SON OF DAVID. DO NOT BE AFRAID TO TAKE MARY AS YOUR WIFE.

BUT SHE IS ALREADY PREGNANT!

– AND SHE WILL HAVE A SON. YOU WILL CALL HIM *JESUS*, FOR HE WILL SAVE HIS PEOPLE FROM THEIR SINS. IT IS THROUGH THE HOLY SPIRIT THAT MARY HAS CONCEIVED.

DO NOT BE AFRAID TO TAKE HER AS YOUR WIFE, SON OF DAVID.

THE PROPHET ISAIAH, HUNDREDS OF YEARS BEFORE HAD SAID THAT A VIRGIN WOULD BEAR A CHILD, WHO WOULD BE CALLED **IMMANUEL**. 'GOD WITH US'.

AND AS THE ANGEL LEFT, JOSEPH KNEW THESE WORDS TO BE TRUE.

AND SO HE MARRIED MARY.

THEIRS WASN'T THE FIRST WEDDING WHERE THE BRIDE WAS OBVIOUSLY PREGNANT, NOR WAS IT THE LAST. BUT JOSEPH TRUSTED THE WORDS OF THE ANGEL, AND TURNED A DEAF EAR TO THE GOSSIP-MONGERS.

JOSEPH TOOK MARY HOME, BUT HE DID NOT SLEEP WITH HIS WIFE UNTIL AFTER HER SON WAS BORN.

THEY BOTH KNEW THAT THIS CHILD WAS SPECIAL...

IN THOSE DAYS, THE ROMAN EMPEROR CAESAR AUGUSTUS ISSUED A DECREE: A CENSUS WAS TO BE TAKEN THROUGHOUT THE EMPIRE, EACH PERSON GOING TO HIS HOME TOWN TO BE REGISTERED.

AND SO JOSEPH TOOK HIS YOUNG WIFE, AND TOGETHER THEY MADE THEIR WAY SOUTH TO THE PLACE WHERE JOSEPH MUST REGISTER; THE TOWN WHERE RUTH HAD MARRIED BOAZ, THE BIRTHPLACE OF KING DAVID...

THE TOWN OF **BETHLEHEM**.

ISRAEL BRISTLED WITH ANGER, RIPE FOR REBELLION UNDER ROMAN RULE.

MANY WAITED FOR THE MESSIAH WHO WOULD RESCUE THEM, RESTORE THEIR FORTUNES, DRIVE THE ROMANS FROM THE LAND.

IT WAS AGAINST THIS BACKGROUND THAT MARY AND JOSEPH LIVED THEIR LIVES.

PLEASE! WE DESPERATELY NEED A ROOM. WE'VE TRIED EVERYWHERE...

SORRY SIR, WE'RE FULLY BOOKED, HAVE BEEN FOR WEEKS. HERE FOR THE CENSUS, ARE WE? WELL, DON'T BLAME ME, BLAME THE ROMANS! IT'S THEIR IDEA!

PLEASE — MY WIFE... THE BABY'S DUE ANY DAY NOW. THERE MUST BE **SOMEWHERE** WE COULD STAY.

IT'S NOT MUCH, I KNOW, BUT IT'S WARM AND DRY, AND MORE TO THE POINT, IT'S ALL I HAVE LEFT.

WE'LL TAKE IT.

WE'LL TAKE IT, JOSEPH! I DON'T THINK I CAN WAIT MUCH LONGER! THE BABY'S COMING!

BUT SURELY THERE MUST BE —

WE'LL TAKE IT!

300 YEARS BEFORE, THE PROPHET MICAH WROTE THESE WORDS: 'FROM YOU, BETHLEHEM, SMALL AS YOU ARE, WILL COME A RULER FOR ISRAEL, WHOSE FAMILY LINE GOES BACK TO ANCIENT TIMES. HE WILL RULE WITH THE STRENGTH THAT COMES FROM GOD... AND HE WILL BRING PEACE.'

TONIGHT, THOSE WORDS WOULD COME TRUE. THE GREATEST KING THE WORLD WOULD EVER SEE, COME AT LAST FOR A PEOPLE WHO HAD CRIED OUT FOR HIM FOR CENTURIES.

BUT NOT IN TRIUMPH AT THE HEAD OF A MIGHTY ARMY, BANNERS IN THE WIND, SHIELDS HELD HIGH.

THE SON OF GOD. THE NEW ADAM. KING OF KINGS AND LORD OF LORDS.

HE CAME INTO THE WORLD A HELPLESS BABY, BORN IN A CATTLE-SHED.

IN THE HILLS ABOVE THE TOWN, A GROUP OF SHEPHERDS WATCHED OVER THEIR SHEEP AS THEIR FOREFATHERS HAD DONE FOR GENERATIONS.

AND AS THEY SAT AROUND THEIR CAMPFIRE THAT NIGHT, THE MOST AMAZING THING HAPPENED...

AN ANGEL OF THE LORD APPEARED, AND GOD'S GLORY SHONE ABOUT THEM. THEY WERE TERRIFIED! BUT THE ANGEL SAID —

DO NOT BE AFRAID! I BRING WONDERFUL NEWS! TODAY IN THE TOWN OF DAVID YOUR SAVIOUR IS BORN: CHRIST, THE MESSIAH! YOU WILL FIND A BABY WRAPPED IN CLOTHS AND LYING IN A MANGER. THEN YOU WILL KNOW!

AND SUDDENLY A GREAT COMPANY OF THE ANGELS OF HEAVEN APPEARED, SINGING PRAISE TO GOD:

GLORY TO GOD IN THE HIGHEST HEAVEN! AND PEACE ON EARTH TO ALL WHO PLEASE HIM.

166

BUT THE WONDERS SURROUNDING THE CHILD'S BIRTH WERE FAR FROM OVER, FOR WHEN THEY TOOK THE CHILD TO THE TEMPLE, AS WAS THE JEWISH CUSTOM...

WE SHOULD HAVE SACRIFICED A LAMB, JOSEPH. HE'S SO SPECIAL, WE SHOULD HAVE DONE *SOMETHING* TO THANK GOD.

PRAISE GOD!

BUT THERE'S NO WAY WE COULD AFFORD IT. TWO PIGEONS IS ALL WE CAN AFFORD RIGHT NOW. WE SHOULD —

HE'S BEAUTIFUL.

THERE WERE ANGELS, HUNDREDS OF THEM, ALL SINGING AND SHINING IN THE DARKNESS. THEY SAID THERE WOULD BE A BABY IN A MANGER, AND LOOK! HERE HE IS!

THEY SAID, 'THIS IS THE ONE YOU'VE BEEN WAITING FOR — THE CHRIST, OUR SAVIOUR'!

I THINK THIS IS *HIM*. I REALLY THINK IT IS!

A MAN CALLED SIMEON, RIGHTEOUS AND DEVOUT, HAD BEEN TOLD BY GOD THAT HE WOULD NOT DIE UNTIL HE HAD SEEN THE MESSIAH. AS SOON AS HE SAW JESUS, HE CRIED ALOUD —

NOW I CAN DIE IN PEACE!

I BEG YOUR PARDON?

WITH MY OWN EYES I HAVE *SEEN* SALVATION! A GREAT *LIGHT* TO SHINE A WAY FOR THE GENTILES, AND BRING GLORY TO *ISRAEL*, GOD'S OWN PEOPLE!

THIS CHILD IS A SIGN FROM GOD, THOUGH MANY PEOPLE WILL SPEAK AGAINST HIM AND SORROW, LIKE A SHARP SWORD, WILL PIERCE YOUR OWN HEART.

MARY REMEMBERED ALL THIS, HOLDING THE WORDS IN HER HEART.

ONE DAY, AS EVENING FELL, A GROUP OF IMPORTANT TRAVELLERS FROM THE EAST ARRIVED AT THE PALACE OF HEROD, THE KING.

ALTHOUGH WEARY FROM THEIR JOURNEY, THEIR GAZE STILL HELD TO THE SKIES, WHERE THE FIRST STARS OF TWILIGHT SHOWED...

GREETINGS. WE HAVE TRAVELLED FROM FAR IN THE EAST, SEEKING THE KING OF THE JEWS.

THEN I FEAR THAT WE HAVE MADE A GRAVE ERROR. WE ARE ASTRONOMERS, OUR LIFE'S WORK THE STUDY OF THE STARS ABOVE.

WE WITNESSED A NEW STAR, A THING **UNHEARD** OF IN OUR OWN TIME. IT LEADS US HERE, TO WHERE THE KING OF THE JEWS IS TO BE BORN AT THIS TIME.

... PERHAPS IT MEANS YOUR SON? IS YOUR WIFE EXPECTING?

AND YOU HAVE FOUND HIM! I AM HEROD, KING OF ISRAEL.

HEROD KNEW THAT THE PROPHETS HAD NAMED BETHLEHEM AS THE BIRTHPLACE OF THE MESSIAH, SO HE DIRECTED THEM THERE.

MAKE A CAREFUL SEARCH FOR THE CHILD. AND WHEN YOU FIND HIM... **TELL** ME WON'T YOU? SO I MAY WORSHIP HIM TOO?

HEROD HAD KEPT POWER UNDER THE ROMANS BY GUILE AND CUNNING, BUT THE STRAIN HAD LEFT HIM DEEPLY PARANOID.

SO HE MADE PLANS TO KILL THE CHILD, IN ORDER TO PRESERVE HIS OWN THRONE.

GOD HAD SPOKEN TO ORDINARY PEOPLE – THROUGH DREAMS, THROUGH ANGELS, THROUGH THE SCRIPTURES – TO ANNOUNCE THE GREAT EVENT.

NOW, AS THE WISE MEN FOLLOWED THE STAR TOWARDS BETHLEHEM, NATURE ITSELF BESPOKE THE CHILD'S BIRTH!

THE WISE MEN FOLLOWED THE STAR, UNTIL IT RESTED OVER THE PLACE WHERE THE CHILD LAY SLEEPING.

THE KING OF THE JEWS – FOUND NOT IN A PALACE OR CASTLE, BUT IN AN ORDINARY HOUSE, IN THE CARE OF ORDINARY WORKING PEOPLE...

WHO'S THAT AT THE DOOR AT THIS HOUR?

I HAVEN'T ASKED ANYONE TO CALL. I WAS ABOUT TO BATHE THE BABY. SEE WHO IT IS, WOULD YOU?

MARY? YOU'RE NEVER GOING TO BELIEVE THIS!

GREETINGS! WE COME LOOKING FOR THE KING OF THE JEWS.

THE WISE MEN DID NOT HESITATE. THEY CAME INTO THIS PLAIN HOUSE BEARING GIFTS FIT FOR A KING — GOLD, INCENSE AND MYRRH.

THEY SAW THE CHILD THEY HAD TRAVELLED SO FAR TO SEE.

AND THEY **WORSHIPPED** HIM.

BE WARNED, JOSEPH. WE HAVE DREAMT OF HEROD, AND DO NOT TRUST HIM! HE EXPECTS US AT HIS PALACE TO BRING NEWS OF... YOUR SON, SHALL WE SAY?

WE INTEND TO RETURN HOME THE LONG WAY, TO AVOID HIM AT ALL COSTS. TAKE CARE, JOSEPH!

THAT NIGHT, JOSEPH HAD A TERRIBLE DREAM. HE MUST TAKE MARY AND JESUS AND LEAVE AT ONCE FOR EGYPT. JOSEPH HAD SEEN SO MUCH THAT HE KNEW THE WARNING WAS NOT TO BE TAKEN LIGHTLY.

THEY CAME AT DAWN.

THIS WAY! I HEARD CRYING!

THIS ONE'S A BOY! KILL IT!

PLEASE! HE'S ONLY A CHILD! HOW CAN YOU DO THIS?

SHUT YOUR MOUTH OR **JOIN** HIM!

EVERY MALE CHILD UNDER TWO YEARS OLD.

THEIR MOTHERS SCREAMED, AND REFUSED TO BE COMFORTED, BUT THERE WAS NOTHING ANYONE COULD DO TO STOP THEM.

IN HIS JEALOUSY, HEROD MURDERED THE INNOCENT TO PROTECT HIS THRONE. WITHIN A YEAR HE HIMSELF WAS DEAD.

AFTER HEROD'S DEATH, AN ANGEL SPOKE IN A DREAM TO JOSEPH. IT WAS SAFE TO GO HOME.

SO JOSEPH TOOK HIS FAMILY, AND RETURNED. NOT TO BETHLEHEM, BUT TO GALILEE, TO THE TOWN OF **NAZARETH**.

EVERY YEAR, MARY AND JOSEPH WENT SOUTH TO JERUSALEM TO CELEBRATE THE PASSOVER. THERE WERE A GREAT MANY PEOPLE ON THE ROADS AT THAT TIME, AND WHOLE COMMUNITIES MIGHT TRAVEL TOGETHER TO WORSHIP GOD.

JOSEPH — HAVE YOU SEEN JESUS? I THOUGHT HE WAS TRAVELLING WITH **BOAZ'S** FAMILY, BUT THEY HAVEN'T SEEN HIM!

BOAZ ?! I THOUGHT HE WAS TRAVELLING WITH **SIMEON'S** FAMILY! I'VE A BAD FEELING ABOUT THIS! I THINK HE'S STILL IN **JERUSALEM** !

JESUS WAS NOW TWELVE YEARS OLD.

I **KNEW** WE SHOULDN'T HAVE LET HIM OUT OF OUR SIGHT !

THE SEARCH TOOK THEM **THREE DAYS**. SICK WITH WORRY, THEY EVENTUALLY THOUGHT TO LOOK IN THE **TEMPLE** ITSELF. AND IT WAS THERE, AMONG THE WISEST MEN IN ISRAEL, THAT THEY WERE TO FIND HIM...

SO WHAT DO YOU THINK THAT MEANS ?

...!?

WELL, IT'S...

JESUS, WHAT ARE YOU **DOING** HERE? THIS IS THE **TEMPLE**! YOUR MOTHER AND I HAVE BEEN WORRIED **SICK** ABOUT YOU !

THE CARAVAN LEFT WITHOUT ME. I KNEW I'D BE SAFE HERE, AND THAT YOU'D COME SOONER OR LATER.

AFTER ALL, DIDN'T YOU KNOW I WOULD BE IN MY **FATHER'S** HOUSE ?

ALTHOUGH IT MADE LITTLE SENSE TO ANYONE AT THE TIME, MARY STORED ALL THESE STORIES IN HER HEART.

AND IN THIS WAY, JESUS GREW IN BODY AND SPIRIT, AND WAS LOVED BY GOD AND PEOPLE ALIKE AS THE YEARS WENT BY...

'A VOICE IS CALLING IN THE DESERT, PREPARE THE WAY FOR THE LORD... THE WHOLE OF CREATION WILL SEE GOD'S SALVATION.'

IN THE FIFTEENTH YEAR OF THE REIGN OF THE ROMAN EMPEROR TIBERIUS CAESAR — WHEN PONTIUS PILATE WAS GOVERNOR OF JUDEA — THE WORD OF GOD CAME TO JOHN, THE SON OF ELIZABETH AND ZECHARIAH.

THE WHOLE COUNTRY CAME **ALIVE** WITH HIS WORDS; AND PEOPLE CAME FROM FAR AND NEAR JUST TO HEAR HIM SPEAK.

CENTURIES EARLIER, THE PROPHET ISAIAH HAD TOLD OF THE STORY NOW UNFOLDING.

YOU BROOD OF **SNAKES**!

DISASTER IS APPROACHING YOU! IT'S NO USE SAYING 'WE'RE **JEWS**! WE HAVE **ABRAHAM** AS OUR FATHER!' THAT WON'T SAVE YOU! GET DOWN ON YOUR KNEES AND **REPENT**!

IF YOU REPENT YOUR LIVES SHOULD SHOW THE **FRUIT** OF THAT REPENTANCE! LOVE! HONESTY! **KINDNESS**!

BE BAPTIZED IN THE RIVER BY ME, AND CHANGE YOUR LIVES WHILE THERE IS STILL TIME!

BUT I AM A **TAX COLLECTOR**! WE'RE HATED BY JEWS FOR SERVING THE ROMANS, AND BY THE ROMANS FOR BEING TRAITORS TO OUR OWN PEOPLE! HOW CAN **WE** EVER LIVE A GOOD LIFE?

EASILY — JUST DON'T COLLECT MORE THAN YOU HAVE TO. BE HONEST.

YOU SOLDIERS — NO MORE EXTORTION OR BRIBERY. DON'T **LIE** ABOUT PEOPLE!

WE HAVE TO ASK YOU, SIR: ARE YOU THE **MESSIAH**?

ARE YOU THE ONE WE'VE BEEN WAITING FOR?

I ONLY BAPTIZE YOU WITH **WATER**. BUT SOMEONE IS COMING SOON WHO IS FAR MORE POWERFUL THAN I! I AM NOT FIT EVEN TO UNLACE HIS SANDALS!

HE WILL BAPTIZE YOU WITH THE **HOLY SPIRIT**! WITH **FIRE**!

AND SO NEWS OF JOHN SPREAD ACROSS THE LAND, AND MANY CAME TO HIM TO BE BAPTIZED.

JESUS. THE MESSIAH.

ARE YOU STILL HERE? THE OTHERS WENT HOME AGES AGO! MOST PEOPLE LEAVE *EARLY* ON THEIR LAST DAY AT WORK!

I WANTED TO FINISH THE JOISTS BEFORE I LEFT. I CAN'T GO OFF AND LEAVE THE JOB HALF FINISHED.

THERE. THAT SHOULD LAST FOR *CENTURIES*.

WELL, WE'RE CERTAINLY GOING TO MISS YOU. I DON'T KNOW, WORKING AFTER HOURS – YOU'RE AS BAD AS YOUR FATHER!

I'LL TAKE THAT AS A COMPLIMENT – ALTHOUGH BEING BAD ISN'T ONE OF HIS TRAITS!

...SORRY?

A JOKE. DON'T WORRY ABOUT IT.

ARE YOU SURE YOU DON'T WANT TO COME *WITH* ME?

I CAN'T. AND I STILL DON'T UNDERSTAND WHY *YOU* OF ALL PEOPLE WANT TO BE *BAPTIZED*! I MEAN, THE PEOPLE WHO COME TO HIM – MURDERERS, THIEVES, LIARS – I'VE KNOWN YOU YOUR WHOLE LIFE, JESUS, AND YOU'RE... YOU'RE *BETTER* THAN THEM!

I'M GOING TO SEE JOHN, AND I'M *GOING* TO GET BAPTIZED. IN FACT I'M LOOKING FORWARD TO IT! GOODBYE!

THE ACT OF BAPTISM WAS A SYMBOL, AN OUTWARD SIGN OF THE PEOPLE WASHING THEIR GUILT AWAY IN FRONT OF GOD.

JESUS WAS DIFFERENT FROM THE CROWDS WHO FLOCKED TO JOHN TO BE BAPTIZED.

172

JESUS **HAD** NO GUILT. NO SIN. NO SHAME. HE WAS BAPTIZED, NOT TO BE MADE CLEAN BEFORE GOD...

BUT TO BE DOWN IN THE WATER, ALONGSIDE THE BROKEN AND THE SINFUL — **THAT** WAS WHY HE CAME.

IS THAT **JESUS**? WHAT'S **HE** DOING HERE?

MAYBE HE'S COME TO HELP JOHN?

BAPTIZE ME, JOHN.

YOU? WHATEVER **FOR**, JESUS? EVERYONE KNOWS YOU'VE DONE NOTHING WRONG YOUR WHOLE LIFE! THIS IS FOR **SINNERS**! IF ANYTHING **YOU** SHOULD BE BAPTIZING **ME**!

TRUST ME, JOHN. THIS IS THE RIGHT THING TO DO.

BAPTIZE ME.

AND SO JESUS WAS BAPTIZED IN THE RIVER JORDAN.

WHEN ASKED ABOUT IT LATER, JOHN DESCRIBED IT IN THESE WORDS:

'I SAW HEAVEN **OPEN**. A VOICE CRIED OUT — '

THIS IS MY SON, WHOM I LOVE; WITH HIM I AM WELL PLEASED!

'I SAW THE HEAVENS TORN OPEN, AND THE HOLY SPIRIT DESCEND ON JESUS LIKE A DOVE!'

'HE IS THE LAMB OF GOD, COME TO TAKE AWAY THE SINS OF THE WHOLE **WORLD**! I SAY IN TRUTH, THAT THIS MAN IS THE LIVING **SON OF GOD**!'

IMMEDIATELY AFTER HE WAS BAPTIZED, THE SPIRIT TOOK JESUS FAR OUT INTO THE DESERT.

THERE, WITHOUT FOOD, HE STAYED FOR FORTY DAYS AND NIGHTS.

HE BURNED BY DAY...

AND HE FROZE BY NIGHT.

AND THEN, WHEN HE WAS AT HIS WEAKEST AND MOST VULNERABLE, HIS TRIALS BEGAN IN EARNEST.

ALONE, AND FAR FROM FRIENDS, JESUS ENCOUNTERED THE **DEVIL**.

WHO TRIED TO **TEMPT** HIM...

I AM SO HUNGRY. LORD GOD, PLEASE HELP ME WITH THIS HUNGER. THE PAIN IS TOO MUCH...

YOU? **HUNGRY**? WHY, JESUS, IF YOU'RE THE SON OF GOD, WHY DON'T YOU COMMAND THE STONES TO BECOME BREAD?

YOU KNOW THEY WILL. YOU KNOW HOW **GOOD** THEY'LL TASTE.

DO IT. DO IT **NOW**!

IT IS WRITTEN: 'MAN DOESN'T LIVE ON BREAD ALONE, BUT BY THE WORDS THAT COME FROM GOD'S MOUTH.' THEREFORE I WON'T USE GOD'S POWER FOR MY OWN NEEDS.

THEN *LOOK.* I WILL GIVE YOU ALL THE KINGDOMS ON EARTH, IF YOU WILL BOW DOWN AND WORSHIP *ME!*

IT IS WRITTEN: 'WORSHIP ONLY GOD, AND SERVE ONLY *HIM!*'

IF YOU *ARE* THE SON OF GOD, WHY NOT THROW YOURSELF FROM THE HIGHEST ROOF OF THE TEMPLE? SURELY GOD WILL SAVE YOU.

YOU COULD DO ANYTHING YOU *WISHED* AND GOD WOULD SAVE YOU! WHY NOT *DO* IT?

IT IS WRITTEN: 'DO NOT PUT THE LORD YOUR GOD TO THE TEST.'

LEAVE ME, SATAN. I WILL NOT TURN FROM GOD.

AND AS THE DEVIL LEFT, *ANGELS* CAME, AND TENDED TO JESUS IN THE DESERT.

HE HAD NOT GIVEN IN AS *ADAM* HAD. JESUS' WORK ON EARTH COULD BEGIN...

JESUS BEGAN TO SEARCH FOR PEOPLE TO HELP HIM IN HIS WORK.

THE FIRST CHOSEN WERE A GROUP OF FISHERMEN, WORKING THE SHORES OF LAKE GALILEE.

ANDREW! PETER!

FOLLOW ME!

AND AT ONCE THE BROTHERS LEFT THEIR NETS AND FOLLOWED JESUS.

WHERE ARE WE GOING, TEACHER? DO YOU NEED US TO HELP YOU FISH?

IN A MANNER OF SPEAKING.

JAMES AND JOHN! FOLLOW ME, AND I WILL MAKE YOU FISHERS OF *PEOPLE*!

WITHOUT A MOMENT'S HESITATION, THE TWO BROTHERS LEFT THEIR FAMILY AND FOLLOWED JESUS.

THE FOUR FISHERMEN WERE JUST THE FIRST OF JESUS' FOLLOWERS. JUST AS THERE WERE TWELVE TRIBES OF ISRAEL, SO JESUS CALLED TWELVE MEN TO FOLLOW HIM CLOSELY AND LEARN FROM HIM.

THEY WERE CALLED HIS **DISCIPLES**.

JUDAS ISCARIOT.

PHILIP.

MATTHEW, A TAX COLLECTOR.

THOMAS.

JAMES, SON OF ALPHAEUS.

BARTHOLOMEW.

SIMON, THE ZEALOT.

JUDAS, SON OF JAMES.

COMING FROM ALL CLASSES AND WALKS OF LIFE, THEY WOULD STAY WITH JESUS FOR THE REST OF HIS LIFE...

AND SO JESUS BEGAN TO TEACH. AND AS HE SPOKE, PEOPLE FLOCKED TO LISTEN IN THEIR *HUNDREDS*.

HE WAS UNLIKE ANYONE THEY HAD EVER HEARD BEFORE...

BLESSED ARE YOU WHO ARE *POOR*. FOR YOURS IS THE KINGDOM OF GOD. BLESSED ARE YOU WHO ARE *HUNGRY* AND WEEP, FOR YOU WILL BE FED AND SHED TEARS OF JOY!

BLESSED ARE YOU WHO ARE *PEACEMAKERS*, FOR YOU WILL BE GOD'S OWN CHILDREN.

I TELL YOU NOW, *LOVE* YOUR ENEMIES. SHOW KINDNESS TO THOSE WHO HATE YOU. TREAT OTHERS IN THE WAY *YOU* WANT TO BE TREATED.

IF SOMEONE STRIKES YOU ON ONE SIDE OF YOUR FACE, SAY 'HERE, HIT THE OTHER SIDE TOO!'

IF YOU CATCH SOMEONE STEALING YOUR CLOAK, THEN SAY 'HERE, HAVE MY TUNIC AS WELL!'

IF YOU'RE ONLY KIND TO THE PEOPLE WHO ARE KIND TO *YOU*, WHAT'S THE GOOD OF THAT? EVEN MURDERERS TREAT THEIR FRIENDS WELL.

DON'T JUDGE PEOPLE, AND *YOU* WON'T BE JUDGED. *FORGIVE* PEOPLE, AND *YOU* WILL BE FORGIVEN.

IF YOU SHOW KINDNESS TO OTHERS, DO IT *QUIETLY*. DON'T ANNOUNCE YOUR GOOD DEEDS WITH *TRUMPETS* LIKE THE HYPOCRITES.

GOD SEES EVERYTHING.

THERE WERE TWO MAIN RELIGIOUS FACTIONS IN ISRAEL, THE **PHARISEES** AND THE **SADDUCEES**. AND JESUS' WORDS DID NOT GO UNNOTICED BY EITHER...

WHY DO YOU LOOK AT THE BIT OF SAWDUST IN YOUR BROTHER'S EYE, AND FAIL TO SEE YOU HAVE A PLANK OF WOOD IN YOUR OWN? YOU HYPOCRITES! FIRST TAKE THE PLANK OUT OF YOUR **OWN** EYE, AND ONLY **THEN** TELL YOUR BROTHER ABOUT THE SAWDUST IN HIS!

AND **WHEN** YOU PRAY, DON'T BE LIKE THE HYPOCRITES WHO LOVE TO PRAY ON STREET CORNERS, WHERE EVERYONE CAN SEE HOW 'HOLY' THEY ARE.

INSTEAD, GO TO YOUR ROOM, CLOSE THE DOOR, AND PRAY TO GOD LIKE THIS:

PSST!... WHAT DO YOU THINK?

I WONDER BY WHAT **AUTHORITY** HE SAYS THESE THINGS. WHO DOES HE REPRESENT? **US**? THE SADDUCEES? THE **ROMANS** EVEN?

DEAR FATHER, HALLOWED BE YOUR NAME. YOUR KINGDOM COME, YOUR WILL BE DONE ON EARTH AS IT IS IN HEAVEN.

GIVE US TODAY OUR DAILY BREAD, AND FORGIVE US OUR SINS, AS WE FORGIVE THOSE WHO SIN AGAINST US. DO NOT LEAD US INTO TEMPTATION, BUT SAVE US FROM EVIL.

I TELL YOU THE TRUTH: IF ANYONE HEARS MY WORDS AND OBEYS THEM, THEN THEY WILL NEVER KNOW DEATH.

NO! HE HAS GONE TOO FAR THIS TIME!

NEVER DIE?! OF **COURSE** THEY'LL DIE!

ABRAHAM DIED! **MOSES** DIED, TOO! IS HE SAYING HE IS GREATER THAN ABRAHAM AND MOSES?!

WHO DOES HE THINK HE IS, SPEAKING THIS WAY?!

I AM THE LIGHT OF THE WORLD. NO ONE WHO BELIEVES IN ME SHOULD HAVE TO LIVE THEIR LIVES IN DARKNESS.

FROM THIS TIME ON, THE RELIGIOUS LEADERS MADE JESUS THEIR ENEMY, AND BEGAN TO PLOT HIS DESTRUCTION...

178

JESUS WENT FROM NAZARETH TO THE TOWN OF CAPERNAUM, TO PREACH IN THE SYNAGOGUE.

PEOPLE WERE AMAZED BY THE THINGS HE SAID.

BEWARE OF FALSE TEACHERS. THEY COME TO YOU AS HARMLESS AS SHEEP, BUT INSIDE THEY'RE *WOLVES*, WAITING TO GET OUT!

HA! I KNOW YOU! I SEE YOU I SEE I SEE I SEE *YOU*!

LOOK AT HIM. DON'T YOU KNOW WHO IT IS?! DON'T ANY OF YOU STUPID, WEAK, *FOOLS* KNOW WHAT IT IS YOU HAVE INVITED INTO YOUR HOUSE?!

HAVE YOU COME TO *DESTROY* US, JESUS OF NAZARETH?

OH YES, I KNOW YOUR *NAME*! I KNOW YOUR *TRUE* NAME, I SEE YOUR - YOUR *TRUE* NATURE! OH I DO, INDEED I DO!

YOU ARE GOD'S HOLY ONE!

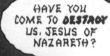

BE QUIET!

COME OUT, DEMON, AND LEAVE THIS POOR MAN ALONE.

NOOOOO! I WON'T GO, I WON'T -

YAAARGGG !!!

PRAISE GOD. MY MIND - IT'S CLEAR! CLEAR AS FRESH AIR!

HAH! - I CAN'T BELIEVE IT! I'M MYSELF AGAIN! PRAISE GOD!

WHO *IS* HE, THIS JESUS? HE GIVES ORDERS EVEN TO EVIL SPIRITS AND THEY *OBEY* HIM?

AND IN THIS WAY, WORD OF JESUS SPREAD THROUGH THE COUNTRY LIKE WILDFIRE.

HIS REPUTATION AS A HEALER AND TEACHER GREW...

MASTER! THANK YOU FOR COMING! IT'S MY WIFE'S MOTHER. I DON'T KNOW WHAT'S WRONG WITH HER.

IS SHE ILL, PETER?

DYING. SHE'S BURNING WITH FEVER — I DON'T THINK SHE WILL LAST THE NIGHT.

I SEE.

JESUS TOUCHED THE WOMAN'S HAND AND THE FEVER LEFT HER.

THERE. HOW DO YOU FEEL?

OH! I FEEL — I FEEL WONDERFUL!

MY! SO MANY GUESTS IN THE HOUSE!

NOW THEN, WHO'S HUNGRY AND WANTS TO JOIN ME IN SOMETHING TO EAT? I'M STARVING!

JESUS STAYED UP ALL THAT NIGHT, HEALING ANYONE WHO WOULD COME TO HIM.

FROM MILES AROUND, PEOPLE BROUGHT THE SICK AND SUFFERING, AND JESUS HEALED THEM ALL.

YOUR GRANDSON WILL BE FINE NOW, BUT YOU MUST TELL NO ONE WHAT HAPPENED HERE TONIGHT.

THEN WHAT THE PEOPLE SAY MUST BE TRUE — YOU ARE THE SON OF GOD!

AGAIN, I TELL YOU, TELL NO ONE ABOUT THIS!

THE JEWS WERE WAITING FOR THE MESSIAH TO OVERTHROW THE ROMANS. JESUS KNEW GOD HAD OTHER PLANS...

NEAR THE SHORES OF THE LAKE THEY WERE MET BY A ROMAN OFFICIAL, SENT BY THE CENTURION OF THE NEARBY GARRISON.

THE CENTURION HAD A SERVANT WHO WAS SICK, AND JESUS HAD BEEN ASKED TO HEAL HIM.

MY MASTER SAYS NOT TO CONCERN YOURSELF WITH MAKING THE JOURNEY TO VISIT US.

WHY NOT? IS THE SICK MAN *WELL* AGAIN?

NO SIR, HE IS *DYING*. BUT MY MASTER GIVES THIS MESSAGE:

'IF YOU SIMPLY SAY THE WORD, MY SERVANT WILL BE HEALED. I TOO AM A MAN UNDER AUTHORITY. IF I TELL A SOLDIER "DO THIS", I KNOW IT WILL BE DONE. I SEE THAT SAME AUTHORITY IN YOU.'

SUCH *FAITH*...

I HAVE NEVER SEEN SUCH FAITH IN ALL OF *ISRAEL*; AND YET HERE IT IS COMING FROM A *ROMAN*...

GO HOME. THE MAN *WILL* BE HEALED JUST AS YOU SAID.

MASTER, I'VE DECIDED TO *FOLLOW* YOU, BUT FIRST LET ME SAY GOODBYE TO MY FAMILY.

NO ONE WHO PUTS A HAND TO THE PLOUGH AND LOOKS BACK IS FIT FOR THE KINGDOM OF GOD.

JESUS DID NOT WANT THE JEWS TO KNOW HIS TRUE IDENTITY, UNTIL THE TIME WAS RIGHT. AS HEIR TO KING DAVID, MANY EXPECTED HIM TO BE *LIKE* KING DAVID – A SOLDIER, LEADING A GREAT ARMY.

THE *ZEALOTS*, A GROUP OF FREEDOM FIGHTERS, WERE PLANNING TO OVERTHROW THE ROMANS AT ANY MOMENT, AND NEWS OF THE MESSIAH WOULD BE THE SPARK THEY NEEDED TO IGNITE THE REBELLION.

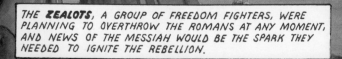

AS THEY LEFT CAPERNAUM, JESUS, WORN OUT FROM THE JOURNEY, FELL INTO A DEEP SLEEP...

WHILE CROSSING THE SEA OF GALILEE, A FIERCE STORM BLEW UP FROM NOWHERE.

SOON EVEN THE HARDENED FISHERMEN AMONG THE DISCIPLES WERE FEARFUL FOR THEIR LIVES!

ANDREW, WE'RE TAKING IN WATER! THE MAST WILL BREAK! WAKE HIM!

YOU WAKE HIM!

UNLESS WE DO SOMETHING WE'LL ALL DROWN! *SOMEONE* HAS TO WAKE THE MASTER!!

HOW CAN HE SLEEP THROUGH THIS?!

JESUS! *SAVE* US! THE BOAT IS GOING DOWN!!

MMPH? WHAT BOAT?

YOU OF LITTLE FAITH, WHY ARE YOU SO AFRAID?

STORM! BE *QUIET!*

HMPH. THAT'S BETTER.

WHAT KIND OF MAN IS THIS?

EVEN THE WIND AND WAVES OBEYED JESUS.

LANDING ON THE FAR SIDE OF THE SEA, JESUS HAD NO SOONER STEPPED FROM THE BOAT, WHEN HE HEARD THE STRANGEST NOISE...

NOISE, WE HEAR.

SHUT UP!

My friends, we have guests!

WORM. YOU WORM.

PEOPLE ON THE BEACH.

I KNOW. I KNOW THERE ARE.

SMASH THEIR BOAT UP!

JESUS! SON OF THE MOST HIGH GOD! WHAT DO YOU WANT WITH US?!!

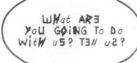

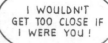

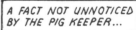

MY PIGS!
MY PIGS!

IT WAS THAT MAN FROM *NAZARETH* THEY'RE TALKING ABOUT – THAT *JESUS*! HE WAS TALKING TO OLD LEGION, AND HE DID SOMETHING TO MY PIGS AND NOW THEY'RE DROWNED!!

I WAS WARNED ABOUT HIM. HE'S CAUSED TROUBLE ALL AROUND GALILEE. WE DON'T WANT HIS SORT *HERE*.

SEE TO IT HE DOESN'T *STAY*, HMM?

RETURNING TO NAZARETH, JESUS WENT TO THE SYNAGOGUE ON THE SABBATH, AS WAS HIS CUSTOM, TO READ ALOUD AND TEACH.

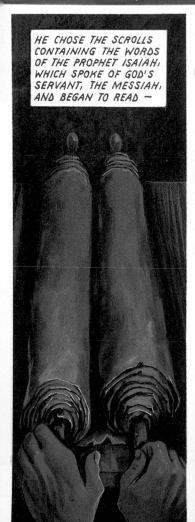

HE CHOSE THE SCROLLS CONTAINING THE WORDS OF THE PROPHET ISAIAH, WHICH SPOKE OF GOD'S SERVANT, THE MESSIAH, AND BEGAN TO READ –

'THE SPIRIT OF THE LORD IS UPON ME, BECAUSE HE HAS CHOSEN ME TO PREACH GOOD NEWS TO THE POOR.'

'HE HAS SENT ME TO ANNOUNCE FREEDOM FOR PRISONERS, AND RECOVERY OF SIGHT TO THE BLIND.'

'TO RELEASE THE OPPRESSED, TO ANNOUNCE THE YEAR OF THE LORD'S FAVOUR.'

THAT'S IT? JUST THAT SHORT SEGMENT?

IT'LL BE INTERESTING TO HEAR WHAT HE HAS TO *SAY* ABOUT IT.

JESUS ROLLED UP THE SCROLL AND BEGAN TO ADDRESS THE PEOPLE.

TODAY THIS PROPHECY HAS COME *TRUE*, AS YOU HEARD IT BEING READ.

WHAT?

TRUE?

HAS HE LOST HIS MIND?!

WAIT A MINUTE, JESUS. ARE YOU SAYING THAT *YOU* ARE THE CHOSEN SERVANT OF GOD?

JESUS, WE'VE KNOWN YOU SINCE YOU WERE A CHILD — YOU BUILT MY HOUSE FOR ME — HOW CAN *YOU* BE GOD'S CHOSEN ONE?

NO PROPHET IS EVER RESPECTED IN HIS HOME TOWN.

WHEN *ELIJAH* PREACHED, THERE WERE *MANY* WIDOWS IN ISRAEL, YET HE HELPED ONE FROM *SIDON*.

WHEN *ELISHA* PREACHED THERE WERE *MANY* LEPERS IN ISRAEL, YET ONLY A *SYRIAN* WAS HEALED.

BLASPHEMY!

HE'S SAYING THAT GOD WILL SEND THE MESSIAH TO *FOREIGNERS* INSTEAD OF JEWS!

KILL HIM!

DON'T LET HIM GET AWAY!

DON'T CARE *WHOSE* SON HE IS!

IT'S *DISGUSTING*! IT'S *OBSCENE*!

STONE HIM!

BUT AS THE CROWD GRABBED AT JESUS, MEANING TO *KILL* HIM, HE WALKED THROUGH THEM COMPLETELY UNHARMED, AND WENT ON HIS WAY.

PHARISEES, TEACHERS OF THE LAW AND ORDINARY PEOPLE CAME FROM ALL OVER JUDEA, EVEN FROM JERUSALEM, TO HEAR JESUS TALK.

AND AS HE TAUGHT, HE HEALED PEOPLE FROM EVERY SICKNESS.

HE'D BETTER *BE* HERE THIS TIME!

IT'S NOT *MY* FAULT WE KEEP MISSING HIM. *YOU* WERE THE ONE WHO SAID WE SHOULD GO TO THE ROMAN GARRISON!

OH NO! THESE PEOPLE HAVE BEEN WAITING FOR *HOURS*. THERE'S NO *WAY* WE'RE GOING TO GET TO SEE HIM!

WELL, THAT'S IT THEN. WE'VE DONE ALL WE CAN.

NO! WE'VE BROUGHT HIM THIS FAR. WE CAN'T JUST GIVE UP NOW. WE'RE SO *CLOSE*!

WAIT! I'VE HAD AN IDEA.

OH PLEASE, NOT ANOTHER ONE.

ALL RIGHT THEN, WE'RE ON THE ROOF. *NOW* WHAT?

YOU'LL *LIKE* THIS PART.

IF WE CAN'T GET HIM IN THROUGH THE *DOOR* THEN WE'LL HAVE TO *MAKE* AN ENTRANCE OF OUR OWN!

BUT JESUS, JOHN'S DISCIPLES FASTED, AND SO DO THE PHARISEES – *YOURS* NEVER STOP EATING AND DRINKING!

DO YOU MAKE WEDDING GUESTS FAST AT A WEDDING RECEPTION? NO, OF COURSE NOT.

BUT BEFORE LONG, THE BRIDEGROOM WILL BE TAKEN AWAY, AND *THEN* THEY WILL FAST!

MORE AND MORE PEOPLE CAME TO SEE JESUS, ASKING HIM TO HEAL THEIR SICK.

MASTER, A MAN CALLED JAIRUS, THE LEADER OF THE LOCAL SYNAGOGUE, ASKS FOR YOU.

MY LITTLE DAUGHTER IS DYING! PLEASE, SHE IS ALL WE HAVE IN THE WORLD. IF YOU PUT YOUR HANDS ON HER I KNOW SHE WILL *LIVE*!

THE DISCIPLES SOON HAD THEIR HANDS FULL CONTROLLING THE CROWDS.

AMONG THE CROWD WAS A WOMAN, WHO HAD SUFFERED FROM CONSTANT BLEEDING FOR YEARS. NO DOCTOR COULD HELP HER. BUT SHE THOUGHT — 'IF ONLY I COULD TOUCH JESUS' CLOAK I WOULD BE WELL AGAIN.'

AND AS SHE BRUSHED HIS CLOAK WITH HER FINGERTIPS —

EVENTUALLY SHE REACHED JESUS...

—SHE WAS *HEALED*.

WHO *TOUCHED* ME?

SOMEONE TOUCHED MY CLOAK. I FELT POWER GO OUT FROM ME.

THE WOMAN, WHO WAS FULL OF FEAR, TOLD JESUS EVERYTHING.

DAUGHTER, YOUR FAITH HAS HEALED YOU.

GO IN PEACE, AND KNOW THAT YOU ARE FREE FROM YOUR SUFFERING.

SEEING THIS ONLY GIVES ME MORE HOPE, JESUS. BUT WE MUST HURRY; PLEASE, COME WITH ME.

JAIRUS! I'M SO SORRY, MY FRIEND, YOUR DAUGHTER HAS DIED. HE CAN'T HELP YOU NOW.

JAIRUS, *LISTEN* TO ME! DON'T BE AFRAID. JUST *BELIEVE* !

JESUS DID NOT LET ANYONE FOLLOW HIM, EXCEPT PETER, JAMES AND JOHN. BUT AT THE HOUSE A CROWD OF MOURNERS HAD GATHERED.

WHAT'S ALL THE COMMOTION ABOUT ? GET OUT! THE CHILD IS NOT DEAD, BUT SLEEPING.

JESUS, LISTEN, PEOPLE ARE *LAUGHING* AT YOU.

MY CHILD, GET UP.

HMM ?

IS IT THAT TIME ALREADY ?

HOW CAN I EVER THANK YOU, JESUS ?

GIVE HER SOMETHING TO *EAT* — SHE MUST BE *STARVING*. AND DON'T TELL ANYONE WHAT HAS HAPPENED.

A CONSTANT STREAM OF PEOPLE CAME TO JESUS TO SEEK HEALING AND COMFORT. AMONG THE CROWD ONE DAY WERE TWO OF JOHN THE BAPTIST'S FOLLOWERS.

TEACHER, TWO OF JOHN'S DISCIPLES ARE HERE TO SEE YOU.

WE HAVE A MESSAGE FROM JOHN IN PRISON: 'ARE YOU THE ONE GOD PROMISED TO US OR SHOULD WE EXPECT SOMEONE ELSE?'

TELL JOHN WHAT YOU'VE SEEN: 'THE BLIND CAN SEE, THE LAME WALK, THE LEPERS ARE CURED, THE DEAF HEAR, THE DEAD ARE RAISED UP AND GOOD NEWS IS PREACHED TO THE POOR.' HE WILL UNDERSTAND WHAT THIS MEANS.

AND SEND JOHN MY GREETINGS...

AS JOHN'S DISCIPLES WERE LEAVING, JESUS BEGAN TO SPEAK TO THE CROWD ABOUT JOHN.

WHEN YOU WENT OUT INTO THE DESERT TO LISTEN TO JOHN, WHAT DID YOU *EXPECT* TO FIND?

A PROPHET? YES, I TELL YOU, AND MORE THAN A PROPHET. THIS IS THE ONE ABOUT WHOM IT WAS WRITTEN: 'I WILL SEND MY MESSENGER AHEAD OF YOU WHO WILL PREPARE YOUR WAY BEFORE YOU.'

I TELL YOU THE TRUTH. JOHN IS THE GREATEST OF ALL THE PROPHETS. AND YET THE VERY *LEAST* PERSON WHO BELIEVES MY WORDS WILL BE GREATER THAN HIM!

JOHN THE BAPTIST HAD SPOKEN OUT AGAINST KING HEROD ANTIPAS, SON OF THE KING WHO HAD ORDERED THE SLAUGHTER OF INNOCENT CHILDREN SOON AFTER JESUS WAS BORN.

JOHN HAD PUBLICLY DENOUNCED THE KING FOR MARRYING HIS BROTHER'S WIFE, HERODIAS, AS THIS WAS AGAINST THE LAW OF MOSES. JOHN WAS DRAGGED OFF TO PRISON THE SAME DAY.

WHILE THE KING DECIDED WHAT TO DO WITH JOHN, HE THREW A PARTY TO CELEBRATE HIS **BIRTHDAY.**

THE MAIN ATTRACTION AT THE PARTY WAS HERODIAS'S DAUGHTER, SALOME, WHO DANCED FOR HEROD AND HIS GUESTS.

ASK ANYTHING OF ME, AND IT SHALL BE YOURS!

ANYTHING?

NAME IT!

VERY WELL.

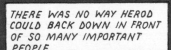

HEROD WAS SO PLEASED WITH SALOME THAT HE MADE A RASH PROMISE TO HER, IN FRONT OF HIS ENTIRE COURT...

GIVE ME THE HEAD OF JOHN THE BAPTIST, HACKED OFF AND ON A SILVER PLATE.

THERE WAS NO WAY HEROD COULD BACK DOWN IN FRONT OF SO MANY IMPORTANT PEOPLE.

DO AS SHE SAYS. HAVE JOHN BEHEADED AND HIS HEAD SERVED ON A SILVER PLATE. HIS DISCIPLES MAY HAVE THE REST OF THE BODY TO BURY AS THEY SEE FIT.

AND BESIDES, HIS WIFE HAD PUT THE GIRL UP TO IT, HE WAS SURE. HERODIAS **HATED** JOHN.

ONE DAY, AS JESUS WALKED ALONG THE SHORES OF LAKE GALILEE, THE CROWDS BECAME SO LARGE HE HAD TO STAND IN A FISHERMAN'S BOAT TO MAKE HIMSELF HEARD.

THE KINGDOM OF GOD IS LIKE THIS:

THERE WAS ONCE A FARMER WHO WENT TO SOW SEED. AS HE SCATTERED THE SEED, SOME FELL ON THE PATH AND BIRDS CAME AND ATE IT UP STRAIGHT AWAY.

'OTHER SEED FELL AMONG THORNS, WHICH CHOKED THE PLANTS BEFORE THEY HAD A CHANCE TO GROW PROPERLY.

'THE SEED IS GOD'S MESSAGE. SOME PEOPLE IGNORE IT; SOME TAKE TO IT AT ONCE, BUT IT NEVER TAKES ROOT. OTHERS BELIEVE FOR A WHILE, BUT LIFE'S WORRIES CROWD IN AND THEY FALL AWAY, BUT OTHERS ALLOW IT TO GROW IN THEIR LIVES AND FLOURISH.'

'SOME SEED FELL ON ROCKY GROUND AND SPRANG UP IN THE THIN SOIL. WHEN THE SUN CAME UP THE PLANTS WITHERED AWAY.

'BUT OTHER SEED FELL ON THE **GOOD** SOIL, WHERE IT PRODUCED A FINE CROP, MANY TIMES OVER.

THE KINGDOM OF HEAVEN IS LIKE THIS: ONCE UPON A TIME A MAN WAS DIGGING IN A FIELD WHEN HE STRUCK A HARD OBJECT...

'THE FIELD WOULD COST ALL HE HAD, SO HE SOLD EVERYTHING TO RAISE ENOUGH MONEY. THE MAN WAS FULL OF JOY FOR THE TREASURE WOULD BE HIS.'

'HE DUG UP A GOLD JAR FULL OF TREASURE – RINGS AND GOLD COINS. IF HE COULD BUY THE FIELDS HE WOULD RIGHTLY OWN THE TREASURE.

LATER, JESUS WAS DINING AT THE HOUSE OF A PHARISEE AND TOLD ANOTHER STORY ABOUT THE KINGDOM OF HEAVEN.

A MAN ONCE THREW A FABULOUS FEAST, A WONDERFUL BANQUET FOR ALL HIS FRIENDS.

'BUT THEY WERE SO SPOILT AND UNGRATEFUL THAT ON THE DAY OF THE FEAST THEY ALL MADE EXCUSES AND DIDN'T COME.

'SO THE MAN SENT HIS SERVANT OUT ONTO THE STREETS TO CALL THE HOMELESS, THE BEGGARS, LEPERS AND CRIPPLES, AND INVITED **THEM** TO HIS HOME FOR THE FEAST.

'THE MAN SAID: "NOT ONE OF THE GUESTS I FIRST INVITED WILL GET EVEN A **TASTE** OF MY BANQUET."'

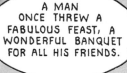

192

AS JESUS' NOTORIETY INCREASED HE WAS INVITED TO THE HOMES OF RELIGIOUS LEADERS WHO WANTED TO HEAR FOR THEMSELVES WHAT HE HAD TO SAY.

ONE EVENING A WOMAN HEARD HE WOULD BE DINING NEARBY AND MADE HER WAY TO THE HOUSE.

SHE WAITED IN THE DOORWAY FOR THE RIGHT MOMENT TO APPROACH JESUS. SHE WAS WELL KNOWN AS A PROSTITUTE AND, AWARE OF HER SHAME, DARED NOT LOOK JESUS IN THE FACE.

INSTEAD, SHE BENT DOWN AND, CRYING BITTERLY, WASHED HIS FEET.

WITHOUT A WORD SHE POURED EXPENSIVE PERFUME ONTO HIS FEET AND DRIED THEM WITH HER HAIR.

DOESN'T HE KNOW WHAT SHE IS, AND HOW SHE GOT THE MONEY FOR THAT PERFUME?

IF HE **WERE** A PROPHET HE WOULD KNOW WHAT KIND OF WOMAN SHE IS — A SINNER.

IF TWO MEN OWED MONEY – ONE MAN A HUGE SUM, THE OTHER MUCH LESS – AND THE DEBTS WERE CANCELLED, WHO WOULD BE THE MOST GRATEFUL?

THIS WOMAN HAS SHOWN *REAL* LOVE. YOU DID NOT EVEN DO ME THE COURTESY OF GIVING ME WATER TO WASH MY FEET, BUT SHE WET MY FEET WITH HER TEARS AND DRIED THEM WITH HER HAIR.

HER MANY SINS HAVE BEEN FORGIVEN – FOR SHE LOVED MUCH. BUT HE WHO HAS BEEN FORGIVEN LITTLE, LOVES LITTLE.

THE WOMAN LEFT KNOWING HER LIFE HAD BEEN CHANGED FOR EVER.

YOUR SINS ARE FORGIVEN. YOUR FAITH HAS SAVED YOU. GO IN PEACE.

CAN YOU BELIEVE HE SAID THAT TO *HER* ?! WHO IS THIS THAT EVEN FORGIVES SINS?

A MAN CALLED NICODEMUS, A PHARISEE AND A MEMBER OF THE RULING COUNCIL, PLUCKED UP THE COURAGE TO GO AND SEE JESUS FOR HIMSELF.

HE WENT IN THE MIDDLE OF THE NIGHT...

WHEN EVERYONE ELSE WAS FAST ASLEEP, AND NO ONE WOULD KNOW WHERE HE'D BEEN.

> YAWN <
A BIT LATE, ISN'T IT?

I HAVE TO *SPEAK* TO YOU. I *KNOW* YOU'VE COME FROM GOD – HOW *ELSE* COULD YOU DO THE MIRACULOUS THINGS YOU'VE DONE?

I TELL YOU THE TRUTH – *NO ONE* CAN SEE THE KINGDOM OF GOD, UNLESS THEY ARE BORN AGAIN.

'BORN' AGAIN? HOW CAN I BE BORN AGAIN AT *MY* AGE? I CAN'T GO BACK TO MY MOTHER'S WOMB.

UNLESS YOU ARE BORN OF WATER AND THE SPIRIT YOU CANNOT ENTER THE KINGDOM OF GOD. FLESH GIVES BIRTH TO FLESH, BUT THE SPIRIT GIVES BIRTH TO SPIRIT.

THE SON OF MAN MUST BE LIFTED UP, SO THAT EVERYONE WHO BELIEVES IN HIM MAY HAVE ETERNAL LIFE.

GOD LOVES THE WORLD SO MUCH, THAT HE SENT HIS ONLY *SON* SO THAT WHOEVER BELIEVES IN HIM WILL NOT DIE, BUT LIVE FOR EVER.

A GREAT LIGHT HAS COME INTO THE WORLD, BUT EVIL PEOPLE LOVE THE DARKNESS, BECAUSE IT HIDES THEIR DEEDS.

BUT IF YOU LIVE BY THE *TRUTH*, YOU WILL COME INTO THE LIGHT, SO THAT ALL CAN SEE WHAT HAS BEEN DONE THROUGH GOD.

JESUS WENT UP TO JERUSALEM, AND WHILE ON HIS WAY TO A PASSOVER FEAST PASSED THE POOL AT BETHESDA. ALL MANNER OF SICK AND DISABLED PEOPLE WERE THERE TO WASH IN THE POOL, BELIEVING THE WATER TO HAVE HEALING POWERS.

IT WAS THE SABBATH, THE DAY OF REST. ONE MAN CAUGHT JESUS' EYE.

YOU HAVE BEEN ILL A LONG TIME. DO YOU WANT TO GET WELL?

OF COURSE I DO! BUT I HAVE NO ONE TO HELP ME INTO THE POOL.

EVERY TIME THE WATERS STIR I TRY TO GET IN, BUT OTHERS GET THERE FIRST.

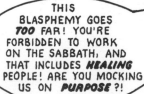

- PICK UP YOUR MAT -

AND WALK.

IN THAT CASE, GET UP!

THIS IS INCREDIBLE! I THOUGHT I'D NEVER WALK AGAIN EVER! NOT EVER!

YOU THERE! JUST WHAT DO YOU THINK YOU'RE DOING?

IT'S THE SABBATH! YOU'RE FORBIDDEN TO DO ANY WORK, AND THAT INCLUDES CARRYING MATS!

BUT THE MAN WHO JUST HEALED ME TOLD ME TO PICK UP MY MAT, AND WALK...

SO I DID - FOR THE FIRST TIME IN 38 YEARS!

THIS BLASPHEMY GOES TOO FAR! YOU'RE FORBIDDEN TO WORK ON THE SABBATH, AND THAT INCLUDES HEALING PEOPLE! ARE YOU MOCKING US ON PURPOSE?!

MY FATHER IS ALWAYS AT HIS WORK, EVEN ON THE SABBATH, AND IN THE SAME WAY I'M AT WORK TOO.

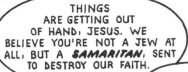

THINGS ARE GETTING OUT OF HAND, JESUS. WE BELIEVE YOU'RE NOT A JEW AT ALL, BUT A *SAMARITAN*, SENT TO DESTROY OUR FAITH.

AND POSSESSED BY A DEMON!

I AM NOTHING OF THE SORT. I KNOW THAT YOUR FATHER *ABRAHAM* LOOKED FORWARD TO THE DAY OF MY BIRTH.

DON'T BE ABSURD! YOU'RE STILL A YOUNG MAN, ABRAHAM HAS BEEN DEAD 2,000 YEARS! ARE YOU TELLING US YOU'VE *SEEN* ABRAHAM?

IF YOU TRULY WERE ABRAHAM'S CHILDREN, YOU WOULD DO THE THINGS *HE* DID. AS THINGS STAND, YOU'RE GOING TO END UP KILLING SOMEONE WHO HAS DONE NOTHING EXCEPT TELL YOU THE *TRUTH*.

TEACHER, WE HAVE A QUESTION. THIS MAN HERE WAS *BORN* BLIND. WHOSE SIN WAS RESPONSIBLE: HIS, OR HIS PARENTS'?

NEITHER.

AS LONG AS THERE IS STILL LIGHT IN THE WORLD, WE MUST DO THE WORK OF HIM WHO SENT ME.

NIGHT WILL BE HERE SOON ENOUGH.

BUT WHILE I AM STILL IN THE WORLD, I *AM* THE LIGHT OF THE WORLD!

WHA-?

MY EYES! WHAT'S HAPPENING TO ME?

GO AND WASH YOUR EYES IN THE POOL NEARBY, AND YOU'LL SEE FOR YOURSELF.

JESUS WENT TO SYCHAR, A TOWN IN SAMARIA NEAR THE LAND WHERE JOSEPH HAD LIVED CENTURIES BEFORE. TIRED FROM HIS TRAVELS, JESUS SAT DOWN BY THE WELL TO REST.

A SAMARITAN WOMAN APPROACHED TO DRAW WATER.

I AM THIRSTY. WOULD YOU BE KIND ENOUGH TO GIVE ME A DRINK?

YOU'RE SPEAKING TO *ME*? THERE'S A FIRST! A JEW TALKING TO A *SAMARITAN*. I THOUGHT IT WAS AGAINST YOUR RELIGION.

IF YOU KNEW WHAT GOD COULD GIVE YOU, YOU WOULD ASK FOR *LIVING* WATER.

ANYONE WHO DRINKS THIS WATER HERE WILL BE THIRSTY AGAIN, BUT WHOEVER DRINKS THE WATER *I* GIVE WILL NEVER BE THIRSTY AGAIN.

PLEASE, *GIVE* ME THIS WATER, SO I WON'T HAVE TO KEEP COMING BACK HERE!

GO, GET YOUR HUSBAND, AND BRING HIM HERE.

I HAVE NO HUSBAND.

YOU'VE HAD FIVE HUSBANDS, AND THE MAN YOU'RE LIVING WITH NOW ISN'T YOUR HUSBAND.

HOW DID YOU *KNOW* THAT? ARE YOU A PROPHET? I KNOW THE *MESSIAH* IS COMING. WHEN HE ARRIVES, HE WILL EXPLAIN EVERYTHING TO US.

I, WHO SPEAK TO YOU NOW, AM HE.

THE WOMAN RAN BACK TO THE TOWN TO TELL THE PEOPLE THERE OF THE MAN SHE HAD JUST MET – A MAN WHO KNEW EVERYTHING ABOUT HER.

MANY OF THE SAMARITANS CAME TO BELIEVE IN JESUS AND ACKNOWLEDGED THAT HE WAS INDEED THE MESSIAH SENT BY GOD.

AT THIS TIME, JESUS APPOINTED ANOTHER SEVENTY-TWO FOLLOWERS AND SENT THEM OUT TWO BY TWO TO EVERY TOWN AND VILLAGE HE WAS ABOUT TO VISIT.

WHEN YOU ENTER A TOWN AND ARE *WELCOMED*, STAY THERE. HEAL THE SICK AND TELL THEM THE KINGDOM OF GOD IS NEAR.

THE HARVEST IS PLENTIFUL, BUT THE WORKERS ARE FEW. GO! I'M SENDING YOU OUT LIKE NEWBORN LAMBS INTO A WORLD FULL OF WOLVES.

WHOEVER LISTENS TO YOU, LISTENS TO ME. WHOEVER REJECTS YOU, REJECTS THE ONE WHO SENT ME!

'IF YOU NEED HELP — ASK!'

'IMAGINE YOU HAVE A FRIEND, AND YOU WAKE THEM UP IN THE MIDDLE OF THE NIGHT AND SAY; "WE'VE HAD UNEXPECTED GUESTS AND HAVE RUN OUT OF FOOD — CAN I BORROW THREE LOAVES OF BREAD?"'

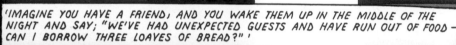

YOUR FRIEND SAYS: 'GO AWAY! WE'RE ALL IN BED AND YOU'LL WAKE THE CHILDREN!' AND YET, IF YOU KEEP ASKING, HE STILL *MAY* GET UP AND GIVE YOU WHAT YOU WANT —

NOT *BECAUSE* HE'S YOUR FRIEND, BUT BECAUSE OF YOUR SHEER *AUDACITY*. BECAUSE YOU KEEP ON ASKING AND WON'T KEEP QUIET!

SO I SAY, *ASK*, AND IT WILL BE GIVEN TO YOU. *LOOK*, AND YOU'LL FIND. *KNOCK*, AND THE DOOR WILL BE OPENED TO YOU.

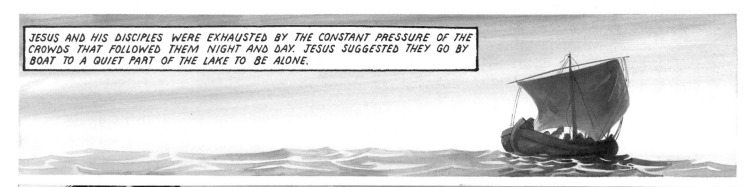

JESUS AND HIS DISCIPLES WERE EXHAUSTED BY THE CONSTANT PRESSURE OF THE CROWDS THAT FOLLOWED THEM NIGHT AND DAY. JESUS SUGGESTED THEY GO BY BOAT TO A QUIET PART OF THE LAKE TO BE ALONE.

BUT SEEING THEM PASS BY, HUGE CROWDS OF PEOPLE BEGAN TO FOLLOW THE BOAT WHEREVER IT WENT.

DESPITE HIS NEED TO REST, JESUS' HEART WAS FILLED WITH COMPASSION, AND HE ASKED FOR THE BOAT TO BE PUT ASHORE SO THAT HE MIGHT HEAL THEIR SICK.

JESUS!

JESUS, MY FATHER IS DYING!

MY BABY! PLEASE HELP ME!

MY WIFE!

PLEASE, LORD! HELP US!

I KNEW YOU WOULDN'T DESERT US!

AFTER HE HAD FINISHED HEALING THEIR SICK, HE TAUGHT THEM ABOUT THE KINGDOM OF GOD, WELL INTO THE EARLY EVENING.

THE CROWD NUMBERED AT LEAST 5,000 PEOPLE.

MASTER, IT'S GETTING LATE. WE'RE IN THE MIDDLE OF NOWHERE AND THESE PEOPLE NEED TO **EAT** SOON. WHY NOT TELL THEM TO GO AND FIND SOME FOOD?

I HAVE A BETTER IDEA. WHY DON'T **YOU** FEED THEM?

HOW MUCH FOOD HAVE WE GOT?

FIVE LOAVES OF BREAD, AND TWO FISH.

THEN THAT WILL HAVE TO BE ENOUGH.

JESUS PRAYED A PRAYER OF THANKS FOR THE FOOD, AND THEN HAD THE DISCIPLES PASS IT OUT TO THE CROWD.

INCREDIBLY, THERE WAS ENOUGH FOOD FOR EVERYONE. THERE WAS SO **MUCH** FOOD, THAT AFTER EVERYONE HAD EATEN UNTIL THEY WERE FULL, THE DISCIPLES WERE ABLE TO FILL A BASKET EACH WITH FOOD THAT WENT UNEATEN.

I'M TELLING YOU, THIS IS **HIM**! THE **MESSIAH**! WHO ELSE COULD DO THIS?

WE SHOULD MAKE HIM OUR KING. WITH HIS POWER WE COULD KICK OUT THE **ROMANS**!

LEAVING THE CROWDS BEHIND, JESUS FINALLY FOUND THE TIME TO BE BY HIMSELF.

SENDING HIS DISCIPLES ON TO THE TOWN OF BETHSAIDA, HE WENT UP INTO THE MOUNTAINS TO PRAY.

IT WAS EARLY EVENING WHEN HE CAME DOWN TO THE LAKE AGAIN, AND SAW THE DISCIPLES SLOWLY MAKING THEIR WAY BY BOAT TOWARDS HIM.

THEY SEEMED TO BE HAVING SOME *DIFFICULTY.*

THE WIND IS *AGAINST* US! I DOUBT WE'LL MAKE IT!

STOP MOANING THOMAS, AND *ROW* HARDER!

STOP FIGHTING, THE *LOT* OF YOU, AND PUT SOME EFFORT INTO IT!

LOOK! IT'S THE MASTER! HE'S —

HE'S WALKING ON THE LAKE!

THAT'S NOT JESUS, IT'S A *GHOST!*

GOD, HELP US! WE'RE DOOMED! HE'LL *DROWN* US ALL!

DON'T BE FRIGHTENED, PETER. IT'S ME, *JESUS.*

IN THAT CASE, I'M GOING TO MEET HIM! HOLD MY CLOAK, JUDAS!

OF COURSE I'M NOT SURE, WHY SHOULD I —

ARE YOU *SURE* ABOUT THIS?

HELP ME! I *CAN'T SWIM!*

YOU'RE SAFE, PETER.

THE WINDS DROPPED. CALM RETURNED. AND AS THE BOAT SLIPPED THROUGH THE WATER THE DISCIPLES WORSHIPPED THEIR LORD, NOW KNOWING FOR SURE THAT HE WAS THE SON OF GOD.

ON REACHING SHORE THEY WERE GREETED BY A CROWD OF PEOPLE, EAGER FOR MORE MIRACLES.

ARE THEY *STILL* HERE?

TEACHER, WHAT DO WE HAVE TO DO IN ORDER TO DO GOD'S WILL?

ALL GOD WANTS IS FOR YOU TO BELIEVE IN THE MAN HE *SENT* TO YOU.

YOU'VE COME BACK TODAY LOOKING FOR MORE BREAD. YOU ATE THE BREAD AND FISH YESTERDAY, AND NOW WANT TO SEE ANOTHER *MIRACLE.*

I AM THE BREAD OF LIFE. WHOEVER COMES TO ME WILL NEVER GO HUNGRY. IF ANYONE EATS THE BREAD I GIVE, HE WILL NEVER DIE – BUT I WILL RAISE HIM BACK TO LIFE ON THE LAST DAY.

COME ON, DO ANOTHER MIRACLE! DO THAT TRICK WITH THE BREAD AGAIN!

YOUR ANCESTORS ATE *MANNA,* WHEN THEY ESCAPED FROM EGYPT – BUT IN THE END DIED, AS ALL PEOPLE DO.

I AM THE *LIVING* BREAD. THE BREAD I WILL GIVE YOU IS MY *FLESH.* WHOEVER EATS MY FLESH AND DRINKS MY BLOOD WILL NOT DIE, BUT LIVE FOR EVER.

THIS IS TOO DEMANDING, TOO DIFFICULT!

MIRACLES OR NO MIRACLES, YOU WON'T CATCH *ME* DOING A THING LIKE THAT!

I CAN'T FOLLOW HIM ANY LONGER – EVEN IF HE CAN PERFORM MIRACLES.

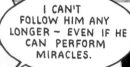

AND WHAT OF YOU *TWELVE?* WILL YOU REJECT ME TOO?

LORD, WHO *ELSE* WOULD WE FOLLOW? WE BELIEVE AND KNOW THAT YOU ARE THE HOLY ONE OF GOD.

AND YET, ONE OF YOU IS A *DEVIL* – ONE OF YOU TWELVE WILL SOON BETRAY ME.

THERE WAS ONCE A MAN WHO HAD TWO SONS. THE YOUNGER SAID, 'FATHER, I CAN'T WAIT UNTIL YOU'RE DEAD. GIVE ME MY SHARE OF YOUR PROPERTY *NOW!*'

'AND SO, WHILE THE ELDER SON WORKED HARD FOR HIS FATHER EVERY DAY AS HE'D ALWAYS DONE, THE YOUNGER SON SOLD THE LAND HE HAD INHERITED.

'ALL HE WANTED WAS THE MONEY, AND AS SOON AS HE GOT HIS HANDS ON IT, HE SET OFF FOR THE BIG CITY, WITHOUT A SECOND THOUGHT FOR THE LIFE HE'D LEFT BEHIND...

'AND THERE HE SPENT THE *LOT* ON DRINK, PARTIES, PROSTITUTES AND GAMBLING. HE LIVED FOR THE MOMENT AND MADE MANY NEW FRIENDS.

'BUT IT DIDN'T LAST. THE MONEY RAN OUT, AND HIS NEW "FRIENDS" DROPPED HIM AS QUICKLY AS THEY HAD TAKEN HIM UP.

'HE WAS LEFT WITH NOTHING.

'IN DESPERATION HE TOOK A JOB LOOKING AFTER PIGS, AND WAS FORCED TO EAT THEIR FOOD JUST TO SURVIVE.

WHAT ARE YOU LOOKING AT?

'EVENTUALLY HE CAME TO HIS SENSES AND REALIZED HE HAD TO RETURN HOME.

'HIS FATHER SAW HIM IN THE DISTANCE AND, FULL OF COMPASSION, RAN TO MEET HIM.

FATHER, FORGIVE ME. I AM NO LONGER WORTHY TO BE CALLED YOUR SON. PLEASE TAKE ME BACK – LET ME WORK AS ONE OF YOUR SERVANTS.

NONSENSE! THIS IS A TIME FOR CELEBRATION – LET'S FEAST! I WANT EVERYONE TO KNOW THE GOOD NEWS.

HOW CAN YOU *DO* THIS? HE'S TREATED YOU LIKE A *FOOL*! NOT *ONCE* HAVE YOU HAD A PARTY FOR *ME*, AND I'VE SERVED YOU *FAITHFULLY*!

BUT THE FATHER SAID, 'MY SON, YOU ARE *ALWAYS* WITH ME, AND EVERYTHING I HAVE IS *YOURS*. BUT WE MUST BE GLAD; YOUR BROTHER WAS DEAD, BUT IS ALIVE AGAIN. HE WAS LOST, BUT NOW IS FOUND.'

YOU HAVE READ THE SCRIPTURES. WHAT DO *YOU* THINK THEY SAY?

YOU SEEM VERY *CONFIDENT*, JESUS. SO *TELL* ME, WHAT MUST *I* DO TO INHERIT ETERNAL LIFE?

'LOVE THE LORD YOUR GOD WITH ALL YOUR HEART, SOUL AND MIND, AND LOVE YOUR NEIGHBOUR AS YOURSELF.'

DO THIS AND YOU WILL LIVE.

BUT WHO *IS* MY NEIGHBOUR?

LISTEN. I'LL TELL YOU.

THERE WAS A MAN, A JEW, TRAVELLING ALONE ON THE STEEP AND DANGEROUS ROAD FROM JERUSALEM TO JERICHO.

'SUDDENLY HE WAS SET UPON BY ROBBERS.

'THEY STOLE ALL HE HAD, BEAT HIM VICIOUSLY AND LEFT HIM FOR DEAD.'

'A *PRIEST* HAPPENED TO PASS BY LATER THAT DAY, BUT DID NOTHING TO HELP THE MAN, NOT WANTING TO GET INVOLVED...

'LIKEWISE, A *LEVITE* CAME BY, BUT CROSSED OVER TO THE OTHER SIDE OF THE ROAD, WANTING NOTHING TO DO WITH THE DYING MAN.

'FINALLY, A *SAMARITAN* PASSED. BREAKING ALL TABOOS HE STOPPED TO HELP...

'AND SAVED THE MAN'S LIFE.

'SEEING HOW BADLY THE MAN WAS HURT, HE TOOK HIM TO THE NEAREST TOWN, AND PAID THE PEOPLE THERE TO CARE FOR HIM.'

SO, WHICH OF THE THREE DO YOU THINK WAS THE INJURED MAN'S NEIGHBOUR?

THE ONE WHO HAD MERCY ON HIM.

GO AND DO LIKEWISE.

GIVE US A *SIGN*, JESUS. GIVE US A SIGN FROM *HEAVEN*. SHOW US WHAT YOU CAN DO.

A *SIGN*?

YOU KNOW THAT RED SKY AT NIGHT MEANS GOOD WEATHER, AND YOU KNOW RED SKY IN THE MORNING MEANS BAD WEATHER.

YOU KNOW HOW TO INTERPRET THE APPEARANCE OF THE *SKY* BUT YOU CAN'T INTERPRET THE SIGNS OF THE TIMES YOU LIVE IN.

THE PEOPLE OF TODAY ARE EVIL AND GODLESS. YOU ASK FOR A *MIRACLE*? THE ONLY MIRACLE YOU WILL BE GIVEN IS THE ONE GIVEN TO *JONAH*. HE WAS IN THE BELLY OF THE WHALE THREE DAYS AND EMERGED ALIVE.

BE CAREFUL OF THE PHARISEES AND SADDUCEES, PETER.

BEWARE OF THEIR TEACHINGS.

TELL ME, WHO DO THE PEOPLE SAY THE SON OF MAN IS?

SOME SAY JOHN THE BAPTIST, THAT HE ESCAPED FROM HEROD.

OTHERS SAY *JEREMIAH.*

OR *ELIJAH*, OR AT THE VERY LEAST ONE OF THE *PROPHETS*, RETURNED TO US.

BUT WHO DO *YOU* SAY I AM?

YOU ARE THE *MESSIAH*, SON OF THE LIVING GOD.

BLESSED ARE YOU, PETER, FOR THIS WAS NOT TAUGHT TO YOU BY *MEN*, BUT BY MY FATHER IN HEAVEN.

YOU WILL BE A ROCK - A ROCK ON WHICH I WILL BUILD MY *CHURCH*. NOT EVEN THE GATES OF *HELL* WILL OVERCOME IT.

I WILL GIVE YOU THE KEYS TO THE KINGDOM OF HEAVEN.

YOU MUST NOT TELL ANYONE WHO I REALLY AM. THERE ARE TERRIBLE TIMES AHEAD. I WILL SUFFER MANY THINGS AT THE HANDS OF THE ELDERS AND CHIEF PRIESTS IN JERUSALEM. I MUST DIE BUT ON THE THIRD DAY I WILL BE RAISED BACK TO LIFE.

NEVER, LORD! THIS CAN'T HAPPEN TO *YOU*.

WE'LL *STOP* THEM SOMEHOW, WE'LL FIND A WAY TO -

ENOUGH!

SUCH TALK IS NOT FROM GOD, BUT THE *DEVIL*!

ANYONE WHO WANTS TO COME WITH ME, MUST FORGET HIS OWN LIFE, TAKE UP HIS *CROSS* AND FOLLOW *ME*.

WHOEVER WANTS TO SAVE HIS OWN LIFE, WILL *SURELY* LOSE IT, BUT WHOEVER LOSES HIS LIFE FOR *MY* SAKE, WILL FIND IT.

WHAT GOOD IS IT IF A MAN WINS THE WHOLE *WORLD*, BUT FORFEITS HIS SOUL?

THE SON OF MAN IS ABOUT TO ENTER HIS FATHER'S GLORY. SOME OF YOU STANDING HERE WILL NOT *DIE* BEFORE SEEING THE COMING OF THE KINGDOM OF GOD.

206

SOME DAYS LATER, JESUS TOOK PETER, JAMES AND JOHN, AND LED THEM UP A NEARBY MOUNTAIN.

ON THE SUMMIT, JESUS BEGAN TO PRAY.

HIS THREE COMPANIONS, EXHAUSTED BY THE CLIMB, HAD OTHER IDEAS.

BUT AS JESUS PRAYED, AN INCREDIBLE **CHANGE** CAME OVER HIM... ONE THE DISCIPLES COULDN'T HELP BUT NOTICE.

... MASTER?

JESUS STOOD BEFORE THEM, HIS FACE SHINING LIKE THE **SUN**, HIS CLOTHES AS BRIGHT AS DAYLIGHT! IT HURT THEIR EYES EVEN TO **LOOK** AT HIM.

ON ONE SIDE OF JESUS STOOD MOSES AND ON THE OTHER THE PROPHET ELIJAH.

THE THREE FIGURES TALKED ABOUT THE WAY THAT GOD WOULD SOON FULFIL HIS PLAN, THROUGH JESUS' DEATH IN JERUSALEM.

MASTER! WHAT CAN I DO? LET ME MAKE THREE SHELTERS, ONE FOR EACH OF YOU!

PETER DIDN'T KNOW WHAT HE WAS SAYING, HE WAS SO OVERCOME WITH SHEER WONDER.

JUST THEN A CLOUD COVERED THE MOUNTAIN, AND A VOICE CAME FROM IT, SAYING:

THIS IS MY **SON** WHOM I LOVE. **LISTEN** TO HIM!

THE DISCIPLES FOLLOWED JESUS BACK DOWN THE MOUNTAIN IN SILENCE.

THEY HAD WITNESSED SOMETHING OF SUCH **ENORMITY**, THAT IT WOULD BE A LONG WHILE BEFORE THEY COULD FIND THE WORDS TO EVEN **BEGIN** TO DESCRIBE IT.

MARY AND MARTHA WERE TWO SISTERS WHO LIVED IN THE TOWN OF BETHANY.

THEIR BROTHER LAZARUS, A CLOSE FRIEND OF JESUS, BECAME CRITICALLY ILL.

THEY SENT WORD TO JESUS. BUT NO REPLY CAME, AND LAZARUS DIED.

PETER, TELL THE OTHERS WE'RE GOING TO BETHANY.

BETHANY? WE WERE DRIVEN OUT OF THERE WITH STONES LAST TIME. ARE YOU SURE?

OUR FRIEND LAZARUS HAS FALLEN ASLEEP, BUT I'M GOING THERE TO WAKE HIM UP SO THAT YOU MAY SEE THE POWER OF GOD.

BUT MASTER, IF HE'S UNWELL THE REST WILL DO HIM GOOD. ISN'T IT BETTER TO LET HIM SLEEP?

I WASN'T SPEAKING LITERALLY, PETER.

HE'S DEAD.

MARTHA –

OH LORD, IF ONLY YOU'D GOT HERE SOONER, YOU'RE A BUSY MAN I KNOW, AND WE ARE GRATEFUL, BUT–

OH I KNOW THAT. ON THE LAST DAY ALL THE DEAD WILL RISE AGAIN.

YOUR BROTHER WILL RISE AGAIN.

I AM THE RESURRECTION, AND THE LIFE. WHOEVER BELIEVES IN ME WILL LIVE EVEN THOUGH THEY DIE.

DO YOU BELIEVE THIS, MARTHA?

MARY! THE TEACHER IS HERE, AND IS ASKING FOR YOU.

MARTHA –

HE HUNG ON TO THE LAST. I TOLD HIM YOU'D COME, BUT HE JUST COULDN'T WAIT...

MARTHA!

YES, LORD – YOU ARE THE CHRIST, THE SON OF GOD.

AND SLOWLY...

FROM THE MURKY DARKNESS OF THE TOMB...

THE DEAD MAN APPEARED.

YOU WERE *DEAD*, BROTHER.

WHAT HAPPENED?

DEAD? AND NOW I AM ALIVE?!

WHAT TRICKERY IS THIS?

BUT I SAW IT MYSELF. THE MAN WAS DEAD AND BURIED!

TAKE OFF HIS GRAVE CLOTHES AND SET HIM FREE!

WE CAN'T LET HIM CONTINUE LIKE THIS. AT THIS RATE THE WHOLE NATION WILL FOLLOW HIM, NOT *US*. WE MUST HANG ON TO WHAT LITTLE POWER THE ROMANS HAVE LEFT US.

JESUS MUST BE STOPPED. AND *SOON*.

THE RAISING OF LAZARUS LED MANY JEWS TO PUT THEIR FAITH IN JESUS. FROM THAT MOMENT ON, THE CHIEF PRIESTS IN JERUSALEM MADE PLANS TO HAVE JESUS KILLED.

AND NOT JUST JESUS, BUT LAZARUS TOO — A WALKING REMINDER OF JESUS' POWER.

ALTHOUGH JESUS KNEW ALL OF THIS, HE LED HIS DISCIPLES TO THE CITY OF **JERUSALEM**.

IT WAS THE TIME OF THE PASSOVER.

YOU TWO, GO TO THE VILLAGE AHEAD. YOU'LL FIND A DONKEY THERE THAT HAS NEVER BEEN RIDDEN. BRING HIM TO ME.

AND SO THE DISCIPLES DID AS HE SAID, TELLING THE OWNER, 'THE MASTER NEEDS HIM,' JUST AS JESUS HAD TOLD THEM.

CENTURIES BEFORE, THE PROPHET ZECHARIAH HAD FORETOLD THESE EVENTS:

'REJOICE, YOU PEOPLE OF JERUSALEM.

'LOOK, YOUR KING HAS COME TO YOU! HE COMES VICTORIOUS, BUT ALSO HUMBLE, RIDING A YOUNG DONKEY.

'HE WILL MAKE **PEACE** BETWEEN THE NATIONS AND RULE FROM SEA TO SEA TO THE ENDS OF THE EARTH.'

THE GREAT CROWD THAT HAD COME TO JERUSALEM FOR THE PASSOVER HEARD THAT JESUS WAS COMING. AS HE ENTERED THE CITY, SHOUTS AND CHEERS FILLED THE AIR: '**HOSANNA! THE PROMISED KING HAS COME!** BLESSED IS HE WHO COMES IN THE NAME OF THE LORD.'

PEOPLE TOOK OFF THEIR CLOAKS AND LAID THEM IN JESUS' PATH. OTHERS LAID PALM LEAVES ON THE GROUND IN FRONT OF HIM.

IT WAS AS IF KING DAVID HIMSELF HAD RETURNED, TO RESTORE ISRAEL TO ITS FORMER GLORY.

WITH ALMOST EVERY PAIR OF EYES AND EARS IN JERUSALEM WAITING TO SEE WHAT HE WOULD DO NEXT, JESUS WENT STRAIGHT TO THE TEMPLE'S OUTER COURT.

HE'S A SCRAWNY THING, I'LL GIVE YOU TEN FOR HIM.

TEN? YOU *INSULT* ME! FIFTEEN, OR NOTHING!

FIFTEEN? ARE YOU *MAD*? WE'LL PAY NO MORE THAN ELEVEN, AND THAT'S GENEROUS.

I NEED TO BORROW MORE MONEY.

THE INTEREST WILL GO UP, YOU KNOW.

MY HOUSE SHOULD BE A HOUSE OF PRAYER FOR ALL NATIONS...

BUT YOU HAVE MADE IT INTO A DEN OF THIEVES!

JESUS THREW OUT ALL THE MONEY-CHANGERS AND STALL-HOLDERS — TO THE HORROR OF THE PRIESTS, WHO THRIVED ON THE TRADE.

DO YOU HEAR THE *NOISE* OUTSIDE? THERE ARE *CHILDREN* SHOUTING '*HOSANNA TO THE SON OF DAVID.*'

FROM THE MOUTHS OF CHILDREN, GOD RECEIVES PRAISE.

THAT'S IT! HE'S GONE TOO FAR THIS TIME!

I DON'T KNOW. JUST *WHO* DOES HE THINK HE IS? ENOUGH IS ENOUGH!

THE HOUR HAS COME FOR THE SON OF MAN TO BE GLORIFIED.

UNLESS AN EAR OF WHEAT FALLS TO THE GROUND AND DIES, IT REMAINS JUST A SINGLE SEED. BUT IF IT DIES, IT PRODUCES MANY SEEDS.

DO NOT LET YOURSELVES BE TROUBLED. I AM GOING ON AHEAD OF YOU TO PREPARE A PLACE FOR YOU. IN MY FATHER'S HOUSE THERE ARE MANY ROOMS.

I AM THE WAY, THE TRUTH AND THE LIFE. NO ONE COMES TO THE FATHER, EXCEPT THROUGH ME. IF YOU LOVE ME, YOU WILL DO WHAT I ASK OF YOU AND I WILL ASK THE FATHER TO SEND YOU A GUIDE WHO WILL BE WITH YOU *FOR EVER* - THE SPIRIT OF TRUTH.

I WILL BE GOING AWAY SOON. THE WORLD MUST SEE THAT I LOVE THE FATHER, AND THAT I WILL DO EXACTLY WHAT MY FATHER ASKS OF ME.

WHILE JESUS WAS SPEAKING ONE OF THE DISCIPLES SNEAKED AWAY...

JUDAS ISCARIOT RAN AS FAST AS HE COULD TO THE CHIEF PRIEST.

SO YOU'VE COME TO YOUR *SENSES* THEN. ARE YOU PREPARED TO TELL US WHERE WE CAN *FIND* HIM?

I WILL. BUT THIS INFORMATION HAS A PRICE.

BUT OF COURSE.

THIRTY PIECES OF SILVER SHOULD BE ENOUGH, I'D SAY. *ENJOY* IT - YOU'VE *EARNED* IT.

BUT THE MONEY WAS TO BRING JUDAS NO PLEASURE. NO PLEASURE AT ALL.

IT WAS JUST BEFORE THE **PASSOVER** FEAST.

JESUS KNEW HIS TIME ON EARTH WAS COMING TO AN END AND THAT HE WOULD SOON RETURN TO HIS FATHER.

IT WAS NOW TIME FOR HIM TO **SHOW** HIS DISCIPLES JUST HOW MUCH HE LOVED THEM.

YOU KNOW THE COMMANDMENTS GIVEN TO MOSES. TODAY I GIVE YOU A **NEW** COMMANDMENT: LOVE ONE ANOTHER AS **I** HAVE LOVED **YOU**. EVERYONE WILL KNOW THAT YOU ARE MY DISCIPLES IF YOU LOVE ONE ANOTHER.

TAKE OFF YOUR SANDALS, AND **WATCH**.

LORD, PLEASE **DON'T** DO THIS! THERE'S NO **NEED**!

PETER, YOU DON'T SEE IT NOW, BUT LATER YOU WILL UNDERSTAND.

UNLESS YOU ALLOW ME TO WASH YOUR FEET, YOU CAN NO LONGER BE MY DISCIPLE.

LORD, IN **THAT** CASE, WASH MY HANDS AND HEAD AS WELL!

YOU ARE ALREADY **CLEAN**.

YOU CALL ME 'TEACHER' AND 'LORD', BUT I HAVE WASHED **YOUR** FEET. IN THE SAME WAY YOU SHOULD WASH EACH **OTHER'S**. I HAVE SET YOU AN EXAMPLE. IT'S ONE YOU SHOULD ALL FOLLOW.

NOW THAT YOU KNOW THESE THINGS, YOU WILL BE BLESSED IF YOU DO THEM.

THIS BREAD –
TAKE AND EAT; THIS
IS MY BODY, GIVEN FOR YOU.
DO THIS IN REMEMBRANCE
OF ME.

TAKE THIS
CUP – DRINK FROM
IT, ALL OF YOU. THIS IS
MY BLOOD, POURED OUT
FOR MANY FOR THE
FORGIVENESS OF SINS.

'I TELL YOU THE TRUTH – I WILL NOT
DRINK THE FRUIT OF THE VINE
AGAIN, UNTIL THE KINGDOM OF
GOD COMES.'

WHEN THEY HAD FINISHED THEIR MEAL, JESUS AND HIS DISCIPLES WENT
OUTSIDE THE CITY WALLS – TO THE MOUNT OF OLIVES – TO PRAY.

SOON YOU WILL ALL RUN AWAY AND LEAVE ME.

IT WAS PROPHESIED, 'GOD WILL KILL THE SHEPHERD, AND THE SHEEP WILL SCATTER.'

NO, LORD! I WON'T LEAVE YOU.

PETER, BEFORE THE COCK CROWS TOMORROW MORNING, YOU WILL DISOWN ME *THREE* TIMES.

NEVER!

TELLING HIS DISCIPLES TO STAY AWAKE AND KEEP WATCH, JESUS WITHDREW TO BE ON HIS OWN. HE WAS FILLED WITH SORROW.

FATHER, I KNOW THAT *EVERYTHING* IS POSSIBLE FOR YOU.

PLEASE, TAKE THIS CUP OF SUFFERING AWAY FROM ME.

YET, NOT WHAT *I* WANT, BUT *YOUR* WILL BE DONE.

ARE YOU ALWAYS SLEEPING? COULDN'T YOU KEEP WATCH FOR ONE HOUR?

OH! WE WERE, ER... JUST ERM...

IT'S TOO LATE NOW. THE HOUR IS HERE.

LOOK. THE SON OF MAN IS BETRAYED INTO THE HANDS OF SINNERS. AND HERE COMES MY BETRAYER.

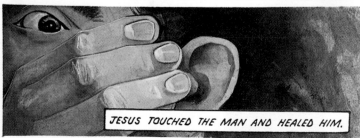

JESUS TOUCHED THE MAN AND HEALED HIM.

WHAT SHOULD WE *DO*, PETER?

I DON'T KNOW. IF WE GET ANY CLOSER, THEY'LL TURN ON *US*.

HEY! AREN'T YOU ONE OF *JESUS'* FRIENDS?

ME? I THINK YOU'VE GOT ME CONFUSED WITH SOMEONE ELSE.

COME ON, LET'S SEE IF WE CAN GET INTO THE COURTYARD. WE MIGHT BE ABLE TO SEE WHAT'S GOING ON.

HEY! THERE'S *ANOTHER* ONE OF HIS FOLLOWERS.

ME? WHAT DO YOU MEAN? *I* DON'T KNOW ANYONE CALLED JESUS. JESUS WHO?

BUT YOUR *ACCENT* — YOU'RE FROM GALILEE.

YOU'RE ONE OF HIS *DISCIPLES* AREN'T YOU? I'VE SEEN YOU WITH HIM!

LOOK, I'M TELLING YOU, I'VE NEVER EVEN *HEARD* OF THE MAN!

WITH THAT THE COCK CROWED.

AND PETER, REALIZING WHAT HE HAD DONE, TURNED AND FLED, TO HIDE HIS BITTER TEARS.

JESUS WAS LED AWAY TO SPEND THE REST OF THE NIGHT IN THE HANDS OF THE TEMPLE GUARDS.

BLASPHEMER!

PROPHESY *NOW*, 'MESSIAH'!

IF YOU'RE A *PROPHET*, TELL US WHO JUST *KICKED* YOU!

AT DAYBREAK, JESUS WAS TAKEN TO THE SEAT OF *REAL* POWER IN ISRAEL...

THE PALACE OF THE ROMAN GOVERNOR, PONTIUS PILATE.

THIS MAN IS GUILTY OF SUBVERTING THE WHOLE *NATION.* HE CLAIMS TO BE KING OF THE JEWS.

I SEE. AND *ARE* YOU? *ARE* YOU THEIR KING?

YOU SAY THAT I AM A KING, BUT MY KINGDOM IS NOT FROM THIS WORLD.

LOOK PILATE, IF HE WERE NOT A CRIMINAL, THEN WE WOULDN'T BE WASTING YOUR TIME.

BUT PILATE COULD FIND NOTHING WRONG WITH HIM.

SO PILATE DECIDED TO LET THE PEOPLE CHOOSE JESUS' FATE. IT WAS A PASSOVER CUSTOM TO RELEASE A CONDEMNED PRISONER.

THE CROWD COULD CHOOSE BETWEEN JESUS OR *BARABBAS* — A MAN CHARGED WITH MURDER FOR HIS PART IN AN UPRISING AGAINST THE ROMANS.

WHO WOULD YOU HAVE ME RELEASE? *BARABBAS*? OR THIS MAN HERE, WHO CLAIMS TO BE YOUR *KING*?

BARABBAS!

BUT WHY? WHAT CRIME HAS HE COMMITTED?

WHAT WOULD YOU HAVE ME *DO* WITH HIM?

CRUCIFY HIM!

CRUCIFY HIM!

CRUCIFY HIM!

CRUCIFY HIM!

CRUCIFY HIM!

CRUCIFY HIM!

THEN I SHALL RELEASE BARABBAS.

I AM INNOCENT OF THIS MAN'S BLOOD. HE IS *YOUR* RESPONSIBILITY.

HAVE HIM FLOGGED AND *CRUCIFY* HIM!

YESSIR.

I HAVE *SINNED*! I HAVE BETRAYED AN INNOCENT MAN! TAKE YOUR MONEY BACK!

BUT *JUDAS*, THAT'S NO CONCERN OF *OURS*. YOU CAME TO *US*, REMEMBER? NO, THE MONEY IS *YOURS*.

JUDAS NEVER LIVED TO ENJOY THE MONEY. HURLING THE THIRTY PIECES OF SILVER INTO THE TEMPLE, HE LEFT THE CITY AND HANGED HIMSELF.

RIGHT THEN. WHO WANTS TO GO *FIRST*?

JUST REMEMBER WE NEED TO LEAVE THIS ONE *ALIVE*. BUT ONLY JUST...

SORRY, YOUR HIGHNESS. THE SCOURGE A LITTLE *HARD* FOR YOUR ROYAL BACK, IS IT?

HERE. WHY DON'T YOU PUT ON THE ROYAL ROBE.

NEVER MIND, YOUR HIGHNESS, YOUR GOD WILL BE ALONG ANY MINUTE. THAT'S WHAT YOU BELIEVE, ISN'T IT?

IF HE'S A *KING* HE NEEDS A *CROWN*! I KNOW...

HAIL KING OF THE JEWS!

WHIPPED, BEATEN, BLEEDING AND COVERED IN SPIT, THE HEIR TO THE THRONE OF DAVID WAS FINALLY CROWNED *KING*. THEN THEY LED HIM AWAY TO CRUCIFY HIM.

THOSE CONDEMNED TO BE CRUCIFIED WERE FORCED TO CARRY THEIR OWN CROSS TO THE PLACE OF CRUCIFIXION.

ALREADY WEAKENED BY BEATINGS, FLOGGINGS AND TORTURE, JESUS COULD SCARCELY *WALK*, LET ALONE CARRY HIS CROSS.

A MAN CALLED SIMON, FROM CYRENE IN NORTH AFRICA, WAS IN THE CROWD. AS JESUS WAS TOO WEAK TO CARRY THE CROSS, THE SOLDIERS FORCED SIMON TO CARRY IT INSTEAD.

IN THIS WAY, WITH SIMON CARRYING THE CROSS AND JESUS STUMBLING ALONGSIDE HIM, THEY MADE THEIR WAY THROUGH THE STREETS UP THE HILL CALLED *GOLGOTHA* – THE PLACE OF THE SKULL.

ALL RIGHT, HOLD STILL.

READY MY SIDE. LET'S DO IT.

TRY NOT TO MOVE.

THE SOLDIERS PUT A SIGN ABOVE HIS HEAD. AND THEN THEY HAULED HIM UPRIGHT.

HERE IS JESUS— KING OF THE JEWS

AND THEY CRUCIFIED HIM.

AS THE LIGHT OF THE WORLD WAS EXTINGUISHED, SO A GREAT DARKNESS FELL OVER THE LAND, SUCH AS HAD NOT BEEN SEEN ON EARTH SINCE CREATION BEGAN.

JOSEPH OF ARIMATHEA, A MEMBER OF THE HIGH COUNCIL, WHO HAD SPOKEN ON JESUS' BEHALF, GAVE HIM HIS OWN TOMB, SAVING JESUS FROM THE MASS GRAVE RESERVED FOR CRIMINALS.

AT SUNRISE ON THE THIRD DAY, MARY MAGDALENE, AND MARY, JAMES' MOTHER, WENT TO THE TOMB WHERE JESUS' BODY HAD BEEN LAID.

THE STONE— IT'S BEEN MOVED!

DO THEY HATE HIM SO MUCH THAT THEY WOULD EVEN DESECRATE HIS GRAVE?

WAIT! ONE OF THEM IS STILL HERE!

BE CAREFUL!

DO NOT BE AFRAID.

YOU ARE LOOKING FOR JESUS, WHO WAS CRUCIFIED. HE IS NOT HERE, BUT HAS RISEN, AS HE SAID HE WOULD.

GO, TELL HIS DISCIPLES HE IS ALIVE AND WILL MEET THEM IN GALILEE.

WHAT'S HAPPENED?

THEY'RE RIGHT, HIS BODY IS GONE.

WHAT CAN IT MEAN?

OH JESUS, WHAT HAVE THEY DONE TO YOU?

...MARY?

MARY, WHY DO YOU LOOK FOR THE LIVING AMONG THE DEAD?

TEACHER!!

DO NOT HOLD ON TO ME, FOR I HAVE NOT YET RETURNED TO MY FATHER.

GO AND TELL THE OTHERS, 'I AM RETURNING TO MY FATHER, WHO IS ALSO *YOUR* FATHER; TO MY GOD AND *YOUR* GOD.'

HE HAD BEEN *DEAD*. THAT WAS WITHOUT QUESTION. SHE HAD *BEEN* THERE AS HE DIED, AND YET HERE HE WAS - ALIVE! *ALIVE!*

MARY RAN AS FAST AS SHE COULD TO TELL THE OTHERS THE *INCREDIBLE* NEWS. *JESUS WAS ALIVE!!*

BUT WHEN THEY HEARD HER SAY THAT JESUS WAS ALIVE AND SHE HAD SEEN HIM THEY DID NOT BELIEVE HER.

WHICH IS WHEN *JESUS* SHOWED UP, IN *PERSON*:

PEACE BE WITH YOU. WHY ARE YOU FRIGHTENED? I *TOLD* YOU WHAT WOULD HAPPEN – THE MESSIAH WOULD BE PUT TO *DEATH*, AND ON THE THIRD DAY RISE *AGAIN*.

WELL DON'T JUST *STAND* THERE. I'D LIKE SOMETHING TO *EAT!*

ALL THE REMAINING DISCIPLES WERE THERE AND *SAW* HIM THAT DAY.

GREETINGS.

AARGGHH!! IT'S A *GHOST*!!!

ALL EXCEPT FOR *THOMAS*, THAT IS...

WELL, *I* DON'T BELIEVE IT.

HE'S *DEAD*, WE ALL *SAW* HIM DIE, AND UNLESS I SEE THE HOLES IN HIS HANDS FOR *MYSELF*, I WON'T BELIEVE A *WORD* OF IT!

THOMAS..!

HERE, FEEL MY HANDS, FEEL THE *HOLES*. FEEL THE SPEAR WOUND IN MY SIDE.

MY *LORD*! MY LORD AND *GOD*!

YOU BELIEVE BECAUSE YOU CAN *SEE* ME. HOW MUCH MORE BLESSED ARE THOSE WHO BELIEVE WITHOUT *EVER* SEEING ME!

JESUS APPEARED TO THE DISCIPLES SEVERAL TIMES OVER THE FOLLOWING DAYS AND WEEKS.

BUT AN ERA HAD COME TO AN END, AND NO ONE SEEMED CERTAIN OF WHAT WOULD HAPPEN NEXT. THIS IN MIND, PETER THOUGHT IT TIME HE PICKED UP HIS LIFE AGAIN.

SO ONE NIGHT PETER AND THE DISCIPLES SET OUT IN THE BOAT TO CATCH FISH — BUT WHEN THE SUN CAME UP, THEIR NETS WERE STILL EMPTY... A FIGURE ON THE SHORE CALLED TO THEM.

FRIENDS, HAVE YOU CAUGHT MANY FISH?

NONE! IT'S AS IF THE SEA IS EMPTY!

THEN WHY NOT CAST YOUR NETS OUT OVER THE RIGHT-HAND SIDE OF THE BOAT? YOU'LL FIND SOME THERE.

TOO TIRED TO ARGUE, THE DISCIPLES DID AS THE MAN SAID. AT ONCE THE NETS BECAME SO FULL OF FISH THAT THEY WERE UNABLE TO HAUL THEM ABOARD.

WHO IS THAT MAN?!

IT'S THE LORD! LOOK! IT'S HIM!

LORD!

PETER, GO BACK AND GET SOME OF THOSE FISH. I'M PREPARING BREAKFAST FOR YOU.

EVERYTHING THE PROPHETS SAID WAS TRUE: 'THE MESSIAH WILL DIE, AND ON THE THIRD DAY RISE FROM THE DEAD.

'IN HIS NAME, FORGIVENESS FOR SINS WILL BE PREACHED TO ALL THE NATIONS ON EARTH, STARTING IN JERUSALEM.'

PETER, DO YOU LOVE ME?

LORD, YOU KNOW I DO. YOU KNOW EVERYTHING.

THEN TAKE CARE OF MY SHEEP FOR ME.

JESUS ASKED PETER THIS QUESTION THREE TIMES. IN THIS WAY JESUS SHOWED PETER HE FORGAVE HIM FOR HIS TRIPLE DENIAL.

PETER'S DAYS AS A FISHERMAN WERE OVER. HE NOW HAD A NEW JOB...

ALL AUTHORITY IN HEAVEN AND EARTH HAS BEEN GIVEN TO *ME*.

GO INTO THE WORLD AND MAKE DISCIPLES FROM ALL NATIONS, BAPTIZING THEM IN THE NAME OF THE FATHER, THE SON, AND THE HOLY SPIRIT.

I AM GOING TO SEND THE ONE MY *FATHER* PROMISED YOU — *THE HOLY SPIRIT*. DO NOT LEAVE JERUSALEM, BUT *WAIT* FOR HIM THERE.

YOU WILL RECEIVE *POWER* WHEN THE HOLY SPIRIT COMES, AND YOU WILL BE MY WITNESSES IN JERUSALEM, JUDEA, AND TO THE ENDS OF THE EARTH! YOUR WORK IS ONLY *BEGINNING*!

AND AS HE STOOD THERE BLESSING THEM, HE WAS TAKEN *UP*, BEFORE THEIR EYES...

UP INTO *HEAVEN*.

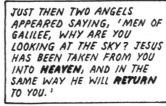

JUST THEN TWO ANGELS APPEARED SAYING, 'MEN OF GALILEE, WHY ARE YOU LOOKING AT THE SKY? JESUS HAS BEEN TAKEN FROM YOU INTO *HEAVEN*, AND IN THE SAME WAY HE WILL *RETURN* TO YOU.'

AND SO THEY RETURNED TO *JERUSALEM*.

AND THERE THEY WAITED...

THE DISCIPLES CONTINUED TO MEET TOGETHER, AND SHARE MEALS, AS THEY HAD DONE WHEN JESUS WAS WITH THEM.

SUDDENLY ONE DAY THERE WAS THE SOUND OF A GREAT AND VIOLENT **WIND.** THE DISCIPLES SAW WHAT LOOKED LIKE TONGUES OF **FIRE** REACH OUT AND TOUCH THEM.

INSTANTLY, THEY WERE ALL FILLED WITH THE **HOLY SPIRIT.**

THEY BEGAN TO PRAISE GOD USING OTHER **LANGUAGES.**

SOON A CROWD OF VISITING JEWS GATHERED, AMAZED TO HEAR THEIR OWN TONGUE SPOKEN SO FAR FROM HOME.

I DIDN'T KNOW YOU UNDERSTOOD LATIN.

THESE PEOPLE ARE **LOCALS.** WHEREVER DID THEY LEARN **OUR** LANGUAGE?

WELL AT LEAST THE LOCAL **WINE** IS GOOD! THIS CROWD MUST HAVE HAD A DOZEN BOTTLES EACH! JUST **LOOK** AT THEM!

THESE MEN ARE NOT **DRUNK!** IT'S ONLY NINE IN THE MORNING! THIS IS HAPPENING JUST AS THE PROPHETS **SAID** IT WOULD!

JESUS OF NAZARETH WAS A MAN USED BY GOD TO DO **MIRACLES** AMONG US! HE WAS PUT TO **DEATH** ON A CROSS, BUT HE ROSE AGAIN! DEATH CANNOT **HOLD** HIM!

I WAS ONE WHO SHOUTED FOR JESUS' DEATH. AND YET I **KNOW** THIS MAN IS TELLING THE TRUTH.

BUT HOW CAN WE EVER PUT THINGS RIGHT AGAIN?

REPENT. APOLOGIZE TO GOD, AND BE **BAPTIZED** IN THE NAME OF JESUS CHRIST AS A SIGN OF GOD'S FORGIVENESS.

AND SO IT BEGAN...

ABOUT 3,000 PEOPLE WERE BAPTIZED ON THAT ONE DAY ALONE. JOINING THE APOSTLES IN THEIR LIFE OF PRAYER, BREAKING BREAD TOGETHER, THEY OPENED THEIR HOMES TO EACH OTHER.

ORDINARY MEN AND WOMEN, COMPLETE STRANGERS, SOLD THEIR POSSESSIONS TO HELP OTHERS IN NEED. EVERY DAY, GOD ADDED MORE TO THEIR NUMBER.

ONE DAY, PETER AND JOHN WENT UP TO THE TEMPLE TO PRAY, AS WAS USUAL.

ANY SPARE CHANGE? CRIPPLED FROM BIRTH, ANY SPARE CHANGE?

I HAVE NO SILVER **OR** GOLD. BUT WHAT I **DO** HAVE, I'LL GLADLY GIVE YOU — AND IT'S THIS:

IN THE NAME OF JESUS CHRIST OF NAZARETH, GET UP AND **WALK.**

I CAN WALK. I CAN **WALK**! FOR THE FIRST TIME IN MY **LIFE**! LOOK, I'M **WALKING**!

WHY DO YOU STARE AS IF IT'S **US** WHO'VE MADE THIS MAN WALK? THE GOD OF **ABRAHAM, ISAAC** AND **JACOB**, THE GOD OF OUR **FATHERS** DID IT, NOT **US**!

MOSES SAID GOD WOULD SEND US ONE FROM OUR OWN PEOPLE, AND HE HAS — **JESUS**. HE DIED BUT LIVES AGAIN AND YOU NEED TO **LISTEN** TO HIM. THROUGH HIM **ALL** PEOPLE ON EARTH WILL BE BLESSED BY GOD!

GUARDS? HAVE THESE BLASPHEMERS THROWN IN JAIL.

THESE ARE DANGEROUS LIES. THIS BLASPHEMY MUST BE STOPPED.

WE CANNOT KEEP QUIET ABOUT THIS AND OBEY GOD.

JOHN IS RIGHT! WE HAVE NO CHOICE BUT TO TELL THE TRUTH!

EVEN THE PRIESTS COULD NOT DENY THAT A MIRACLE HAD OCCURRED, SO PETER AND JOHN WERE RELEASED, FOR THE TIME BEING AT LEAST...

THE NUMBER OF BELIEVERS CONTINUED TO GROW SO FAST THAT THE DISCIPLES SOON APPOINTED ANOTHER SEVEN LEADERS TO CARE FOR THE WIDOWS AND THOSE IN NEED.

ONE OF THESE WAS STEPHEN, A MAN OF GREAT FAITH.

STEPHEN, IT'S ONE THING TO GO AROUND DISTRIBUTING FOOD, BUT THESE MEN SAY YOU ARE GUILTY OF BLASPHEMY. IS THIS TRUE?

THROUGHOUT HISTORY, WE HAVE IGNORED GOD'S MESSENGERS. WE HAVE MURDERED THOSE WHO PREDICTED THE COMING OF THE MESSIAH, AND NOW WE HAVE KILLED HIM AS WELL!

I TELL YOU, I CAN SEE HEAVEN FROM HERE! AND I SEE JESUS STANDING AT GOD'S RIGHT HAND!

ENOUGH!! WILL THIS BLASPHEMY NEVER END!?

TAKE HIM! STONE HIM! HAVE HIM STONED TO DEATH!

DO NOT HOLD THIS CRIME AGAINST THEM. LORD JESUS RECEIVE MY SPIRIT.

HE'S DEAD.

GOOD. IT'S WHAT HE DESERVES.

MANY PERSECUTED THE NEW BELIEVERS, BUT THE MOST RUTHLESS WAS A MAN CALLED SAUL, FROM TARSUS.

SEARCHING JERUSALEM HOUSE TO HOUSE, SAUL HAD THE BELIEVERS DRAGGED THROUGH THE STREETS TO PRISON, AND ALTHOUGH THE JAILS WERE SOON FULL, SAUL WAS STILL NOT SATISFIED.

WITH THE RULING COUNCIL'S PERMISSION, HE SET OFF TO NEIGHBOURING **DAMASCUS**, TO ARREST THE FOLLOWERS OF JESUS LIVING THERE.

THE JOURNEY WAS TO BE THE MOST IMPORTANT OF HIS LIFE.

HURRY IT UP. THE LONGER WE DELAY, THE MORE CHANCE BLASPHEMY HAS TO BREED. *FASTER!*

SAUL!

SAUL, WHY DO YOU PERSECUTE ME?

WHO **ARE** YOU, LORD?

I AM *JESUS!* YOU ARE PERSECUTING *ME*, SAUL, BY ATTACKING MY FOLLOWERS!

GET UP AND GO TO THE CITY. I WILL *TELL* YOU *THERE* WHAT YOU MUST DO!

WHERE DID THAT VOICE COME FROM?

I, I CAN'T... WHAT... I... SOMEONE TAKE MY HAND. *I'M BLIND!*

SAUL SAT ON HIS OWN, IN DARKNESS, FOR THREE DAYS, REFUSING FOOD AND DRINK.

EVERYTHING HE HAD HELD TO BE TRUE, HIS WHOLE LIFE LONG, HAD BEEN SHATTERED. JESUS WAS **ALIVE**, AND SPEAKING WITH THE VOICE OF **GOD**.

IN ATTACKING THE DISCIPLES, SAUL HAD ATTACKED... GOD?

THERE LIVED IN DAMASCUS A MAN CALLED **ANANIAS**, AND GOD TOLD HIM TO FIND SAUL AND HEAL HIM.

ANANIAS WAS NOT **STUPID**. HE KNEW OF SAUL'S REPUTATION, AND WHY HE HAD COME TO DAMASCUS IN THE FIRST PLACE. BUT HE WENT ANYWAY.

GOD HAD CHOSEN SAUL, OF ALL PEOPLE, TO CARRY THE MESSAGE OF JESUS TO THE OUTSIDE WORLD, AND ANANIAS HAD THE JOB OF BREAKING THE NEWS TO HIM.

BROTHER SAUL, THE LORD *JESUS*, WHO YOU HAVE NOW MET, HAS SENT ME SO YOU MIGHT *SEE* AGAIN, AND BE FILLED WITH THE HOLY SPIRIT.

I REALLY *DO* HOPE THIS ISN'T A TRAP!

MY *EYES*. I CAN *SEE YOU*. THANK YOU, MY... FRIEND.

FROM THAT DAY ON SAUL BECAME A FANATICAL FOLLOWER OF JESUS. HIS NEXT STOP WAS THE LOCAL SYNAGOGUE...

FELLOW JEWS, *LISTEN* TO ME! AS YOU ARE NO DOUBT AWARE, I CAME HERE TO ARREST THOSE WHO SAY JESUS IS THE SON OF *GOD*.

INCREDIBLE AS IT MAY SEEM, I HAVE TO TELL YOU THEY ARE *RIGHT*! EVERYTHING THEY HAVE SAID ABOUT HIM IS *TRUE*! THE MESSIAH HAS COME, AND HAS RISEN FROM THE GRAVE!

HAS THE STRAIN DRIVEN HIM *MAD*?! HE WAS SUPPOSED TO ARREST THESE PEOPLE, NOT *JOIN* THEM!

WHILE DAMASCUS AND JERUSALEM SHOOK WITH NEWS OF SAUL'S CHANGE OF HEART, PETER TRAVELLED TO THE PORT OF *JOPPA*.

PETER STAYED AT THE HOUSE OF SIMON, HEALING THE SICK AND RAISING THE DEAD. A GREAT MANY PEOPLE CAME TO BELIEVE IN JESUS AS A RESULT.

ABOUT NOON ONE DAY PETER WENT UP ON TO THE ROOF TO PRAY. AS HE STOOD THERE A PICTURE CAME INTO HIS MIND.

HE SAW EVERY TYPE OF FOOD FORBIDDEN TO JEWS, AND HE HEARD A VOICE TELLING HIM TO EAT IT, SAYING 'NOTHING GOD HAS MADE CLEAN IS UNCLEAN.'

PETER WAS TROUBLED BY THE VISION. WAS GOD TELLING HIM THE JEWISH FOOD LAWS WERE WRONG? OR WAS THERE SOME *DEEPER* MEANING?

WHILE STILL PUZZLING OVER THIS, PETER RECEIVED A VISITOR...

SIMON PETER? WE HAVE BEEN SENT BY *CORNELIUS*, THE CENTURION IN CAESAREA. YESTERDAY AN *ANGEL* APPEARED TO HIM AND TOLD HIM TO BRING YOU TO HIS HOUSE.

THERE ARE MANY PEOPLE *EAGER* TO HEAR WHAT YOU HAVE TO SAY.

I SEE. VERY WELL, ROMAN. LEAD THE WAY.

PLEASE, PLEASE, *STAND UP*. I'M ONLY A *MAN*, THERE'S REALLY NO NEED TO *KNEEL*! NOW THEN, WHAT IS IT YOU WISHED TO SEE ME ABOUT?

SIR, THANK YOU FOR COMING, I —

YOU DO **KNOW** THAT IT IS AGAINST JEWISH LAW FOR ME TO ASSOCIATE WITH GENTILES, OR EVEN **VISIT** THEM?

...NOW I SEE WHAT THE VISION MEANS: **NOTHING** GOD MAKES CLEAN IS UNCLEAN. GOD HAS NO FAVOURITES, BUT WILL ACCEPT **ANYONE** WHO BELIEVES IN HIM.

I DO. BUT I WAS PRAYING WHEN AN **ANGEL** TOLD ME TO SEND FOR YOU. ALL THESE PEOPLE ARE DESPERATE TO HEAR WHAT YOU HAVE TO SAY THAT IS SO IMPORTANT.

I KNOW YOU HAVE HEARD WHAT'S BEEN HAPPENING IN JUDEA, AND OF JESUS OF NAZARETH. **EVERYONE** WHO BELIEVES IN HIM RECEIVES FORGIVENESS OF SINS — AND THAT INCLUDES YOU. YOU MUST BE BAPTIZED TOO!

IT WAS JUST AS BEFORE: GOD SENT HIS HOLY SPIRIT, AND PEOPLE SPOKE IN OTHER LANGUAGES. BUT **THIS** TIME, IT WAS NOT **JEWS** WHO RECEIVED GOD'S SPECIAL GIFT, BUT GENTILES!

PETER DECIDED TO RETURN TO JERUSALEM TO LET THE JEWISH CHURCH KNOW HIS ASTOUNDING NEWS.

THERE KING HEROD AGRIPPA WAS TRYING TO MAKE HIMSELF POPULAR WITH JEWISH LEADERS BY JOINING THE PERSECUTION.

JAMES, ONE OF THE DISCIPLES, WAS PUT TO THE **SWORD** AT HEROD'S REQUEST. NOW ONLY **TEN** OF THE TWELVE DISCIPLES REMAINED.

PETER WAS HAULED BACK TO JAIL TO AWAIT TRIAL AND ALMOST CERTAIN EXECUTION.

LORD GOD, THERE IS STILL SO MUCH WORK TO BE DONE. SAVE ME FROM THIS, SO I CAN CARRY THE NAME OF **JESUS** TO THE WORLD.

I KNOW **NOTHING** IS IMPOSSIBLE FOR YOU.

HUH? WHAT'S THAT NOISE? IT SOUNDS LIKE...

WITHOUT EVEN PAUSING TO OPEN THE DOOR THE GIRL RUSHED TO TELL THE OTHERS THE AMAZING NEWS.

238

THE CHURCH IN **ANTIOCH** HAD MANY PROPHETS AND TEACHERS.

AS THE COMMUNITY PRAYED ONE DAY THE HOLY SPIRIT SPOKE, SAYING 'SET APART **SAUL** AND **BARNABAS** FOR THE WORK I HAVE CHOSEN FOR THEM.'

AND SO IT WAS THAT SAUL AND BARNABAS SET OFF TO TAKE NEWS OF JESUS TO THE GENTILES. THEIR FIRST STOP WAS THE ISLAND OF CYPRUS.

TRAVELLING ACROSS THE ISLAND, THEY EVENTUALLY MADE THEIR WAY TO THE TOWN OF PAPHOS, AND THE COURT OF THE ROMAN PROCONSUL, SERGIUS PAULUS.

THE PROCONSUL HAD AN ATTENDANT – **BAR-JESUS** – WHO WAS A SORCERER AND A FALSE PROPHET. SERGIUS HAD A KEEN AND CURIOUS MIND, AND WISHED TO HEAR WHAT THE TRAVELLERS HAD TO SAY.

GREETINGS, IN THE NAME OF OUR RISEN LORD, JESUS CHRIST.

PROCONSUL, DON'T LISTEN TO THESE **LIES**! THESE MEN ARE NOT ONLY **HERETICS**, BUT **FRAUDS**! SHOW ME ONE PIECE OF EVIDENCE THAT PROVES THIS JESUS CAME BACK FROM THE DEAD!

YOU WANT PROOF? YOUR 'POWERS' ARE CONJURING TRICKS AND NOTHING MORE. YOU HAVE NO REAL POWER, NO REAL AUTHORITY.

YOU ARE A CHILD OF THE **DEVIL**! YOU PERVERT ANYTHING THAT IS GOOD AND TRUE.

GOD IS **AGAINST** YOU! IT WILL BE A LONG TIME BEFORE YOU SEE THE SUN AGAIN!

I'M BLIND! SOMEONE HELP ME!

SORRY ABOUT THAT, PROCONSUL. NOW, AS I WAS SAYING ...

SERGIUS BELIEVED FROM THAT MOMENT ON.

LEAVING SERGIUS, THEY MADE THEIR WAY AROUND THE TOWNS OF THE EASTERN MEDITERRANEAN.

IT WAS AT THIS TIME THAT SAUL TOOK THE NAME **PAUL**, THE GENTILE VERSION OF HIS NAME.

AMONG THE TOWNS THEY VISITED TO TELL PEOPLE ABOUT JESUS WAS LYSTRA.

SIR? CAN YOU HELP ME, SIR?

YOU SEE, I HAVE NEVER BEEN ABLE TO *WALK*, AND I COULDN'T HELP BUT HEAR YOU SAY THIS JESUS CAN MAKE LAME PEOPLE WALK AGAIN.

YOUR *FAITH* HAS MADE YOU ASK THIS. AND YOUR FAITH WILL *SAVE* YOU.

STAND UP!

LOOK! LOOK AT *THIS*!

I CAN *WALK*!

LOOK AT ME! HE MADE ME *WALK*! I CAN *WALK*!

THIS IS A MIRACLE! SURELY THE *GODS* HAVE COME TO VISIT US!

YOU ARE SURELY *HERMES*, MESSENGER OF ZEUS, FOR YOU BRING ZEUS'S POWER!

YES! AND YOUR FRIEND MUST BE MIGHTY ZEUS HIMSELF!

NO! NO! NO! PLEASE *STOP* THIS!

HERE! ACCEPT OUR SACRIFICE OF THIS BULL, MIGHTY HERMES!

WHAT? ARE YOU *MAD*?

AHH! YOU MEAN IT'S NOT *BIG* ENOUGH? *QUICK* - FETCH MORE!! *BIGGER* ONES!

moo?

PLEASE JUST *LISTEN* TO US! WE ARE *NOT* GODS! I AM PAUL, A *JEW*. I MAKE *TENTS* FOR A LIVING!

AND MY FRIEND BARNABAS IS MOST DEFINITELY *NOT* ZEUS! BELIEVE ME!

YOU HAVE LIVED YOUR LIVES WORSHIPPING EMPTY, WORTHLESS *THINGS*. BUT WE BRING NEWS OF THE *LIVING* GOD, WHO MADE HEAVEN AND EARTH!

IT'S NO USE, PAUL. THEY'RE TOO SET IN THEIR WAYS.

ENEMIES OF PAUL AND BARNABAS SOON STIRRED UP TROUBLE FOR THEM IN LYSTRA. PAUL WAS DRAGGED OUT OF THE CITY, STONED AND LEFT FOR DEAD.

BUT GOD WAS WITH PAUL. THE NEXT DAY PAUL AND BARNABAS WERE ABLE TO LEAVE LYSTRA. THEY WERE NEEDED IN JERUSALEM.

THE BELIEVERS THERE WERE DISCUSSING ISSUES THAT WOULD HAVE A BEARING ON PAUL'S JOURNEYS. PAUL TOLD OF THE MANY CHURCHES NOW GROWING WITHIN THE ROMAN EMPIRE.

IF THE GENTILES ARE TO JOIN US JEWS, THEN THE LAW OF MOSES CLEARLY STATES THEY *MUST* BE *CIRCUMCISED*!

PETER, YOU *CANNOT* DENY THIS!

GOD HAS ACCEPTED THESE PEOPLE BECAUSE OF THEIR *FAITH*. SO WHY SHOULD WE BIND THEM WITH RITUAL, WHEN GOD HAS ALREADY MADE THEM *FREE*?

IT IS THROUGH OUR LORD, *JESUS CHRIST*, THAT WE ARE SAVED. WHAT DO YOU SAY, *JAMES*?

THE PROPHETS SAW THIS DAY COMING. THEY KNEW GOD WOULD USE GENTILES TO CARRY HIS NAME OUT INTO THE WORLD.

IF GOD HAS MADE A WAY FOR THEM TO COME TO HIM, LET *US* NOT MAKE IT HARDER FOR THEM!

PAUL MADE SEVERAL JOURNEYS AROUND THE MEDITERRANEAN.

ON HIS SECOND JOURNEY SILAS JOINED HIM TO HELP AND AS PAUL SPOKE, PEOPLE *BELIEVED*, AND SMALL COMMUNITIES OF BELIEVERS GREW INTO *CHURCHES*.

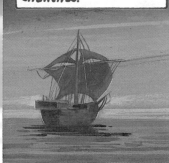

ONE SUCH PLACE WAS *PHILIPPI*, IN NORTHERN GREECE.

PAUL MET WITH A WOMAN CALLED *LYDIA*, A DEALER IN CLOTH. AS HE SPOKE, LYDIA'S HEART BECAME OPEN TO GOD, AND SOON SHE, AND HER ENTIRE HOUSEHOLD, WERE BAPTIZED AS FOLLOWERS OF CHRIST.

BUT NOT ALL CONVERSIONS WERE TO BE SO STRAIGHTFORWARD...

IT'S THAT SLAVE-GIRL AGAIN. SHE'S POSSESSED BY A SPIRIT THAT TELLS THE FUTURE.

TELLING THESE PEOPLE H HOW TO BE SAVED. GOD, TELLING YOU H THESE PEOPLE ARE: TO BE SAV

REETINGS. I —

YES. I COME TO —

LOOK!, I —

SPIRIT! IN THE NAME OF JESUS CHRIST, I *COMMAND* YOU TO LEAVE THIS WOMAN *AT ONCE*!

..?

THAT'S BETTER. WE CAN HEAR OURSELVES *THINK*.

HER MIND IS HER OWN AGAIN. SHE'S *FREE* NOW.

FROM THE *SPIRIT* PERHAPS, BUT I DON'T KNOW WHAT HER *OWNER* WILL SAY ABOUT IT! HE MADE A LOT OF MONEY FROM HER FORTUNE TELLING.

THESE JEWS ARE CAUSING *CHAOS* WHEREVER THEY GO! THEY'RE GOING AGAINST ROMAN LAW!

YOU'RE JUST ANGRY BECAUSE YOU'VE LOST YOUR MONEY-MAKING SCHEME!

THEY'VE *STOLEN* MY LIVELIHOOD! CALL THE GUARDS! WE ARE *ROMAN CITIZENS*! WE NEED PROTECTION FROM THEM!

PRISON AGAIN. NOW WHAT?

WE SHOULD *SING*, SILAS. SING TO OUR GOD AND PRAY. IT WILL HELP PASS THE LONG NIGHT.

NEARLY MIDNIGHT AND STILL SINGING – NOW THEY'RE MAKING *HUMMING* NOISES! THEY *ARE* AS MAD AS PEOPLE SAY.

WAIT A MINUTE... HUMMING??? THAT'S NOT THE PRISONERS – THAT *NOISE*, IT'S...

TAKE *COVER*! IT'S AN *EARTHQUAKE*!

THE PRISONERS! IF THEY'RE NOT DEAD, THEY WILL HAVE ESCAPED...

GREAT MITHRAS, TAKE MY SOUL. I MUST DIE FOR FAILING MY EMPEROR AND GOD, MY CAESAR!

THERE'S REALLY NO *NEED* FOR THAT, YOU KNOW. WE'RE STILL HERE!

SIR! I–I DON'T KNOW WHAT TO *SAY*! YOUR GOD HAS FREED YOU. HOW CAN I HAVE SUCH A GOD ON *MY* SIDE?

BELIEVE IN THE LORD, JESUS CHRIST.

THAT MORNING THE JAILOR AND HIS WHOLE FAMILY WERE BAPTIZED, BECOMING FOLLOWERS OF JESUS. PAUL AND SILAS WAITED THERE, EATING AT THE JAILOR'S TABLE, UNTIL THE MAGISTRATES ARRIVED.

ALL CHARGES AGAINST YOU HAVE BEEN DROPPED. YOU'RE BOTH FREE TO LEAVE... QUIETLY.

WHAT? AFTER YOU'VE GIVEN US A PUBLIC BEATING – WITHOUT *TRIAL* – EVEN THOUGH WE'RE ROMAN CITIZENS? NO. WE WANT A *PUBLIC* APOLOGY.

FEARFUL OF THE CONSEQUENCES, THE ROMAN OFFICIALS APOLOGIZED, RELEASED THE PAIR AND ASKED THEM TO LEAVE THE CITY. AS PAUL AND SILAS WENT FREE FROM PHILIPPI, THEY LEFT BEHIND THEM A SMALL *CHURCH*.

A MERCHANT WOMAN, A ROMAN JAILOR, AND THEIR FAMILIES, WOULD BECOME THE FOUNDERS OF THE CHURCH THAT WOULD GROW AND GROW IN THE TOWN.

PAUL TRAVELLED THROUGHOUT GREECE, MAKING A LIVING FROM HIS SKILLS AS A TENTMAKER. HE PREACHED AND TAUGHT FROM TOWN TO TOWN ESTABLISHING SMALL CHURCHES WHEREVER HE WENT.

HE EVENTUALLY ARRIVED AT THE INTELLECTUAL HEART OF THE GREEK WORLD — *ATHENS* ITSELF.

WELCOME TO THE AREOPAGUS. WE WOULD BE INTERESTED IN HEARING THIS NEW TEACHING OF YOURS, PAUL. IT'S BEEN AGES SINCE WE HAD ANYTHING *NEW* TO AMUSE US.

I HEAR YOU'RE IN FAVOUR OF CERTAIN *FOREIGN* GODS, YET YOU HAVE NO LIKENESSES TO SHOW US. WHY IS THIS?

YOU KNOW, I REALLY DO BELIEVE ATHENS TO BE THE MOST *RELIGIOUS* CITY ON EARTH. I SEE STATUES *EVERYWHERE*. GODS FOR THIS, GODS FOR THAT. I EVEN SAW ONE STATUE ' *TO AN UNKNOWN GOD.*'

WHAT YOU WORSHIP AS UNKNOWN, I WILL NOW *MAKE* KNOWN TO YOU.

THE GOD WHO MADE ALL OF CREATION HAS SET A DAY WHEN HE WILL JUDGE THE WHOLE WORLD THROUGH THE ONE MAN HE HAS CHOSEN — JESUS CHRIST. AND HE HAS GIVEN *PROOF* OF THIS BY RAISING HIM FROM THE DEAD.

AS THE CROWDS LEFT THE AREOPAGUS THERE WAS MUCH DISCUSSION OF PAUL'S WORDS.

MANY OF THE PHILOSOPHERS DERIDED HIM, BUT NOT ALL.

SOME TOOK HIS WORDS TO HEART, AND BELIEVED FROM THAT MOMENT ON.

PAUL LEFT ATHENS KNOWING THAT ANOTHER CHURCH HAD BEGUN TO GROW.

BUT HIS MISSION WAS FAR FROM OVER. PAUL'S TRAVELS TOOK HIM THROUGH CORINTH TO THE CITY OF EPHESUS.

HE TAUGHT THERE FOR SEVERAL MONTHS, BUILDING UP THE FAITH OF THE NEW CHRISTIANS.

THE NEW FAITH TOOK HOLD. PEOPLE TURNED AWAY FROM WORSHIPPING IDOLS AND DESTROYED THEIR GOLD AND SILVER STATUES. PAUL PREACHED OPENLY AGAINST THE IDOLATRY HE SAW EVERYWHERE.

NONE OF WHICH WENT UNNOTICED BY THE WEALTHY BUSINESSMAN **DEMETRIUS**.

HE WAS A **SILVERSMITH** WHO PROFITED FROM MAKING IDOLS, AND THE CHRISTIANS WERE THREATENING HIS **LIVELIHOOD**.

WITHIN A FEW SHORT WEEKS, EPHESUS WAS A CITY IN **RIOT**.

DEMETRIUS USED HIS CONSIDERABLE INFLUENCE TO STIR FEELINGS AGAINST WHAT HE SAW AS A NEW JEWISH SECT. A CULT WHICH THREATENED THEIR RELIGION, THEIR GODS, THEIR VERY **CULTURE**.

ABOVE ALL, IT WAS BAD FOR **BUSINESS**.

LET ME GO AND **SPEAK** WITH THEM! I MAY BE ABLE TO —

— TO GET YOURSELF **LYNCHED**, PAUL? NO, WE'RE STAYING OUT OF THE WAY UNTIL THIS BLOWS OVER!

TIME TO MOVE ON. THINGS WILL SETTLE DOWN ONCE I'VE GONE.

PAUL TRAVELLED THROUGH MACEDONIA AND GREECE, BUT HIS ULTIMATE GOAL WAS JERUSALEM.

HE HAD RECEIVED WORD OF A **PROPHECY**, THAT THERE HE WOULD BE CAPTURED BY THE JEWS AND HANDED TO THE GENTILES.

ALTHOUGH HE WAS **WILLING** TO DIE FOR HIS FAITH IF NEED BE, HE SET SAIL WITH A HEAVY HEART.

THE CHURCH IN JERUSALEM WELCOMED PAUL WITH OPEN ARMS, AND SOON HE JOINED THEM IN PRAYER AND TEACHING. BUT THERE WERE OTHER FACTIONS IN THE TEMPLE WHO WEREN'T SO PLEASED TO SEE HIM.

THERE HE IS! I SAW HIM IN ASIA, SPREADING HIS BLASPHEMIES! AND LOOK! HE'S BROUGHT GREEKS IN HERE WITH HIM!

OUTSIDE! NOW, BLASPHEMER!

WAIT! WILL YOU JUST LISTEN TO ME?! THEY'RE NOT GREEKS, THEY'RE JEWS!

HOW DARE YOU!? HOW DARE YOU SHOW YOUR FACE IN HERE?!

LOOK, IF YOU WOULD JUST LISTEN. THERE'S NO NEED FOR THIS!

ALL RIGHT, THAT'S ENOUGH! WHAT'S GOING ON HERE?

THIS MAN HAS DEFILED THE TEMPLE, BROKEN THE STRICTEST LAW!

THEN LET US DEAL WITH HIM.

COME ON, ON YOUR FEET, JEW.

WAIT! LET ME SPEAK TO THEM.

MY FELLOW JEWS, HEAR ME! MY NAME IS PAUL, OF TARSUS. I TRAINED UNDER THE RABBI GAMALIEL, TO BE AS ZEALOUS AS ANY OF YOU!

TO PROTECT OUR FAITH AS JEWS, I HAD CHRISTIANS ARRESTED, AND ARRANGED THEIR DEATHS, MEN AND WOMEN BOTH! I STOOD HERE IN JERUSALEM AND WATCHED STEPHEN DIE IN FRONT OF MY EYES, GLADLY.

I WENT SO FAR AS TO ASK PERMISSION OF THE HIGH PRIEST TO TRAVEL TO DAMASCUS TO PERSECUTE THE CHRISTIANS LIVING THERE.

BUT ON THE JOURNEY THE LORD JESUS SPOKE TO ME, SAYING THE GOD OF OUR FATHERS HAD CHOSEN ME TO BE A WITNESS TO WHAT HE IS DOING IN THESE DAYS.

AND SO HE SENT ME TO TEACH THE GENTILES...

YOU HEAR HIM?! HE ADMITS IT!!

YOU'RE DEAD, PAUL! YOU HEAR ME?! A DEAD MAN!

THAT'S ENOUGH. I DON'T WANT A RIOT ON MY HANDS.

HAVE HIM FLOGGED, AND QUESTIONED.

246

ARE YOU SURE IT'S *LEGAL* TO FLOG ROMAN CITIZENS WITHOUT TRIAL?

NO ONE SAID ANYTHING ABOUT YOU BEING A *CITIZEN*.

HOW DID YOU GAIN CITIZENSHIP? I HAD TO PAY *DEARLY* FOR MINE.

I WAS *BORN* A CITIZEN. AND I KNOW THE LAW WELL ENOUGH TO KNOW THAT YOU CAN'T FLOG A CITIZEN WITHOUT TRIAL.

TO PREVENT HIM BEING TORN APART BY THE MOB, THE COMMANDER OF THE GARRISON HAD HIM PLACED IN PROTECTIVE CUSTODY. BUT GOD HAD SPOKEN TO PAUL, SAYING, 'JUST AS YOU WERE MY WITNESS IN JERUSALEM, SO WILL YOU BE IN *ROME*.'

IT SEEMED PAUL WAS TO SPEND THE REST OF HIS LIFE AS A *PRISONER*.

BUT A SMALL GROUP OF JEWS TOOK A SOLEMN VOW NOT TO EAT OR DRINK UNTIL PAUL WAS DEAD.

THEY ASKED THE JEWISH COUNCIL TO SEND FOR PAUL.

ONCE HE'S LEFT THE PALACE, WE'LL KILL HIM.

THEIR PLOT WAS OVERHEARD BY PAUL'S NEPHEW. WHEN THE ROMAN COMMANDER GOT TO HEAR OF IT HE DECIDED TO GET PAUL OUT OF JERUSALEM AT ONCE.

IN THE DEAD OF NIGHT PAUL WAS ESCORTED FROM THE FORT TO TRAVEL TO THE ROMAN HEADQUARTERS AT CAESAREA.

PAUL WAS CALLED TO DEFEND HIMSELF BEFORE THE ROMAN GOVERNOR, BUT HIS CASE WAS NEVER SETTLED. HE WAS RUNNING OUT OF PATIENCE.

TAKE DOWN THIS MESSAGE.

I APPEAL TO CAESAR. I AM A ROMAN CITIZEN AND I WISH TO EXERCISE MY RIGHT TO HAVE MY CASE HEARD IN ROME BY THE EMPEROR HIMSELF.

AND SO, JUST AS HAD BEEN PROPHESIED, PAUL SET SAIL FOR THE VERY HEART OF THE WORLD, AND OF THE GREATEST EMPIRE EVER SEEN.

ROME.

THE JOURNEY WAS NOT AN *EASY* ONE.

A FIERCE STORM STRUCK IN THE MEDITERRANEAN. FOR DAYS THEY WERE BATTERED BY THE SEA. IN DESPERATION THE CAPTAIN RAN THE SHIP AGROUND.

IN SUCH CIRCUMSTANCES IT WAS USUAL TO KILL THE PRISONERS, BUT THE CAPTAIN WAS A LENIENT MAN.

I CAN'T SWIM! WE'LL BE *DROWNED*!

NO! LAST NIGHT *GOD* APPEARED TO ME. HE TOLD ME THAT WE WILL *ALL* SURVIVE! *SO STOP SHOUTING AND KICK!*

I DON'T KNOW *HOW*, BUT WE'RE SAFE. ALL 276 OF US!

I *TOLD* YOU. GOD HAS OTHER PLANS.

THE ISLAND THEY WASHED UP ON TURNED OUT TO BE *MALTA*.

AS SOON AS THE STORM ABATED, THE ISLANDERS CAME TO HELP THE SURVIVORS, BRINGING FOOD AND DRY CLOTHING.

THEY WERE TO SPEND THREE MONTHS ON MALTA, BEFORE A SHIP COULD BE FOUND TO TAKE PAUL ON THE FINAL STEP OF HIS JOURNEY.

THE ALEXANDRIAN VESSEL SOON ARRIVED AT ROME'S SEA PORT.

CHRISTIANS IN ROME HAD HEARD OF PAUL'S JOURNEY, AND TRAVELLED DOWN TO MEET HIM.

PAUL, WE MEET AT LAST! THE CHURCH HERE OWES YOU SO MUCH.

MY FRIENDS, I HAVE WORRIED ABOUT YOU ALL FOR SO LONG. *DESPITE* BEING A PRISONER, I AM HAPPIER THAN I CAN SAY TO BE HERE WITH YOU.

IT IS BECAUSE OF THE *HOPE* OF ISRAEL THAT I AM A PRISONER BEFORE YOU. GOD'S SALVATION *HAS* BEEN SENT TO THE GENTILES, AND BELIEVE ME, THEY *WILL* LISTEN.

PAUL WAS NOT ONLY A SPEAKER, BUT A MAN OF LETTERS. DURING HIS JOURNEYS HE HAD WRITTEN LONG LETTERS TO THE CHURCHES THROUGHOUT THE EMPIRE. NOW HE WAS UNDER HOUSE ARREST IN ROME, HE HAD MORE TIME TO DEVOTE TO WRITING.

PAUL WAS GREEK-EDUCATED, JEWISH BY BIRTH, AND A ROMAN CITIZEN INTO THE BARGAIN. THERE WAS NO ONE AS QUALIFIED TO CARRY GOD'S MESSAGE THROUGHOUT THE ROMAN WORLD.

FROM MOUTH TO MOUTH, HEART TO HEART, THE NAME OF JESUS SPREAD ALONG THE ARROW-STRAIGHT ROADS OF THE EMPIRE.

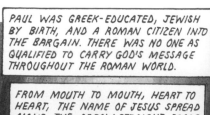

INDEED, IT WAS **BECAUSE** OF THE CLOSELY KNIT EMPIRE THAT THE MESSAGE SPREAD SO FAST.

BUT THE ROMANS WERE AS CRUEL AS THEY WERE CIVILIZED, THEIR CREATIVE MINDS TURNING TO TORTURE AS READILY AS TO ENGINEERING OR PHILOSOPHY.

THE EMPEROR **NERO**, SEEKING SCAPEGOATS FOR THE GREAT FIRE OF ROME, HURLED THE BLAME SQUARELY AT THE FEET OF THE CHRISTIANS.

MANY MET THEIR DEATHS IN THE ARENA, SOME EATEN ALIVE BY WILD ANIMALS, SOME SLAUGHTERED BY GLADIATORS.

THE ROMANS TOOK SUCH DELIGHT IN WATCHING AGONIZING, HUMILIATING DEATHS THAT BEING THROWN TO THE LIONS WAS FAR FROM THE **WORST** DEATH POSSIBLE.

OF THE FINAL END OF THE DISCIPLES, NO **OFFICIAL** RECORDS SURVIVE THOSE DARK DAYS. SOME LEGENDS SAY THAT THOMAS MADE IT AS FAR AS **INDIA**, AND PAUL TO **SPAIN**, ONLY TO BE EVENTUALLY BEHEADED BY THE ROMANS.

PETER WAS ALSO CAPTURED. DYING ON A ROMAN CROSS, HIS LAST REQUEST WAS THAT HE BE CRUCIFIED UPSIDE DOWN, CONSIDERING HIMSELF **UNWORTHY** OF EVEN THE SAME **DEATH** AS HIS BELOVED JESUS.

IN 70AD, SOME JEWS — NOT BELIEVING THE MESSIAH HAD BEEN AND GONE — GREW TIRED OF WAITING AND ROSE UP IN ARMS AGAINST THE ROMAN OCCUPIERS.

HALF-TRAINED ZEALOTS WERE NO THREAT TO THE MOST DISCIPLINED, WELL-TRAINED FIGHTING MEN THE WORLD HAD SEEN. THE BATTLE QUICKLY BECAME A **MASSACRE**.

IN THE ENSUING CHAOS, THE TEMPLE IN JERUSALEM WAS DESTROYED, AS HAD BEEN PREDICTED. IT REMAINS A RUIN TO THIS DAY.

OF THE MEN WHO HAD KNOWN JESUS IN HIS TIME ON EARTH, **ONE** STILL LIVED — A **PRISONER** IN THE WORK CAMP ON THE ISLAND OF **PATMOS**.

HIS NAME WAS **JOHN**. AND IT IS FROM HIM THAT THE LAST STORY OF THEM ALL COMES. FOR JUST AS ADAM SAW THE WORLD WHEN IT WAS NEW, SO GOD ALLOWED JOHN TO SEE IT AT ITS **END**.

IT WAS EARLY IN THE MORNING. I, JOHN, THE LAST OF THE DISCIPLES WHO SAW GOD WALK ON EARTH, STOOD AT THE EDGE OF THE SEA, AND FELT THE DESPAIR WELL UP IN ME.

THERE ON PATMOS, BETWEEN THE LAND AND SKY, I STOOD AND WEPT, NOT KNOWING WHY OUR GOD HAD NOT YET RETURNED TO US.

SURELY IF HE WERE EVER TO RETURN IT WOULD BE *NOW*, I THOUGHT. YET HE HAD NOT.

HOW LONG WOULD WE HAVE TO WAIT? MONTHS? YEARS? CENTURIES? *MILLENNIA*?

BUT THEN I *HEARD IT...* A *VOICE.*

A VOICE BEHIND ME, AS LOUD AS *TRUMPETS*! AS LOUD AS *THUNDER*!

AND THE VOICE SAID:

'WRITE DOWN ALL YOU SEE AND SEND IT TO THE CHURCHES. DO NOT BE AFRAID! I AM THE *FIRST*, AND THE *LAST.* I WAS DEAD, BUT NOW I AM ALIVE *FOR EVER*!'

I SAW A GREAT *SCROLL*, FASTENED WITH SEVEN SEALS, BUT THERE WAS NO ONE *WORTHY* ENOUGH TO BREAK THEM, EXCEPT ONE.

I SAW THE ONE PERSON WHO HAD WON THE RIGHT – THE SON OF DAVID. HE SEEMED TO ME TO BE AS POWERFUL AS A *LION* ONE MOMENT, AND YET AS MEEK AS A *LAMB* THE NEXT.

HE BROKE THE FIRST FOUR SEALS, ONE BY ONE, AND OUT RODE FOUR TERRIFYING *HORSEMEN.* THERE WOULD BE NONE ON EARTH WHO COULD *STOP* THEM...

THE FIRST RODE A HORSE AS WHITE AS *DISEASE*, AS COLD AS *DESPAIR.* HE WENT OUT TO CONQUER THE WORLD IN THE NAME OF GOD'S *ENEMIES.*

THE SECOND WAS AS RED AS *BLOODSHED*, AS RED AS *ANGER.* HE HELD A TERRIBLE SWORD, AND BROUGHT WAR AND VIOLENCE TO ALL THE EARTH.

THE THIRD HORSE WAS AS BLACK AS *MURDER*, AS DARK AS *HUNGER.* THE RIDER HELD HIGH A PAIR OF SCALES, AND SPREAD STARVATION AND FAMINE WHEREVER HE WENT.

AND AS FOR THE FOURTH RIDER... THE FOURTH WAS *DEATH*, AND WHERE THE OTHER THREE WENT, HE FOLLOWED IN THEIR WAKE.

AND THEN THE FIFTH SEAL BROKE, AND I HEARD THE VOICES OF ALL THOSE WHO HAD BEEN MURDERED BECAUSE THEY SPOKE THE TRUTH ABOUT GOD.

WITH ONE VOICE THEY CRIED OUT TO GOD: 'HOW LONG BEFORE OUR DEATHS ARE AVENGED?'

AS THE SIXTH SEAL BROKE, THE SUN BECAME **BLACK.**

THE MOON TURNED BLOOD-RED AND THE STARS FELL FROM THE SKY.

MASSIVE EARTHQUAKES SHOOK EVERY MOUNTAIN AND ISLAND FROM ITS PLACE.

ALL PEOPLE, FROM THE HIGHEST TO THE LOWEST, RAN TO HIDE FROM THE AWESOME WRATH OF GOD.

I SAW FOUR ANGELS STANDING AT THE FOUR CORNERS OF THE WORLD, HOLDING BACK THE FOUR WINDS.

AND THERE WAS A VAST CROWD OF PEOPLE, SO MANY THAT I COULD NOT **COUNT** THEM.

FROM EVERY COUNTRY, EVERY STATE, CITY, TRIBE AND NATION, THEY STOOD IN FRONT OF THE LAMB OF GOD, SHOUTING **'SALVATION BELONGS TO OUR GOD! AND IT COMES FROM THE LAMB OF GOD!'**

AND THEN THE SEVENTH SEAL WAS OPENED.

THERE STOOD BEFORE ME A **WOMAN** IN LABOUR, WHO CRIED OUT, FOR SHE WAS SOON TO GIVE BIRTH.

AND THEN I **SAW** IT.

THE **DRAGON.** THE SEVEN-HEADED, HORNED SERPENT, **SATAN,** IN ITS TRUE FORM. IT TRIED TO EAT THE CHILD AS IT WAS BORN, BUT THE CHILD WAS RESCUED AND TAKEN TO GOD.

AND THERE WAS WAR IN HEAVEN.

THE ARCHANGEL MICHAEL AND HIS ANGELS ATTACKED THE SERPENT, WHO FOUGHT BACK WITH **HIS** ANGELS.

AND I SAW **BABYLON**, AND I WATCHED IT BURN. AND UNDERSTOOD WHY IT WAS THAT THE DRAGON HAD SEVEN HEADS, FOR THE CITY THAT I WATCHED BURNING WAS THE HEART OF THE EVIL **EMPIRE**, AND ALSO SAT ON SEVEN **HILLS**.

AND THEN... OH! **HEAVEN** OPENED, AND I **SAW** HIM!! I SAW HIM AGAIN WITH MY OWN **EYES**!

IT WAS THE **LORD**, AND HE CAME RIDING A WHITE HORSE, WITH ALL THE ARMIES OF HEAVEN BEHIND HIM, BRINGING **JUSTICE** FOR ALL.

THEN I SAW MICHAEL, THE ARCHANGEL, COMING DOWN FROM HEAVEN HOLDING IN HIS HAND THE KEY TO HELL AND CARRYING A GREAT CHAIN.

THE DEVIL WAS BOUND AND THROWN INTO A BOTTOMLESS PIT, AND IT WAS LOCKED AND SEALED SO THAT HE MIGHT DECEIVE NO MORE.

THEN I LOOKED AGAIN AND SAW EVERYONE WHO HAD EVER LIVED, STANDING BEFORE THE LORD. THE HISTORIES OF THEIR LIVES WERE READ, AND THEY WERE JUDGED ON HOW THEY HAD LIVED; THE EVIL DESTROYED, THE GOOD SAVED.

AND WHEN THEY HAD BEEN JUDGED **DEATH ITSELF** WAS DESTROYED TOO.

AND AS I STOOD THERE IN THAT PLACE THAT KNEW NO DEATH, I LOOKED *UP*...

I LOOKED AND I SAW A NEW HEAVEN AND A NEW EARTH, FOR THE OLD HEAVEN AND THE OLD EARTH HAD BEEN DESTROYED. AND I SAW THE HOLY CITY, *JERUSALEM*, COMING DOWN OUT OF HEAVEN LIKE A BRIDE DRESSED FOR HER WEDDING DAY!

NOW GOD'S HOME WILL BE WITH HIS PEOPLE *FOR EVER*! THEY WILL BE HIS PEOPLE, HE WILL BE THEIR GOD, AND HE WILL WIPE AWAY EVERY TEAR FROM THEIR EYES.

NO MORE DEATH. NO MORE PAIN. NO MORE EVIL. THE *OLD* THINGS OF THE WORLD HAVE GONE FOR EVER.

I AM JOHN. OF THE DISCIPLES WHO SAW GOD WALK ON EARTH, ONLY I SURVIVE. AND I SAW ALL THIS WITH MY OWN EYES...

JOHN.

THERE IS STILL MUCH TO SEE. COME WITH ME.

LOOK AGAIN. SEE THE DOORS TO THE CITY THAT ARE NEVER SHUT. THERE IS NO NEED, FOR THE NIGHT IS GONE FOR EVER. THEY WILL NOT NEED THE SUN TO SEE BY DAY OR LAMPS BY NIGHT, FOR GOD WILL LIVE WITH THEM AND HE WILL BE THEIR LIGHT.

SEE. THE RIVER OF *LIFE* FLOWS OUT FROM THE CITY, AND ON ITS BANK STANDS THE TREE OF LIFE – THE FRUIT TAKEN AWAY FROM HUMANKIND IN EDEN IS NOW RETURNED TO YOU.

JOHN! WHOEVER STANDS BY ME WILL INHERIT ALL OF THIS. I WILL BE THEIR GOD, AND THEY WILL BE MY CHILDREN.

AT THIS I WAS SO OVERCOME, I FELL DOWN AT THE FEET OF THE ANGEL TO WORSHIP, BUT HE SHOUTED OUT –

NO! WORSHIP ONLY *GOD*!

FOR EVER.

AMEN.